Mahdis and Millenarians

Mahdis and Millenarians is a discussion of Shīʿite groups in
eighth- and ninth-century Iraq and Iran, whose ideas reflected a mixture of indigenous non-Muslim religious teachings
and practices in Iraq in the early centuries of Islamic rule.
These ideas demonstrate the fluidity of religious boundaries
of this period. Particular attention is given to the millenarian expectations and the revolutionary political activities of
these sects. Specifically, the author's intention is to define
the term "millenarian," to explain how these groups reflect
that definition, and to show how they consequently need to
be seen in a much larger context than Shīʿite or even simply
Muslim history. The author concentrates, therefore, on the
historical-sociological role of these movements. The central
thesis of the study is that they were the first revolutionary
chiliastic groups in Islamic history and, combined with the
later influence of some of their doctrines, contributed to the
tactics and teachings of a number of subsequent Shīʿite or
quasi-Shīʿite sectarian groups.

William F. Tucker is Associate Professor of History at the
University of Arkansas and holds an A.B. degree in European history from the University of North Carolina, an M.A.
in Balkan and Middle East history, and a Ph.D. in Middle
Eastern history, the last two from Indiana University. He has
authored multiple articles and book chapters on Shīʿism,
Kurds, Mamluk history, and the history of natural disasters
in the Middle East between 600 and 1800.

T0382511

Mahdis and Millenarians

Shī'ite Extremists in Early Muslim Iraq

WILLIAM F. TUCKER
University of Arkansas

CAMBRIDGE UNIVERSITY PRESS
Cambridge, New York, Melbourne, Madrid, Cape Town,
Singapore, São Paulo, Delhi, Tokyo, Mexico City

Cambridge University Press
32 Avenue of the Americas, New York, NY 10013-2473, USA

www.cambridge.org
Information on this title: www.cambridge.org/9780521178372

First published 2008
First paperback edition 2011

A catalog record for this publication is available from the British Library

Library of Congress Cataloging in Publication data
Tucker, William Frederick, 1941–
Mahdis and millenarians : Shi'ite extremists in early Muslim Iraq / William F. Tucker.
p. cm.
Includes bibliographical references and index.
ISBN 978-0-521-88384-9 (hardback)
1. Shi'ah – Iraq – History.   2. Shi'ah – Iran – History.   3. Islam – Iraq – History.
4. Islam – Iran – History.   5. Islamic fundamentalism – Iraq – History.   6. Islamic
fundamentalism – Iran – History.   I. Title.
BP192.7.17T83   2008
297.8′20956709021 – dc22   2007020994

ISBN 978-0-521-88384-9 Hardback
ISBN 978-0-521-17837-2 Paperback

Contents

Acknowledgments

The present book has taken many years to formulate and produce, primarily because I became convinced years ago that Middle Eastern and Islamic history should be embedded within the larger context of world history and, in particular, comparative historical and sociological analysis of religion. In determining the requisite knowledge and methodology to use in this study, I have incurred many intellectual and personal debts, and I would like to take this opportunity to thank a series of individuals and institutions who had major roles in my scholarly, educational, and personal life.

First of all, I want to thank my good friend and colleague Evan B. Bukey for all of his emotional and professional support for decades here at the University of Arkansas. Without his encouragement, advice, and occasional scolding, this book would not be appearing now or, perhaps, ever. Similarly, I have no doubt that without years of friendly support and intellectual input from Michael Morony, valued friend and distinguished scholar at UCLA, and Fred McGraw Donner, equally valued friend, premier scholar, and supportive colleague at the University of Chicago, I would not have been able to produce this study, or, for that matter, many of the articles I have published over the years. The same holds true for my cherished friend of many years, Robert W. Olson, distinguished scholar at the University of Kentucky.

Professor Olson has been a major source of intellectual and emotional sustenance since our days as graduate students in Bloomington, Indiana. His advice and insights, especially on the history of the Kurdish people (an area of mutual interest), have been invaluable in my understanding and teaching of Middle Eastern history. Paul Walker at the University of Chicago, the preeminent scholar of Isma'ilism, tendered valuable counsel and shared materials with me, for which I am most grateful. In addition, I would like to remember with great fondness two immensely learned friends who helped my work in numerous ways: the late G. Martin Hinds and Michael W. Dols.

Going back many years, I owe a tremendous debt to a number of teachers and scholars for their instruction and guidance in the discipline of history. I will always be indebted to Herbert L. Bodman and Josef Anderle for starting me on the path of historical studies so many years ago in idyllic Chapel Hill. Similarly, I can never repay the intellectual guidance and support of the two people who most shaped my ideas about historical analysis and the study of world cultures: the late Wadie Jwaideh and my first graduate mentor, Charles Jelavich. Professor Jwaideh made me really aware of the riches of Middle Eastern and Islamic cultures and societies and, among other issues, afforded me valuable insights into the history of Iraq (his natal country), Shi'ism, and the Kurdish people. In addition, he offered great personal and psychological support to his other students, and to me. Similarly, Charles Jelavich was a guide and inspiration in my educational and professional maturation. Professor Jelavich led me through the intricacies of Balkan civilization and cultures and, in so doing, enabled me to see the historian's craft and methodology at their best.

I would also be remiss if I did not acknowledge the scholarly guidance and influence of a series of specialists who taught me medieval East European and Byzantine histories: Glanville Downey, George Soulis, Gustav Bayerle, Barisha Krekic (for many years now at UCLA), and Donald Nicol (University of

Edinburgh). I benefited immeasurably from their instruction, which helped me to place the Middle East within a larger and comparative context.

My appreciation also goes to a number of colleagues, former colleagues, and friends here at Arkansas, beginning with Joel Gordon, a premier historian, who has been encouraging and collegial in his time here in Fayetteville. I also wish to thank Linda Schilcher and Gwenn Ohkruhlik for their support and friendship. Thanks, similarly, to my colleagues Thomas Kennedy, Daniel Sutherland, Donald Engels, Walter L. Brown, David Sloan, and Henry Tsai for their friendly interest over the years. I hope that this book will stand as a tribute to the memories of Robert Reeser, Gordon McNeil, George Ray, Timothy Donovan, and Stephen Strausberg. Nor could I omit mention of my friends John Ryan (my mathematician friend, who tolerates my math ignorance), Patrick Conge, Bob Stassen (fun to argue politics with), Tatsuya Fukushima, Myron Brody, Gerald Sloan (esteemed musician friend), Conrad and Ann Waligorski, Joseph and Anne Marie Candido, James S. Chase, Rick Sonn and Mary Neligh, and Anne and James Vizzier. Special mention should also be made of my friend and former colleague Jim Jones, distinguished scholar of American history, and Larry Malley, Director of the University of Arkansas Press and fellow lover of the Tarheels and Chapel Hill. My appreciation goes to Suzanne Wall and Jane Rone, who, along with a number of other office personnel over the years, have made my life at Arkansas infinitely easier and more pleasant. The able assistance of Roger Henry helped me immensely when I prepared my manuscript in final form.

It goes without saying that a considerable number of libraries and librarians have made this book possible. I would therefore like to thank the staffs of the following libraries: Bibliothèque Nationale in Paris, the Bodleian Library of Oxford University, the India Office Library in London, the Istanbul University Library, the Nuri Osmaniye Mosque Library in Istanbul, the Suleymaniye

Central Library in Istanbul, and the University Research Library of Cambridge University. In the United States, I owe a great deal to the libraries of the following institutions: Columbia University, Cornell University, Duke University, Harvard University, Indiana University, the University of Arkansas, the University of Chicago, the University of Michigan, and the University of North Carolina at Chapel Hill, among others. In Canada, particular thanks and best wishes go to Steve Millier and the fine staff of the Islamic Institute Library, McGill University, in Montreal, who have made my research trips there both productive and enjoyable.

Of course, I am perhaps most indebted to the reference, acquisitions, and interlibrary loan departments of my own library, Mullins Library, University of Arkansas. Specifically, my heartfelt gratitude goes to the following people: Anne Marie Candido, Steve Chism, Doris Cleek, Judy Culberson, Donna Daniels, Phillip Jones, Beth Juhl, Elizabeth McKee, Debbie Miller, Necia Parker-Gibson, Karen Myers, Robin Roggio, and Michele Tabler. Any mention of Mullins Library, of course, must include a tribute to the man who did so much to make it into a serious research facility: the late John Harrison. John was a learned man, a fellow book and music lover. Along with many others, I owe him a great deal and miss him profoundly.

I have enjoyed substantial assistance and support for years from a number of graduate students and research assistants. Special thanks go to the following people: Karim al-Ghamedi, Rakan al-Mutairi, Charles Argo, Michael Bracy, the late Bill Dederich, Teresa Farah, Dorianne Gould, Lahmuddin, Gabriel Lahoud, Matt Parnell, Valor Pickett, Patricia Singleton, Monica Taylor, Stephanie Wade, Christopher Wright, and most particularly Ahmet Akturk and Farid al-Salim, both of whom have done much hard work for me. Ali Sadeghi, manager of the University of Arkansas Bookstore, has been of great help in deciphering some difficult Persian texts, and I want to thank him for his generous assistance.

Portions of this book have been published previously in different forms. I would like, therefore, to thank the editors and staffs of the following journals for permission to reprint, with modifications, the following studies: "Bayān ibn Samʿān and the Bayāniyya: Shīʿite Extremists of Umayyad Iraq," *Muslim World*, LXV (1975); "Rebels and Gnostics: al-Mugīra ibn Saʿīd and the Mugīriyya," *Arabica*, XXII (1975); "Abu Mansūr al-ʿIjli and the Mansūriyya: A Study in Medieval Terrorism," *Islam*, 54 (1977); and "ʿAbd Allāh ibn Muʿāwiya and the Janāhiyya: Rebels and Ideologues of the Late Umayyad Period," *Studia Islamica*, LI (1980).

I, of course, owe much gratitude and affection to my family and family friends. My late grandparents, Neil and Pearl F. Thompson; my late uncle Gilbert Cour, a proud son of Swansea, Wales, and surrogate father; and my aunt Annie Reid Cour, all of whom quite simply made my life possible and immeasurably better. Thanks to Mildred Walker, my relative and benefactor, as well as to her son Larry, with whom I grew up. Special mention, also, goes to Sara Cartrette and Dr. Bill Avant, both of whom have been friends and supporters for many years, as well as Linda Rethmeyer, Penny and Fred Carson, Susan Staffa, and the late Etta Perkins, all friends from Bloomington days. I would also like to express deepest affection for a family friend, indeed, a member of our extended family, Nongphot Sternstein, a great lady and my son's "virtual" mother and Thai language teacher at the University of Pennsylvania. Deepest affection and thanks, also, go to my sisters, Cecilia Burtnett (a fellow historian) and Cynthia Phillips, as well as to my nieces and nephew and their families.

Finally, my love and gratitude go to my greatest supporters and inspiration, my wife, Janet G. Tucker, world-class scholar of Russian literature and best friend of forty years; my marvelous son Robert E. Tucker, anthropologist and scholar of Southeast (especially Thailand) and South Asian societies; and my beautiful and beloved daughter-in-law Charoensri Supattarasakda.

To Lewis Bateman and Eric Crahan, my editors at Cambridge University Press, Kate Queram, as well as all of the other Cambridge staff and support personnel, many thanks for your assistance and your patience in this process. Sincere thanks also to the anonymous readers who recommended this book for publication.

Preface

With the advent of the Iranian Revolution in 1978, the Western
world became aware to a much greater extent than before of
the significance and the emotional and intellectual power of
Shī'ite Islam. Serious students and observers of world affairs at
that time began to cast about for Western-language studies of
Shī'ite history, only to find that there was much less scholarly work
available than might have been anticipated. Aside from the studies of Hamid Algar, Alessandro Bausani, Henri Corbin, Michel
Mazzaoui, and, somewhat later, Shahrough Akhavi, Michael
Fischer, Said Arjomand, and Abdulaziz Sachedina, one could
find few substantial examinations of "Twelver" (*Imāmī* or "moderate") Shī'ism in Iran for the past four centuries.[1] This was true

---

[1] Hamid Algar, *Religion and State in Iran, 1785–1906: The Role of the Ulama in
the Qajar Period* (Berkeley, Calif., and Los Angeles, 1969); Alessandro Bausani,
Persia Religiosa (Milan, 1959); Henri Corbin, *En Islam Iranien*, Vols. I–IV (Paris,
1971–1972); Michel Mazzaoui, *The Origins of the Safawids: Shī'ism, Sūfism, and
the Ghulāt* (Wiesbaden, 1972). Later important works include the following:
Shahrough Akhavi, *Religion and Politics in Contemporary Iran: Clergy-State Relations in the Pahlavi Period* (Albany, N.Y., 1980); Michael M. J. Fischer, *Iran:
From Religious Dispute to Revolution* (Cambridge, Mass., 1980). On Safavid and
Qajar Shī'ism, see Said Arjomand, *The Shadow of God and the Hidden Imam: Religion, Political Order and Societal Change in Shī'ite Iran from the Beginning to 1890*
(Chicago, 1984). For an important study of the "Twelver" *Mahdī* concept, we

in spite of the fact that it has been the state religion of Iran since the beginning of the sixteenth century. Since the Iranian Revolution, not surprisingly, a number of important works have appeared, for example, those of Yann Richard, Heinz Halm, Moojan Momen, and Hossein Modarressi, just to mention a few, which have given us a much better understanding of Shī'ism in Iran and, in some cases, elsewhere.[2] Now, happily, one may also point to a number of studies of non-Twelver Shī'ism (e.g., Ismā'īlism), for example, the works of Farhad Daftary, Paul Walker, Abbas Hamdani, Wilferd Madelung, Heinz Halm, and Ismail Poonawala.[3]

have Abdulaziz Sachedina's *Islamic Messianism: The Idea of the* Mahdī *in Twelver Shī'ism* (Albany, N.Y., 1981).

[2] Yann Richard, *Shī'ite Islam: Polity, Ideology, and Creed,* trans. Antonia Nevill (Oxford, 1995); Heinz Halm, *Shiism,* trans. Janet Watson (Edinburgh, 1991); Moojan Momen, *An Introduction to Shī'i Islam: The History and Doctrines of Twelver Shī'ism* (New Haven and London, 1985); Hossein Modarressi Tabataba'i, *An Introduction to Shī'i Law* (London, 1984). One may multiply the number of such works, especially those of Nikki Keddie (for example, *Iran and the Muslim World: Resistance and Revolution* [New York, 1995]) but, in the interest of space and time, other writings on various aspects of Twelver Shī'ism will be included in the bibliography, where one will also find more recent studies of Shī'ism outside Iran, especially in Iraq and Lebanon.

[3] Two works by Farhad Daftary, *The Ismā'īlīs: Their History and Doctrines* (Cambridge, 1990), and his edited book *Medieval Ismā'īlī History and Thought* (Cambridge, 1996); Paul E. Walker, *Early Philosophical Shī'ism: The Ismā'īlī Neoplatonism of Abū Ya'qūb al-Sijistānī* (Cambridge, 1993) and *Abū Ya'qūb al-Sijistānī: Intellectual Missionary* (London and New York, 1996); Abbas Hamdani, "Evolution of the Organisational Structure of the Fatimi Da'wah," *Arabian Studies,* 3 (1976), 85–114 and numerous other articles by the same author; Heinz Halm, *Kosmologie und Heilslehre der Frühen Ismā'īlie: Eine Studie zur islamischen Gnosis* (Wiesbaden, 1978); Ismail K. Poonawala, numerous articles, including, most recently, "Ismā'īlī *ta'wīl* of the Qur'ān," in *Approaches to the History of the Interpretation of the Qur'ān,* ed. A. Rippin (Oxford, 1988), 199–222. One may also find a reference to his excellent bio-bibliography of Isma'ili literature in the bibliography of this work. The Nizārī Ismā'īlīs, of course, were examined many years ago in two classic studies, that of Marshall G. S. Hodgson, *The Order of the Assassins* (The Hague, 1955), and Bernard Lewis, *The Assassins: A Radical Sect in Islam* (New York, 1968).

From a casual reading of the aforementioned scholars, it is clear that the history of Shī'ite Islam is a very long, controversial, and complicated one, and it is certainly not the purpose of this work to present an exhaustive history of Shī'ism. In spite of all of the emphasis upon Iranian Shī'ism, it is crucial to understand that Shī'ite history has its roots in the wider history of the early Muslim community and that it is not specific to one ethnic or linguistic group. The pluralistic nature of early Shī'ism constitutes the starting point for the present study, devoted to an examination of certain "extremist" Shī'ite organizations that originated in early Muslim Iraq (i.e., seventh–eighth century A.D.) and that had an impact upon later religious groups, whether Shī'ite, non-Shī'ite, or even quasi-Shī'ite. Whereas a long exposition of the broad patterns of Shī'ite history is beyond the scope of the present study, certainly that history can be better understood through elucidating the evolution of four early extremist Shī'ite groups whose ideas and tactics had a substantial impact upon later Shī'ites ("moderate" and "extremist"[4]), non-Shī'ite groupings, and quasi-Shī'ite religious movements. Such an investigation is necessary for an understanding of the origins and development of Shī'ism and other facets of the Islamic faith.

The groups to be examined in this book include the followers of Bayān ibn Sam'ān, al-Mughīra ibn Sa'īd, Abū Mansūr al-'Ijli, and 'Abd Allāh ibn Mu'āwiya. These sectarian leaders all led uprisings against the Umayyad Caliphs (who ruled from 661 to 750 A.D.) during the first half of the eighth century. In addition to their seditious activities aimed at the ruling elite, these individuals and those who followed them developed religious doctrines and tactics destined to have a lasting influence upon groups all the way to the present. Their doctrines were to affect moderate Shī'ites, extremist Shī'ites (the Nusayris or 'Alawis of present-day Syria), quasi-Shī'ite sects such as the Druze and the

---

4 The issue of "extremism" or *Ghulāt* among the Shī'ites is examined in note 11.

Ahl-i Haqq (Kurdish sectarians), and even non-Shī'ites, for example, the Sunni-affiliated Sufis. The organization and techniques
employed by at least two of the four groups were later used with
telling effect against their religious-political opponents.

Important factors to be emphasized include the understanding of these groups as belonging to a milieu of religious dissent
and also, especially, to a fluidly conceived community in the process of defining its parameters and its governing paradigm. In
other words, it is vital to understand that our received notions of
Islamic thought and institutions were in the process of formation
at the time these groups were active. They may be seen as religious dissenters whose vision of reality was violently suppressed
and unacceptable to the larger community, but it is particularly
important that their ideas were not eradicated and, in fact, came
to play an important role in some of the groups mentioned above
and to be referred to again by those who incorporated these concepts into an evolving, dissenting body of belief. One must also
be cognizant of the fact that, as always, these groups were not
solely "religious." As is always the case, religious groups or sects,
however one chooses to label them, exist in the world, that is,
they relate in some way or other to social, political, or even economic realities surrounding them. As we shall see, this was most
certainly the case with the movements to be examined here.

In the present study, the ideas and activities of the Bayāniyya
(followers of Bayān), the Mughīriyya (the followers of al-
Mughīra), the Mansūriyya (Abū Mansūr's partisans), and the
Janāhiyya (the sect forming around Ibn Mu'āwiya) will be analyzed in terms of origins, evolution, and the nature of their impact
upon later Islamic sects or groups. In particular, an attempt will
be made to delineate the original contributions of each of the
four groups. The present volume, it should be emphasized, must
not be construed as an exercise in comparative religion or the
history of religion. The approach adopted here, quite frankly,
is to treat religious ideas as a form of ideology that shapes the

behavior of its adherents. Furthermore, it should be noted that the organizational structure of this monograph is conceived in a manner calculated to actually present the subject matter as well as the results of the research, particularly because there is disagreement and a lack of clarity about just who believed what, and how those beliefs originated and were transmitted.

Ultimately, the most significant goal here is to show that these four sects were the first millenarian movements (groups expecting total, imminent, and collective salvation *in this world*) to appear in the Muslim world. In a sense, the inspiration for this project lies not in any of the synthetic or monographic studies of Shi'ism, however excellent and provocative, but rather in a book that the present author read many years ago as a young man. When I first encountered Norman Cohn's brilliant *The Pursuit of the Millennium: Revolutionary Millenarians and Mystical Anarchists of the Middle Ages*, I felt that it was one of the most penetrating analyses of religious dissent that I had ever encountered and, quite frankly, one of the most interesting books of history in any field with which I was familiar. It was controversial; the author made dangerous and tenuous connections between Reformation religious groups and modern political movements; but for all of its radical interpretations, it seemed to penetrate to the heart of what religious dissent, involving violence and/or revolutionary politics, was about. The importance of its insights and methodology came to be readily seen in the series of conferences, volumes of collected essays, and journals devoted to comparative millenarism that it stimulated (references to these can be found in the bibliography). It has continued to generate books and articles about millenarism.

When I began to examine the various volumes and essays devoted to this subject, I was struck by the absence of any serious and systematic studies from Islamic history. This situation has not changed over the decades since I first began working with this subject. To be sure, one sees the term "millenarian" employed in various studies, but, with the exception of Said A. Arjomand, scholars of Islam seem to feel no need to explain exactly what this term involves. At the very least, a millenarian movement is a group or sect expecting total, imminent, and collective salvation in this world. This may or may not involve the intervention of some messianic figure. One may speak of a millenarian paradigm, but the varied nature of the phenomenon has to be kept in mind. The groups to be examined here possess many of the characteristics that are seemingly a part of this type of sociopolitical religious movement, regardless of time or location. Such characteristics as militant elitism, reversal of status, antinomianism (not simply vulgar libertinism), and, frequently, a sense of relative deprivation or *perceived* injustice are often associated with millenarian movements and are demonstrably present within the groups constituting the subject of this study. In this sense, hopefully, one will gain some understanding of the millenarian impulse in early Shī'ite and Muslim history generally. It is also to be hoped that this analysis will show the similarity of the sects under examination to other groups in other religious traditions, at other times and places, that is to say, that this research will be of potential value for comparative studies, whether by anthropologists, sociologists, or historians of comparative religion. It must be reiterated, however, that this book is not, *per se*, a study in comparative religion. Furthermore, in the interest of clarity and coherence, I propose to reserve the millenarian analysis for a separate chapter. One might argue that it would be preferable to treat the topic group by group in each of the relevant chapters, but it seems to me that technical problems with sources and analysis of the groups' ideas would obscure their millenarian features, in addition to which these features are best understood by analyzing them within the context of the groups taken together, instead of in isolation. One of the most obvious reasons for this is that the four groups under consideration evolved over a period of years in which survivors of one suppressed group went on to join and to take their ideas with them into another.

The book consists of six chapters. Chapter 1 is devoted to an examination of ʿAbd Allāh ibn Saba' and his followers, as well as to the rebellion of al-Mukhtār and the Kaisāniyya. Special emphasis is placed upon the impact of Ibn Saba' and al-Mukhtār upon the four sects constituting the primary focus of this study. Chapters 2 through 5 deal with Bayān, al-Mughīra, Abū Mansūr, ʿAbd Allāh ibn Muʿāwiya, and their respective followers. Chapter 6 focuses upon the millenarian features of the four groups, considers the impact of the four groups on later movements, and also points to parallels with non-Islamic millenarians outside the Middle East. A short conclusion offers final thoughts about the nature of the four sects examined in the body of the text.

In the first five chapters the organization is essentially the same. Each chapter consists of four basic divisions. The first part contains information about the leader of the particular group. Next, the membership of each sect is examined. This is followed in each instance by an enumeration and discussion of the religious ideas. In the final paragraphs of the individual chapters, an attempt is made to assess the contributions and the significance of each sect.

There is little in the way of secondary literature devoted specifically to these groups, the best study undoubtedly being that by Heinz Halm, entitled *Die Islamische Gnosis: Die Extreme Schīʿa und die ʿAlawiten*.[5] Halm's study traces the nature of gnostic thought from the early extremist Shīʿites through the Nusayris (still extant, of course, in Syria). He provides the reader with invaluable historiographical materials gleaned from heresiographers and, of greater import, examines and translates into German

---

5 Heinz Halm, *Die Islamische Gnosis: Die Extreme Schīʿa und die ʿAlawiten* (Zurich and Munich, 1982).

the major texts of the various groups themselves. In spite of its signal importance, Halm's book does not address certain major historical, sociological, or political issues surrounding these sects. One of the most useful book-length treatments of the sects is still the Ph.D. dissertation of the late W. W. Rajkowski, which unfortunately has remained unpublished and which suffers from a lack of systematic comparison of the source materials, as well as a failure to adequately explore the intellectual relationships among the groups.[6] In addition, it is dated in some respects with regard to the sources the author utilized. In spite of all of this, it remains one of the clearest, most detailed, and most coherently organized examinations of not only the four sects relevant to the present volume, but, indeed, of early Shī'ism in Iraq generally. S. H. M. Jafri's *Origins and Early Development of Shī'ite Islam* contains mention of the groups but only as they related to the 'Alids and only in a fashion calculated to minimize their importance and to distance them from moderate Shī'ism.[7]

Another brief but well-formulated treatment of at least two of the four sects can be found in Wadād al-Qādī's definitive study of the rebellion of al-Mukhtār and the rise of the Kaisāniyya Shī'a. Al-Qādī conceives of the sects she examines as branches or off-shoots of the Kaisāniyya, and, even though valid in at least one case, this approach does not take into account the original ideas of the four groups and the ways in which they differed from the partisans of Mukhtār.[8]

Among the books mentioning the four sects, Henri Laoust's study of what he refers to as "schisms" in Islam does little more than summarize their ideas in passing and so is of little use to the serious investigator of their historical role.[9] W. Montgomery

---

[6] W. W. Rajkowski, "Early Shī'ism in Iraq," Ph.D. diss. (London University, 1955).

[7] S. Husain M. Jafri, *Origins and Early Development of Shī'ite Islam* (London, 1979).

[8] Wadād al-Qādī, *al-Kaisāniyya fī Ta'rīkh wa al-Adab* (Beirut, 1974).

[9] Henri Laoust, *Les Schismes dans l'Islam* (Paris, 1965).

Watt's *The Formative Period of Islamic Thought* has a section on the groups, but it is short and seems to add little to his earlier treatment of Umayyad Shī'ism in an article mentioned later in this chapter.[10] Moojan Momen offers some interesting and useful remarks in his large synthesis, *An Introduction to Shi'i Islam*, cited previously, but his treatment is brief, centers upon Islamic conceptual categories, such as *Ghulāt* ("extremists"), and thereby fails to address the sociopolitical aspects of the sects. As the important article of Wadād al-Qādī demonstrates, the term "*Ghulāt*," indicating extremism or exaggeration, was a fluid one for Islamic authors and could mean different things in different accounts.[11] For this reason, the term "*Ghulāt*" in this study will be used to indicate sects possessing at least one of the following characteristics: deification or supernatural status of 'Alī and other Shī'ite *Imāms*, belief in transmigration of souls, the concept of God becoming incarnate in any given person, and the expectation that a person will experience reincarnation.

In an important study of the spiritual and esoteric nature of the early Shī'ite *Imāms*, Mohammad Alī Amīr-Moezzi refers marginally to some of these groups but, interestingly enough, seems to use primarily research that I had published some years ago. The same secondary treatment is true of an outstanding study of the relationship between Jewish and Shī'ite sectarian movements, published by Steven Wasserstrom in 1995. Wasserstrom's book, incidentally, is an intriguing examination of comparative religious techniques and the influence religions can have on one another. The crucial concept of the *Mahdī* (saviour figure), which plays a central role in Shī'ism generally, is treated with great insight and depth by Abdulaziz Sachedina, in his work

---

[10] W. Montgomery Watt, *The Formative Period of Islamic Thought* (Edinburgh, 1973).

[11] Wadād al-Qādī, "The Development of the Term *Ghulāt* in Muslim Literature with Special Reference to the Kaysāniyya," in *Akten des VII. Kongresses für Arabistik und Islamwissenschaft* (Göttingen, 1974), 295–319.

cited previously, but he addresses the issue for later, Twelver, thought using classical Shīʿite texts, and therefore sheds no real light upon how the four sects and other early groups understood the concept. Other brief remarks about these groups are to be found in the work of Hossein Modarressi, *Crisis and Consolidation in the Formative Period of Shīʿite Islam: Abū Jaʿfar ibn Qiba al-Rāzī and His Contribution to Imāmite Shīʿite Thought.* Finally, among books and monographs, I would like to take special note of the as-yet-unpublished dissertation of L. N. Takim, which, though devoted to an investigation of the early Shīʿite *Rijal*, refers in a few places to individuals associated with extremist Shīʿite sects. It is to be hoped that this important study will soon appear in print.[12]

An examination of the periodical literature also offers a number of worthwhile, albeit limited, studies, but in at least some cases one encounters problems of narrow scope and peripheral treatment. Probably the best short study of these extremist sects is the second part of a two-article series by Heinz Halm, which appeared in *Der Islam* in 1981. In essence, however, it is a summary minus translations of his already-cited volume on Islamic gnosis, which appeared the following year. In 1984, Mohamed Rekaya examined the groups briefly in an important article devoted to the so-called *Khurramite* movements active in early ʿAbbāsid Iran. His remarks, however, were taken largely from my own published studies. In the next year, Steven Wasserstrom contributed a stimulating, award-winning essay to the journal *History of Religions*, which treated the gnostic features of al-Mughīra ibn Saʿīd's

---

[12] Mohammad Ali Amir-Moezzi, *The Divine Guide in Early Shiʿism*, trans. David Streight (Albany, N.Y., 1994); Steven Wasserstrom, *Between Muslim and Jew: The Problem of Symbiosis under Early Islam* (Princeton N.J., 1995); Abdulaziz Sachedina, *Islamic Messianism*; Hossein Modarressi, *Crisis and Consolidation in the Formative Period of Shīʿite Islam: Abu Jaʿfar ibn Qiba al-Razi and His Contribution to Imamite Shīʿite Thought* (Princeton, 1993); L. N. Takim, "The *Rijal* of the Shiʿi *Imāms* as depicted in *Imāmi* Biographical Literature," Ph.D. diss. (London University, SOAS, 1990).

teachings and showed how they were rejected by the community. This remains one of the best studies of any *Ghulāt* group down to the present.[13]

In addition to these more recent essays, there are several older periodical treatments that continue, in my opinion, to be of great merit and usefulness. Probably one of the best of these is the study published by Israel Friedlaender more than seventy years ago in the commentary to his translation of Ibn Hazm's treatise on the Shī'ites. This commentary is cited elsewhere and referred to on a number of occasions in the following pages. It is seen to be of particular value in suggesting possible origins of important concepts associated with the four sects and other early Shī'ite circles.

One of the most stimulating analyses of the nature and classification of the groups is to be found in Sabatino Moscati's "Per una Storia dell' Antica Sī'a," which was published in 1955. The article begins with an excellent discussion of the sources. The author points out the problems involved in the use of those works treating Islamic heresies. The main difficulties, he suggests, are the obvious prejudices of the Muslim authors against "heretical" groups, their resort to stereotypes or clichés in presenting the doctrines of the heretics, and the chronological confusion arising from the arrangement of the heresies by grade rather than time period or stages of development.[14] He leaves little doubt, however, as to the necessity of using such sources carefully and systematically.

---

[13] Heinz Halm, "Das 'Buch der Schatten': Die Mufaddal-Tradition der *Gulāt* und die Ursprünge des Nusairiertums. II. Die Stoffe," *Der Islam*, 58 (1981), 15–86; Mohamed Rekaya, "Le *Khurramādin* et les mouvements khurramites sous les 'Abbasides," *Studia Islamica*, 60 (1984), 5–57; Steven Wasserstrom, "The Moving Finger Writes: Mughīra ibn Sa'īd's Islamic Gnosis and the Myths of Its Rejection," *History of Religions*, 25 (1985), 1–29.

[14] Sabatino Moscati, "Per una Storia dell' Antica Sī'a," *Rivista degli Studi Orientali*, XXX (1955), 253.

Moscati classifies the groups as being either primarily "religious" or "political." He suggests that movements emphasizing religious dogma included predominantly non-Arabs. Other groups that he considers to have been motivated mainly by political goals were, according to his line of reasoning, essentially Arab movements. The latter type, he argues, more often included 'Alids in its positions of leadership or its ranks. The "religious-oriented" group, by contrast, was promoted by non-'Alids, who began by championing 'Alid claims and ended by advancing their own claims to leadership.[15] Whereas there is some merit in this classification scheme, the research for this study demonstrates that the movements dealt with here were both "political" and "religious" and included both Arabs and non-Arabs. Moscati's twofold classification will not, therefore, be utilized in this book. Professor W. Montgomery Watt's study of Umayyad Shī'ism has proved to be of greater use in matters of detail and interpretation.[16] Generally, though, his treatment of the groups with which we are concerned is too brief to be overly helpful. His remarks about the Aramaean *Mawālī* are of interest, although the presence and role of the Aramaeans in Iraq has now been more rigorously examined by Michael Morony in his *Iraq After the Muslim Conquest.*[17] Watt's remarks about the South Arabian complexion of early Shī'ism are also in need of qualification, as this study indicates the presence of other elements in these movements.

The late Marshall G. S. Hodgon's investigation of the sectarian beginnings of Shī'ism has been valuable because of his statements concerning a possible relationship between the speculation of the early *Ghulāt* ("extremist" or "exaggerating") Shī'ites and that

[15] Ibid., 263–264.
[16] W. Montgomery Watt, "Shī'ism under the Umayyads," *Journal of the Royal Asiatic Society* (1960), 158–172.
[17] Michael G. Morony, *Iraq After the Muslim Conquest* (Princeton N.J., 1984).

of the later Ṣūfis.[18] These suggestions have proved to be useful in tracing the impact of the groups studied here and will be referred to again.

The books and articles just mentioned are the only noteworthy treatments of the early Shīʿite extremists that have appeared to date. Other works have mentioned them briefly or given a synopsis of their beliefs without, however, examining them closely. Furthermore, and more importantly, no one has investigated the four groups upon which this study is concentrated within the framework of millenarian sectarianism. Hopefully, the present treatment will provide the detailed examination heretofore lacking.

The transliteration system is that employed by most English-language journals of Islamic studies at present, especially the *International Journal of Middle East Studies*. Technical names and personal names are rendered within the strictures of this system, whereas place names such as Mecca or Medina are instead spelled in accordance with current common English usage.

[18] Marshall G. S. Hodgson, "How Did the Early Shīʿa Become Sectarian," *Journal of the American Oriental Society*, 75 (1955), 1–13.

Mahdis and Millenarians

Introduction

Historical Background – Umayyad Rule

In order to gain a clearer understanding of the conditions that led to the emergence of the sects that form the subject of this study, it is necessary to examine briefly the nature of Umayyad rule in Iraq and especially the problems at Kufa and its surroundings. Beginning with the reign of the Umayyad dynastic founder, Mu'āwiya ibn Abī Sufyan, the ruling circles in Damascus experienced hostility and intransigence on the part of many of the inhabitants of Iraq. Anti-Umayyad outbreaks became a permanent feature of the Iraqi milieu. These movements of protest stemmed from problems of assimilation with non-Arabs, religious conflicts, and social stratification and polarization in Kufa. The economic and social grievances associated with stratification were particularly bitter and troublesome for those seeking to govern Iraq. It was inevitable that the situation resulting from prolonged struggle would, in the long run, serve only to increase the obstinacy of the Iraqis, on the one hand, and the severity of the Umayyad rulers, on the other.

Since the publication of M. A. Shaban's *Islamic History A.D. 600–750 (A. H. 132): A New Interpretation*, scholars of early Islamic history have begun to revise their views of one of the most important features of early Iraqi history: tribal rivalries among the Arabs living in that region. Earlier scholars such as Julius Wellhausen, Ignaz Goldziher, and others argued that early Muslim history,

1

especially in Iraq, was shaped to a great extent by rivalry between
North Arabs, Qaysites, and Southern Arabs, known in the sources
as Yamanis. According to this line of reasoning, the Umayyad
dynasty became embroiled in a blood dispute going all the
way back into pre-Islamic days. Although the sympathies of the
dynasty shifted according to ruler, essentially the Umayyads gradually came to be looked upon, particularly in Iraq, as partisans of
the Mudar branch of North Arabs and thereby alienated for good
the Rabī'a branch of the North Arabs, as well as the South Arabs.
As Shaban has pointed out, what seems to have been at work was
a difference between "Qaysites" and "Yamanites" over the policy
to be followed with regard to the role of non-Arab Muslims in
the Islamic state. The Qaysites and the Umayyads apparently
fought against a policy of assimilating and conciliating non-
Arabs, whereas the Yamanites, in the interest of settled life and
trade, opted for a policy of assimilation and cooperation. When
the Umayyads sought to maintain Arab hegemony and non-
assimilation, the Rabī'a and the Yaman adopted a policy of opposition and enmity toward the ruling dynasty.[1]

More recently, Patricia Crone, in an interesting rebuttal of
Shaban's thesis, argues that the Qays-Yaman conflict did not
result from a conflict between two political parties bearing those
names. She maintains, rather, that the Qays-Yaman antagonism
was primarily a military phenomenon involving rivalries for
positions within the provinces. Most importantly, and, in some
respects, reflective of the older pre-Shaban arguments, she suggests that the rivalry took the form of *'asabiyya,* in other words, the
involved parties conceived of their identities as lineage-based.[2]

---

[1] M. A. Shaban, *Islamic History A.D. 600–750 (A. H. 132): A New Interpretation*
(Cambridge, 1971), 120–124, 128–130.
[2] Patricia Crone, "Were the Qays and Yemen of the Umayyad Period Political
Parties?" *Der Islam,* 71 (1994), 1–57.

Whatever the truth of the matter, the evidence forthcoming with respect to the four sects considered in this book clearly shows that both Arabs and non-Arab Muslims, or *Mawālī*, fought side by side in these anti-Umayyad efforts. Whether this reflected a desire for Arab and non-Arab assimilation is open to question. Factors of political and economic justice, factional rivalries, and religious conviction all undoubtedly played a major role in this cooperation.

Similar factors may have been at work in the rise of religious opposition groups, which troubled the Umayyads from the time of their accession to power. The Kharijites, for instance, engaged in anti-government activities for the duration of Umayyad rule. Their agitation was especially intense in Iraq at the time of the early Umayyad caliphs. From the beginning of Mu'āwiya's reign in 661 down to the year 680, there were sixteen Kharijite revolts, most of them around Basra or Kufa.[3] The Kharijite emphasis doctrinally, as is well known, was upon the piety and the deeds of the individual, leadership of the religious community being the prerogative of the most pious and egalitarian member of that community. They were the uncompromising foes of Umayyad rule, which in their way of thinking consisted of the centralized control of governing power by a secular hereditary ruler.

In addition to the Kharijite opposition, the Shī'ites, partisans of 'Alī ibn Abī Tālib and his descendants, were quite active in the anti-Umayyad movements. This party was particularly strong in Iraq, primarily in the city of Kufa and its hinterland. Since this Shī'ite activity constitutes the focal point of the present study, further remarks will be reserved for the following chapters. Here it is sufficient to note that the proto-Shī'ites formed another active opposition movement to Umayyad rule.

---

[3] W. Montgomery Watt, "Kharijite Thought in the Umayyad Period," *Islam*, XXXVI (1961), 216–217.

The social and economic grievances of at least some non-Arab Muslims, the *Mawālī*, served to add these people to the ranks of the anti-Umayyad movements. In upholding a policy of non-assimilation, the Umayyads not only condoned discrimination against non-Arabs; a number of the caliphs and their entourages actively engaged in it. The *Mawālī*, for example, received harsh treatment at the hands of the Umayyad governor al-Hajjāj ibn Yūsuf. He is known to have forced converts who had moved to the cities to return to their lands and to pay the *Jizya* (head tax), which was in theory imposed only upon non-Muslims.[4] His severe treatment of those *Mawālī* who had fought on the side of ʿAbd al-Rahmān ibn al-Ashʿath stands in glaring contrast to his more generous attitude toward certain Arabs who had also followed Ibn al-Ashʿath.[5] Not all *Mawālī* flocked to the anti-Umayyad cause, but enough did so that Shīʿism after 685 begins to take on a definite *Mawālī* coloration, as even the most recent research tends to confirm. Further information about the situation of the *Mawālī* will be given in Chapter 6. We may simply note here their presence among the most bitter opponents of the Damascene regime.

Iraqi anti-Umayyad feeling also appears to have been a reflection of anti-Syrian regional feeling. As Wellhausen pointed out years ago, the Iraqis resented the transfer of the capital from

---

[4] Surprisingly enough, given his importance, we possess no recent study of the career of al-Hajjāj in a European language. There is the considerably dated work of Jean Perier, *Vie d'al-Hadjdjadj Ibn Yousof s'après les Sources Arabes* (Paris, 1904), 262–263. More recently and importantly, we have the numerous references to al-Hajjāj included in the following: ʿAbd al-Ameer ʿAbd Dixon, *The Umayyad Caliphate 65–86/684–705 (A Political Study)* (London, 1971); G. R. Hawting, *The First Dynasty of Islam – The Umayyad Caliphate A.D. 661–750* (Carbondale, Ill., 1987), esp. 70; A. Dietrich, "al-Hadjdjādj B. Yūsuf B. al-Hakam B. ʿAkīl al-Thakafī, Abū Muhammad," in *Encyclopædia of Islam*, III (2nd ed., Leiden, 1971), 39–43.

[5] For a detailed treatment of the Ibn al-Ashʿath rebellion, see Redwan Sayed, *Die Revolte des Ibn al-Asʿat und die Koranleser* (Freiburg, 1977); note especially 276–369. For the *Mawālī* issue, see Hawting, *First Dynasty*, 69–70. One may also consult L. Veccia Vaglieri, "Ibn al-Ashʿath," *E.I.2*, III (Leiden, 1971), 719.

Kufa to Damascus with the resulting loss of status and power for the Iraqi city and its inhabitants. The severity of the Umayyad governors in Iraq and the introduction of Syrian garrisons into that region are perhaps the clearest proof of Iraqi resistance to Syrian centralized rule. Strong measures were necessary in order to control the Iraqis' striving for autonomy. This fierce regional sentiment was to find full expression in the revolt of Yazīd ibn al-Muhallab. Francesco Gabrieli has pointed out that it was the Muhallabid attempt to intertwine their personal fortunes with Iraqi regional feeling that caused the Umayyads to exterminate this important family. He goes on to say that it is that attempted identification of interests that gives the Muhallabid revolt its historical significance. Had it been merely a matter of family ambition, he argues, the revolt would not have been of such importance.[6] Iraqi anti-Syrian feeling may very well have had some place in the motives of those Arabs who joined the groups to be examined in the subsequent chapters.

In view of the Iraqi attitude toward the Umayyad government, it is not surprising that the latter should have entrusted the governorship of an unruly province to individuals of a rather stern and forceful nature. It was obvious to the central government that Iraq, for strategic and economic reasons, had to be ruled firmly. This posed a considerable dilemma for the Umayyads, however. The problem was to strike a balance between the necessary firmness and undue severity, which could only reinforce discontent. In several cases the harsh policies of the Umayyad governors exacerbated the situation and intensified anti-Umayyad feeling and activity.

Some governors were able to find the right mix between persuasion and power. Ziyād ibn Abīhī, Muʿāwiya's adopted brother

---

[6] Francesco Gabrieli, "La Rivolta dei Muhallabiti nel Iraq e il nuovo Baladuri," *Atti della Accademia Nazionale dei Lincei. Rendiconti: Classe Scienze Morali, Storiche e Filologiche*, Ser. VI, Vol. XIV (1938), 235.

and his governor of Iraq, ruled the province with strength but, at the same time, managed to avoid unnecessary violence. In order to establish order in Basra, he initiated a curfew and had violators summarily executed.[7] On the other hand, he did not seek to subdue the tribes by mass executions. His solution to tribal unruliness was to locate different tribes in one quarter, to name a chieftain to head each of these quarters, and to make him responsible for their good behavior.[8] He was able to establish security in his domains without resorting to extreme harshness. The same thing applies to the governorate of Khālid ibn 'Abd Allāh al-Qasrī. He was one of the most able and, simultaneously, one of the most moderate governors of Iraq. It is interesting to note that the revolt of al-Mughīra ibn Sa'īd and Bayān ibn Sam'ān took place during Khālid's relatively benign rule.

Al-Hajjāj ibn Yūsuf, Umayyad governor of Iraq from 695 to 714, is perhaps the best example of the authoritarian, overly severe official. Whereas it is true that he was able to maintain Umayyad control over Iraq, it is also true that his methods raised enemies for the Umayyad dynasty. His implacability, which has become proverbial among the Arabs, was no doubt responsible for many anti-government outbursts, the most serious of which was that of Ibn al-Ash'ath. His treatment of the *Mawālī* intensified the hatred of many of them for the Syrian dynasty and its representatives. A clear indication of this is to be found in the presence in the ranks of Ibn al-Ash'ath's rebel force of a large number of Persian *Mawālī*.[9] Whereas it is necessary to allow for the prejudice of the sources, there can be no doubt that al-Hajjāj, although an able and dedicated official, was excessively stringent in the discharge of his official duties.

---

[7] Henri Lammens, "Ziād ibn Abīhī, vice-roi de l'Iraq," *RSO*, IV (1911–1912), 41–42.

[8] Ibid., 658–659.

[9] Hawting, *First Dynasty*, 69–70; Sayed, *Die Revolte*, Ch. 5 passim; Perier, *al-Hadjdjadj ibn Yousof*, 201.

Another Umayyad governor who seems to have done much to heighten anti-government feeling in Iraq was Yūsuf ibn ʿUmar. During his term in office, he acquired the general reputation of a bloodthirsty tyrant.[10] Certainly his senseless vengeance against Khālid al-Qasrī did much to crystallize anti-Umayyad feeling among the Yamanite Arabs who were supporters or associates of Khālid in Iraq and Syria. As will be seen, it was during his rule that Abū Mansūr al-ʿIjli and the Mansūriyya appeared in Iraq.

Finally, it must be stressed that the emergence of the four sects was a reflection mainly of problems at Kufa that had arisen before the first half of the eighth century. There was by the 730s extreme social fragmentation at Kufa among the many tribal groups. There was an early end to significant territorial expansion by the Kufan army, which meant that there were few rewards from booty or the administration of new territory after 650 compared to Basra, Syria, or Egypt. The pressures were transferred to the *Sawād* of Kufa and its peasants, where the tax base was insufficient to support the military population at Kufa, and this was in turn aggravated by its alienation as land grants to favored individuals beginning in the time of ʿUthmān and continuing into the Marwānid period. By the time of Muʿāwiya, the Arab population of Kufa was polarized and stratified, and the emergence of the Kharijites and the Shīʿites at least partially resulted from internal social conflicts in that city. By the early eighth century, the Kufans were largely demilitarized as well as stratified. The *Ashrāf* (Islamic notables) had been replaced by a new elite of Marwānid princes and protégés, who monopolized the rewards of administration and economic development in Iraq. Those who could escape migrated from Kufa to find new economic opportunities in western Iran. It is not, therefore, surprising to find disenchanted

---

[10] K. V. Zettersteen, "Yūsuf ibn Omar," in *E.I.*, III (Leiden, 1934), 1177.

Arabs and *Mawālī* engaging in common anti-regime activities by
that time. As one scholar has written:

Such polarization also enhanced the attraction of religious piety as an
alternative source of status and to express disapproval of worldly success.
The piety of the Khawarij was both a matter of religious status and
justification for revolt while the Messianic elite of the Kaysāniyya Shī'a
invented their own alternate status.[11]

For all of the preceding reasons, then, the Umayyad rulers faced
almost constant challenges in the Iraqi provinces. Individuals and
groups resisting the Damascene dynasty were never lacking. The
groups to which this study is devoted were only a small portion of
the rebellious movements that appeared between 661 and 750.
Although the movement that finally overturned the Umayyads
(the 'Abbāsids) began in the eastern provinces, it is clear that
the forces culminating in this revolt had their ultimate origins in
turbulent Iraq.[12]

---

[11] Quoted with the permission of the author from Michael G. Morony, "Status
and Stratification in the Iraqi Amsar" (Paper presented to the Thirteenth
Annual Meeting of the Middle East Studies Association at Salt Lake City, Utah,
on November 10, 1979.). Further details were provided to me in a personal
communication from Professor Morony, and I am grateful to him for this
information. For an exhaustive treatment of these social issues in Iraq, see his
study, *Iraq after the Muslim Conquest*, cited previously.

[12] For the 'Abbasid revolution and its Iraqi element, see the study of Moshe
Sharon, *Black Banners from the East. The Establishment of the 'Abbasid State –
Incubation of a Revolt* (Jerusalem, 1983), passim. Now one should consult Salah
Said Agha, *The Revolution Which Toppled the Umayyads: Neither Arab Nor Abbasid*
(Leiden, 2005).

1

Earlier Movements

In view of the emphasis placed upon sectarian or group structure in this study, the most logical starting point is an examination of the earliest Shī'ite or proto-Shī'ite group, known as the Saba'iyya, whose name comes from its founder, one 'Abd Allāh ibn Saba', a contemporary of 'Uthmān and 'Alī. There has been much disagreement and uncertainty surrounding the life of this individual and the nature of the movement named for him. Although there has been some doubt as to whether Ibn Saba' ever existed, information found in reliable sources seems to indicate his presence among the partisans of 'Alī.[1] Still one of the best presentations of the source materials for the activities and beliefs of Ibn Saba' and his followers, as well as a detailed and skillful analysis of these materials, is the study of Israel Friedlaender, entitled "'Abd Allāh ibn Saba', der Begrunder der Shī'a, und sein Judischer Ursprung."[2] Although some of Friedlaender's views require modification, perhaps, his general conclusions concerning the activities and beliefs of Ibn Saba' and the Saba'iyya seem to be

---

[1] Abū 'Uthmān 'Amr ibn Bahr al-Jāhiz, *Kitāb al-Bayān wa al-Tabyīn*, II (Cairo, 1949), part III, 81; G. Levi della Vida, "Il Califfato di 'Ali secondo il Kitāb Ansab al-Asraf di al-Baladuri," *RSO*, IV (1914–1915), 495.

[2] Israel Friedlaender, "'Abdallah b. Saba', der Begrunder der Shi'a, und sein judischer Ursprung," *Zeitschrift für Assyriologie*, XXIII (1909), 296–327, IIXIV (1910), 1–46.

9

substantially correct. The significant result of Friedlaender's work is that it demonstrates in a rather conclusive manner that Ibn Saba' and the Saba'iyya did, in fact, exist, at least from the time of 'Alī, and that they came to entertain religious beliefs, at least some of which were adhered to by the groups that are the subject of this study. The reliability of Friedlaender's study has been attested to by Sabatino Moscati, who made substantial use of it in his treatment of the Saba'iyya in an article about the early Shī'a.[3] More recently, Halm has discussed the Saba'iyya issue, especially with emphasis upon the religious facets of Ibn Saba's movement.[4] The following discussion, therefore, will be derived largely from the works of Friedlaender and Halm, with supplementary materials from other sources introduced where necessary.

Traditionally 'Abd Allāh ibn Saba' is said to have been a converted Jew from the Yaman.[5] Based upon his research, G. Levi Della Vida has denied this, maintaining that Ibn Saba' was an Arab. His name, according to this account, was 'Abd Allāh ibn Wahb al-Hamdāni.[6] Friedlaender advances the hypothesis that he was the son of an Ethiopian Falasha woman, adducing this from the information that he is sometimes called Ibn as-Sawda.[7] The heresiographer al-Baghdādī maintains that Ibn Saba' and Ibn as-Sawda were two different individuals.[8] This seems to be the only source to make such a distinction, however. It is quite possible that the imputation of Jewish ancestry to Ibn Saba' on

[3] Sabatino Moscati, "Antica Sī'a," 256.

[4] Halm, *Islamische Gnosis*, 33–42.

[5] Marshall G. S. Hodgson, "'Abdallāh ibn Saba'," in *E.I.*, I (2nd ed., Leiden, 1960), 51.

[6] Levi della Vida, "Califfato di 'Alī," 495.

[7] Friedlaender, "'Abdallah b. Saba'," XXIV, 22–31. This hypothesis is unlikely. The woman might just as easily have been an East African slave. Halm has referred to this issue, but his conclusions regarding Friedlaender's "hypothesis" are unclear. Halm, *Islamische Gnosis*, 41–42.

[8] 'Abd al-Qāhir ibn Tāhir ibn Muhammad al-Baghdādī, *Moslem Schisms and Sects* (*al-Fark bain al-Firak*), trans. A. S. Halkin (Tel Aviv, 1935), 42–43.

his father's side, as well as the attribution of black descent on his mother's side, was designed to discredit his credentials as a Muslim Arab and thus stigmatize all ideas associated with him.

Whatever is the case regarding his ethnic identity, it is quite probable that Ibn Saba' was a Yamanite, and that he came from a Jewish milieu and may have been exposed to Monophysite ideas.[9] If, as Levi della Vida maintains, Ibn Saba' was an Arab, it would appear, on the basis of Levi della Vida's source, that he belonged to the Bānu Hamdān, a tribe that may have accepted Judaism at the time of Dhū Nuwas.[10] The fact that his religious ideas bear close resemblance in some respects to those of Christianity may be explained in any one of three ways. The form of Judaism adopted in the Yaman was probably different from the official Judaism of the time.[11] In addition, as noted previously, Monophysite Christianity seems to have been present in the Yaman from an early date.[12] This may have had an impact upon the form of Judaism practiced. Finally, the close contacts with Ethiopia may have exposed the people of Yaman to Ethiopian Monophysitism or even the doctrines of the Falashas, whose religious views bear certain similarities to Monophysite beliefs.[13] We should also note at this point that Ibn Saba' may very well have come under the

---

[9] Friedlaender, "'Abdallah b. Saba'," XXIV, 27–31. Monophysitism and Nestorianism appear in South Arabia at an early date. There were Nestorian churches and bishops in Sanā', for example. For Monophysitism consult the following: Ernest Honigmann, *Eveques et Eveches Monophysites d'Asie Anterieure au IVe siècle* (Louvain, 1951), 129–130; anon., *The Book of the Himyarites*, trans. Axel Moberg (Leipzig, 1924), lii; Philip K. Hitti, *History of the Arabs* (8th ed., New York, 1963), 61. Concerning the Nestorians, particularly in Sanā', consult Thomas, Bishop of Marga, *The Book of Governors*, II, trans. E. A. W. Budge (London, 1893), 448; A. S. Atiya, *History of Eastern Christianity* (Notre Dame, Ind., 1968), 259; Bertold Spuler, *Die Gegenwartslage der Ostkirchen in ihrer volkischen und staatlichen Umwelt* (Wiesbaden, 1948), 124.

[10] J. Schleifer and W. Montgomery Watt, "Hamdān," *E.I.*2, III, fasc. 41–42 (Leiden, 1965), 123.

[11] Friedlaender, "'Abdallah b. Saba'," XXIV, 26–27.

[12] Hitti, *Arabs*, 61.

[13] Friedlaender, "'Abdallah b. Saba'," XXIV, 28–31.

influence of other religions after his arrival in Iraq, where it would seem that he was located, at least at the time of 'Alī's caliphate.

Some have argued that Tabarī's account of Ibn Saba's conspiracy against 'Uthmān is a fabrication of Sayf ibn 'Umar. It has been suggested, in fact, that Sayf was generally unreliable.[14] One cannot sustain this opinion, however. Although Sayf may have been something less than a scrupulously accurate *Hadīth* scholar, this does not detract from his overall reliability as an *Akhbārī*, in other words, a transmitter of historical information rather than religious traditions.[15]

There is no doubt that Sayf had certain biases. His work reflects the Iraqi point of view with a strong Tamīmī coloring. This is not unusual, however; the work of other *Akhbāris*, such as Abū Mikhnaf, 'Awānah ibn al-Hakam, Nasr ibn Muzāhim, and al-Haytham ibn 'Adī was also influenced by tribal, regional, political, and sectarian considerations.

Friedlaender argues that Sayf's account of Ibn Saba' was invented for the purpose of finding a scapegoat for the troubles surrounding 'Uthmān. He suggests that Sayf sought to cast the blame on Ibn Saba' in order to absolve the Companions of any complicity in the strife resulting in the death of the third caliph.[16] Whereas this may have been the case, there is no concrete evidence to support such a contention. Even if Sayf's treatment of Ibn Saba' was a fabrication, the question arises as to whether Sayf himself was responsible for it. He appears to have been only the transmitter of the story and, thus, not necessarily the ultimate source of it. It would seem, however, that the accounts of Ibn Saba' and the Saba'iyya to be found in the sources devoted to

---

[14] Hodgson, "Ibn Saba'," 51.

[15] With respect to Sayf's role as an historian, as opposed to a transmitter of *Hadīth*, see Ella Landau-Tasseron's nuanced treatment in "Sayf ibn 'Umar in Medieval and Modern Scholarship," *Der Islam,* 67 (1990), 1–26.

[16] Friedlaender, "'Abdallah b. Saba'," XXIII, 315.

the heresies are more complete in doctrinal and historical information, particularly for the Saba'iyya.

As to the report that 'Alī is supposed to have had Ibn Saba' and his followers burned for declaring him to be God, one strongly suspects that this is an invention. In the first place it is highly doubtful that he deified 'Alī, a point that will be examined later. More significantly it is quite impossible that Ibn Saba' should have died before 'Alī, since this would completely negate the doctrines that he and the Saba'iyya appear to have professed. The entire burning incident is perhaps a projection into the past of the execution of *Ghulāt* figures by Khālid ibn 'Abd Allāh al-Qasrī and Yūsuf ibn 'Umar.[17] What is likely is that 'Alī banished Ibn Saba' to Madā'in because of the latter's excessive veneration of him.[18] Beyond the fragments of information mentioned in the previous pages, nothing is known of Ibn Saba's origins and activities.

Fortunately, more information is available for the religious ideas of the man and his followers. They are said to have deified 'Alī, for which he put them to death. As has been indicated, this is probably not true. In the first place the manner in which this account is presented is very reminiscent of the story about the Rāwandiyya and their encounter with Abū Ja'far al-Manṣūr.[19] One is led to believe that the sources have wrongly attributed such a belief to the Saba'iyya and have invented the execution, the episode of the Rāwandiyya and al-Manṣūr serving as the model for this fiction. Friedlaender argues that this may have been an invention of moderate Shī'ites seeking to cast 'Alī in the role of the foremost enemy of the *Ghulāt*.[20] If one considers that the Sa'baiyya were probably the first proto-Shī'ite sect (as opposed

[17] Ibid., 318.
[18] A. S. Tritton, *Muslim Theology* (London, 1947), 20; Guy Le Strange, *The Lands of the Eastern Caliphate* (New York, 1966), 33.
[19] Friedlaender, "'Abdallah b. Saba'," XXIII, 317.
[20] Ibid., 316–318.

to a pro-ʿAlī political faction or individual ʾAlid supporters), one
may speculate that Sunni authors sought to attribute the Incarnation idea, one of the cardinal tenets of many *Ghulāt*, to this
early group. The intention here would be to discredit Shīʿism
generally by arguing that it contained extremist ideas from its
inception.[21]

In reality, the basic tenet of the religious system of Ibn Sabaʾ
and his followers appears to have been the denial of ʿAlī's death.
They are supposed to have said that ʿAlī had not died, that a
devil had assumed his form and died in his place.[22] This is
strikingly similar to a belief of some early Christian groups,
which taught that Christ had suffered only in appearance, not in
reality.[23] There are traces of this idea, known as *Docetism*, in the
New Testament and in the works of the Apostolic Fathers.[24] It
was quite prevalent among the Gnostics, assuming various forms.
According to the Valentinians (second century A.D.), for example, the body of Jesus was a heavenly psychical formation that
sprang from the womb of Mary in appearance only. Saturninus denied the birth of Christ, whose physical embodiment, he
believed, was only a phantom.[25] A view nearer to that of Ibn
Sabaʾ was held by Basilides, who believed that Christ had been
made manifest in human form. He had descended to the earth

---

[21] Ibid., 319.
[22] Ibid., 326. Cf. al-Baghdādī, *Schisms* (trans. Halkin), 42; al-Hasan ibn Mūsā al-
    Nawbakhtī, *Firaq al-Shīʿa* (Najaf, Iraq, 1959), 43–44; French trans. by Muham-
    mad J. Mashkūr, "Al-Nawbakhti. Les Sectes Shiʿites," *Revue de l'Histoire des
    Religions*, CLIII (1958), 199.
[23] anon., "Docetism," in *The Oxford Dictionary of the Christian Church* (London,
    1958), 409. See also the comments of Kurt Rudolph in *Gnosis: The Nature and
    History of Gnosticism*, trans. and ed. Robert M. Wilson (San Francisco, 1983),
    157–158.
[24] Adrian Fortescue, "Docetism," in *Hastings Encyclopædia of Religion and Ethics*,
    IV (New York, 1961), 832.
[25] Adolph Harnack, *History of Dogma*, I, trans. from the German 3rd ed. Neil
    Buchanan (Boston, 1905), 259–260.

and worked miracles, but he had not suffered. At the moment of his crucifixion, one Simon of Cyrene had been substituted for him, and he had ascended to Heaven.[26] Manichaean religious doctrines also included the denial of the actual crucifixion and suffering of Christ.[27] Finally, one may note that according to the Qur'ān, Jesus was not killed on the cross but was raised to Heaven by Allāh. One traditional Muslim interpretation has been that Jesus was in a place of concealment, and that one of his companions was crucified in his place.[28] One may conclude that there are a number of possible sources for Ibn Saba's view of 'Alī's disappearance. Probably it is a reflection of the Qur'ānic idea.

The refusal of the Saba'iyya and Ibn Saba' to believe in 'Alī's death is not surprising. One may recall that 'Umar ibn al-Khattāb would not believe that the Prophet had died and violently rebuked those who declared this. It is even said, according to an account in Tabarī, that he expected Muhammad to return, like Moses, after forty days.[29] The main source for Ibn Saba's disbelief in 'Alī's death is Jāhiz's *Bayān wa Tabyīn*. According to this account, Ibn Saba', after having been informed that 'Alī had been severely wounded, stated that he would not believe that 'Alī had died before "driving you with his stick" even if his brains were brought to him (Ibn Saba') in a hundred bags.[30] When this

---

[26] G. Bareille, "Docetisme," in *Dictionnaire de Théologie Catholique*, IV, part II (Paris, 1939), cols. 1490–1491.

[27] A. A. Bevan, "Manichaeism," in *E.R.E.*, VIII (New York, 1961), 398. See, more recently, Hans-Joachim Klimkeit, trans. and ed. *Gnosis on the Silk Road: Gnostic Texts from Central Asia.* (San Francisco, 1993), 16; and also the excellent essay of Geo Widengren, "Manichaeism and its Iranian Background," in *The Cambridge History of Iran*, III, part 2 (Cambridge, 1993), 984.

[28] Geoffrey Parrinder, *Jesus in the Qur'an* (New York, 1965), 108–109.

[29] Abū Ja'far Muhammad ibn Jarīr al-Tabarī, *Ta'rīkh al-Rusūl wa al-Mulūk*, I (Leiden, 1964), 1815–1816; Israel Friedlaender, "The Heterodoxies of the Shi'ites in the Presentation of Ibn Hazm: Commentary," *JAOS*, 29 (1908), 24.

[30] al-Jāhiz, *Bayān*, II, part III, 81.

notice is compared with information afforded by other sources, it becomes clear that Ibn Saba' and the Saba'iyya refused to believe that 'Alī had been killed.[31]

Ibn Saba' and his followers maintained that instead of dying, 'Alī had ascended to Heaven, where he resided "in the clouds." The Saba'iyya are said to have believed, moreover, that the thunder was 'Alī's voice and the lightning his whip.[32] This belief that 'Alī was in the clouds may have been a popular one among the early Shī'a. One indication of that may be seen in the report that the poet Ishāq ibn Suwayd al-'Adawī ridiculed those people who gave greetings to the clouds at the mention of 'Alī's name.[33]

Finally Ibn Saba' and the Saba'iyya appear to have affirmed that 'Alī was a messiah who would return to the earth to establish the reign of righteousness and justice, "driving the Arabs with his stick."[34] As one scholar has pointed out, such a view finds support in the presence among the earlier Shī'a of a view according to which the *Dabbat al-'Ard* (Beast of the Earth) occurring in Muslim eschatology referred to 'Alī, who was expected to return to earth before the Day of Judgment.[35] Other evidence for a belief in 'Alī's return comes from al-Madā'inī, who reports that al-Hasan ibn 'Alī protested against the teaching that his father would return to this earth before the time of the resurrection, an idea espoused by

[31] Friedlaender, "'Abdallah b. Saba'," XXIII, 324–326.
[32] Muhammad ibn 'Abd al-Karīm al-Shahrastānī, *al-Milal wa al-Nihal*, I (Cairo, 1961), 184.
[33] Friedlaender, "Ibn Hazm: Commentary," 42–43.
[34] Friedlaender, "'Abdallah b. Saba'," XXIII, 327; Hodgson, "Early Shī'a," 2–3; Tritton, *Theology*, 20.
[35] Frants Buhl, "Alidernes Stilling til de Shi'istke Bevaegelser under Umajjaderne," *Oversigt over de Kgl. Danske Videnskabernes Selskaba Forhandlingen*, 5 (Copenhagen, 1910), 326 (8 of the offprint). A more recent and significant treatment of the issue of the *Dabbat al-'Ard* is presented by Muhammad Osman Salih in his fascinating and definitive dissertation "Mahdiism in Islam up to 260 A. H./847 a.d. and Its Relation to Zoroastrianism, Jewish, and Christian Messianism," Ph.D. diss. (University of Edinburgh, 1976), 113–120.

certain people of the time.[36] It should be noted in passing that the belief in *Raj'a* (return from the dead) appears to have been held by some Arabs in pre-Islamic times.[37]

There seem to be several possible sources for Ibn Saba''s messianic concept. One may be termed, broadly speaking, Yamanite. Under this name one might include Yamanite Judaism and Monophysite Christianity. Friedlaender considers the Falasha messianic doctrine the chief influence in this area.[38] This seems a rather remote possibility. In view of the mixture of religious currents in the Yaman, it is impossible to state with any certainty that the idea is derived from any one religious community. An alternative possibility is that the idea stems from the Zoroastrian *Saoshyant*, the world restorer who is to appear in the last days.[39] Perhaps Ibn Saba' encountered such an idea through the Persian influence in Yaman or through the Persians in Kufa or Madā'in.

It is also possible that the Saba'iyya messianic idea grew out of messianic expectations current among at least a segment of the South Arabians at an early date. It has been suggested recently that the earliest mention of the *Mahdī* with the connotation "saviour" or "deliverer" comes from Ka'b al-Ahbar, a South

---

[36] M. J. de Goeje, "Al-Beladhori's Ansab al-Aschraf," *Zeitschrift der Deutschen Morgenlandischen Gesellschaft*, XXXVIII (1884), 391.

[37] E. W. Lane, "Raj'ah," in *Lane's Arabic-English Lexicon*, book I, part III (New York, 1961), 1040; Marshall G. S. Hodgson, "Ghulāt," *E.I.*2, II (Leiden, 1965), 1094.

[38] Friedlaender, "'Abdallah b. Saba'," IIXIV, 37.

[39] Said A. Arjomand, "Religion and the Diversity of Normative Orders," in *The Political Dimensions of Religion*, ed. Said A. Arjomand (Albany, N.Y., 1993), 53–60; R. N. Frye, *Heritage of Persia* (New York, 1962), 237; A. C. Christensen, *L'Iran sous les Sassanides* (2nd ed. rev., Copenhagen, 1944), 148; Cl. Huart, *Ancient Persia and Iranian Civilization* (New York, 1927), 177; J. W. Waterhouse, *Zoroastrianism* (London, 1934), 125; R. C. Zaehner, *The Teaching of the Magi* (New York, 1956), 85. In his work, *The Zoroastrian Faith: Tradition & Modern Research* (Montreal and Kingston, 1993), 94, S. A. Nigosian points out that the *Saoshyant* is actually the third of three saviour figures to appear before the end of the world.

Arabian. It is possible that he was reflecting a view held by at least a portion of his fellow South Arabians[40] Perhaps this is the genesis of the South Arabian *al-Qaḥṭānī*, the tribal messiah. This figure is more clearly defined by the time of Abū Hurayra al-Yamani (d. 679), who relates a tradition that says that the hour of resurrection will not arrive until a man from Qaḥṭān comes, "driving the people."[41] The *Qaḥṭānī* idea seems to have reached its full development by the time of the revolt of ʿAbd al-Rahmān ibn al-Ashʿath, who proclaimed himself the awaited *al-Qaḥṭānī*.[42] Possibly, then, the *Qaḥṭānī* idea was one of the sources for Ibn Sabaʾ's messianism.

In evaluating the contributions of Ibn Sabaʾ and the Sabaʾiyya, it seems evident that they were the first to introduce into Shīʿism certain concepts of fundamental importance. The first of these, noted previously, was Docetism. Also numbered among their beliefs was the *Ghayba* (concealment) of the religious leader.[43] This idea was to have particular significance among both the moderate and extreme Shīʿa. The followers of al-Mughīra ibn Saʿīd and ʿAbd Allāh ibn Jaʿfar were to include it among their doctrinal systems. The return (*Rajʿa*) of a *Mahdī* (messianic figure) was to be of paramount importance for later Shīʿism.[44] We see the central position of this last doctrine in the religious beliefs of the Bayāniyya, the Mughīriyya, the Mansūriyya, and the Janāhiyya. Although Ibn Sabaʾ spoke about a messiah, he does not appear,

[40] C. L. Geddes, "The Messiah in South Arabia," *Muslim World*, CVII (1967), 319. An excellent account of the *Qaḥṭānī* and related apocalyptic prophecies among the South Arabians can be found in Wilferd Madelung's article, "Apocalyptic Prophecies in Hims in the Umayyad Age," *Journal of Semitic Studies*, XXXVI, part 2 (1986), 141–185, especially 151–156.

[41] Ibid., 313.

[42] Ibid., 315; Cf. B. van Vloten, *Recherches sur la Domination Arabe, le Chiʿitisme et les Croyances Messianiques sous le Califat des Omayyades* (Amsterdam, 1894), 61.

[43] Moscati, "Antica Sīʿa," 256.

[44] Abū al-Hasan ʿAlī ibn Ismāʿīl al-Ashʿarī, *Maqālāt al-Islāmiyyin*, I (Cairo, 1954), 85; Shahrastānī, *Milal*, I, 184.

it should be noted, to have used the word *"Mahdī"* as a designation for this figure.

al-Mukhtār and the Kaisāniyya

One of the most important of all early Shī'ite movements was that of al-Mukhtār ibn Abī 'Ubayd al-Thaqafī. Surprisingly enough, there is no recent, in-depth Western-language historiographical analysis of this man and the events surrounding him in late seventh-century Kufa. Fortunately, one does have the dissertation of Michael Fishbein, "The Life of al-Mukhtār b. Abī 'Ubayd in Some Early Arabic Historians," which offers us translations and critiques of the relevant sources for this subject. Fishbein has also translated the important volume of Tabarī, which is relevant here as well.[45] There is also Wadād al-Qāḍī's important study of the Kaisāniyya, referred to in the preface, but, unfortunately, it has not yet been translated into a Western language. Although a detailed discussion of the background and activities of al-Mukhtār is outside the scope of this study, it is necessary to note briefly some of the more important events of his life. Particular attention will be given to the great rebellion he raised in Kufa, ideas crystallized by him or others during the course of this uprising, and, especially, the nature of the sectarian movement that it spawned.

Al-Mukhtār was the son of Abū 'Ubayd al-Thaqafī, who was martyred at the Battle of the Bridge (634). He is reported to have been born in 622, but this date is uncertain. Very little is known of his early life. He is said to have behaved badly toward al-Hasan ibn 'Alī when the latter took refuge from Mu'āwiya in the

---

45 Michael Fishbein, "The Life of al-Mukhtār ibn Abī 'Ubayd in Some Early Arabic Historians," Ph.D. diss. (The University of California at Los Angeles, 1988); Abū Ja'far Muhammad ibn Jarīr al-Tabarī, *Ta'rikh al-rusūl wa al-Mulūk*, Engl. trans.: *The Victory of the Marwanids*, vol. 21, trans. Michael Fishbein (Albany, N.Y. 1990).

home of al-Mukhtār's uncle, Sa'd ibn Mas'ūd, who had adopted
his orphaned nephew. By 680 or 681, however, al-Mukhtār had
undergone a change of heart, for he is known to have collaborated with Muslim ibn 'Aqīl. Because of this he was imprisoned,
regaining his freedom only after the death of al-Husayn.[46]

After this, al-Mukhtār appears to have attached himself to
'Abd Allāh ibn al-Zubayr, who had installed himself as the anti-
Umayyad champion. In 684 al-Mukhtār traveled to Kufa. Upon
his arrival in this city, he began to seek the support of the Shī'a,
at that time under the influence of one Sulaymān ibn Surad. Ibn
Surad and his followers, known as the *Tawwabūn* (Penitents),
fought to demonstrate their repentance for having deserted al-
Husayn in his time of need. They pledged themselves to avenge
his death.[47] Belittling the leadership of Ibn Surad, al-Mukhtār
began to win over the Shī'a, calling upon them to recognize the
Imāmate of Muhammad ibn al-Hanafiyya, a son of 'Alī named after
his mother's tribe.[48] Al-Mukhtār, like Ibn Surad, called upon the
people to avenge the blood of al-Husayn, and this became one
of the primary themes of his movement.[49] All of this activity
led the Zubayrid governor, 'Abd Allāh ibn Yazīd al-'Ansārī, to
imprison him. At the beginning of 685, Ibn Surad and his adherents met an Umayyad army under 'Ubayd Allāh ibn Ziyād at a
place called 'Ayn Warda, near Ra's al-'Ayn (in the region of Upper
Mesopotamia).[50] The Penitents were thoroughly defeated, and
Ibn Surad lost his life. At this point al-Mukhtār was released from

[46] G. Levi della Vida, "*Mukhtār*," in *E.I.*1, III (Leiden, 1936), 715–716.
[47] Watt, "Umayyad Shī'ism," 158.
[48] Levi della Vida, "*Mukhtār*," in *E.I.*1, III, 715–716.
[49] Ahmad ibn Da'ūd Abū Hanīfa Dīnawārī, *Akhbār al-Tiwāl* (Cairo, 1960),
288; Ahmad ibn Muhammad ibn 'Abd al-Rabbīhī, *Al-'Iqd al-Farīd*, I (Cairo,
1884/1885), 267; Nawbakhtī, *Firaq*, 45 (trans. Mashkūr), 201; Shahrastānī,
Milal, I, 148.
[50] Julius Wellhausen, *The Arab Kingdom and its Fall*, trans. M. G. Weir (Beirut,
1963), 185; Le Strange, *Lands*, 95.

prison upon giving his word not to take up arms against the Zubayrid government.

As soon as he had been released, al-Mukhtār returned to his anti-Zubayrid activities. He was able to attract to his cause Ibrahim ibn Malik al-ʿAshtar, the son of the able general who had fought for ʿAlī. Late in 685 al-Mukhtār and his supporters rose against ʿAbd Allāh ibn Mutīʿ al-Qārashi, the Zubayrid governor, and expelled him from Kufa. Al-Mukhtār now became the master of the city and extended his power throughout Mesopotamia and the eastern regions.[51]

The base of support for al-Mukhtār came, as has frequently been noted, from the *Mawālī*. He seems to have relied upon them to a considerable degree. He is accused of having favored them over the Arabs, and it is certain that he did much to improve their situation.[52] For this reason, they flocked to him in large numbers.[53] Many of the Kufan Arabs became angered at the unprecedented favor shown the *Mawālī*, and, taking advantage of the absence of Ibrahim ibn Malik al-ʿAshtar and his army, they attempted to overthrow al-Mukhtār.[54] Al-Mukhtār managed to recall Ibrahim ibn Malik al-ʿAshtar, who quickly put down the counterrevolution. Al-Mukhtār now lost no time in initiating his program for avenging al-Husayn. Many people who were alleged to have had a hand in the death of al-Husayn or who had neglected to aid him were put to death.[55]

Whereas the *Mawālī* were the mainstay of al-Mukhtār's movement, one should not forget that several Arab tribes were to be

[51] Levi della Vida, "Mukhtār," in *E.I.*1, III, 716.
[52] ʿIzz al-Dīn ibn al-Athīr, *al-Kāmil fī al-Taʾrīkh*, IV (Beirut, 1965), 231; Tabarī, *Taʾrīkh*, II, 650–651.
[53] Dīnawārī, *Akhbār*, 288, 293; Cf. N. V. Pigulevskaja, A. Ju. Jakubovskij, et al., *Istorija Irana s drevnejšix vremën do konca XVIII veka* (Leningrad, 1958), 97.
[54] Ibid., 299.
[55] Ahmad ibn Yahyā al-Balādhurī, *Kitāb al-Ansāb wa al-Ashrāf*, V (Jerusalem, 1936), 236–241; Ibn al-Athīr, *al-Kāmil*, IV, 241–244.

found in his ranks. The Banū Hamdān, a South Arabian tribe, were strong supporters of al-Mukhtār.[56] Groups belonging to this tribe were involved in an episode concerning a chair that was alleged to have belonged to ʿAlī. Those involved were the clans of Shibām, Khārif, and Shākir.[57] Also numbered among the supporters of al-Mukhtār and noted, too, for their role in the incident of the chair were the Banū Nahd, another South Arabian tribe.[58] This is of particular interest, because, as we shall have occasion to point out, Bayān ibn Samʿān seems to have been a member of this tribe.[59] Some elements of the Banū Kinda appear to have been among the adherents of al-Mukhtār. They are said, for instance, to have fought in the army of Ibrahim at the Battle of the Khāzir.[60] Here again this is of special interest, because the Kinda are said to have been prominent in the movements of al-Mughīra ibn Saʿīd and Abū Mansūr.[61] The same is true in the case of some sectors of the Bajīla, who fought for al-Mukhtār at the disastrous battle at Madhār.[62] It is interesting to note that all of these tribes are South Arabian. On the basis of this information, then, it is clear that al-Mukhtār's movement was far from being a purely *Mawālī* affair.

Having rid himself of the major opposition within Kufa, al-Mukhtār turned his attention to external threats. An Umayyad army, led by ʿUbayd Allāh ibn Ziyād, was making its way toward Kufa. Al-Mukhtār now dispatched Ibrahim and his army to intercept the Umayyad force. In August 686 (10 Muḥarram 67 A.H.)

---

[56] Balādhurī, *Ansāb*, V, 242.

[57] Balādhurī, *Ansab*, V, 242; W. Caskel, *Gamharat an-Nasab des Genealogische Werk des Hisam Ibn Muhammad al-Kalbi*, I (Leiden, 1966), tables 227, 228, 230.

[58] Balādhurī, *Ansāb*, V, 242.

[59] Nawbakhtī, *Firaq*, 49 (trans. Mashkūr), 206.

[60] Tabarī, *Ta'rīkh*, II, 702; Balādhurī, *Ansāb*, V, 248.

[61] Abū Muhammad ʿAbd Allāh ibn Muslim ibn Qutayba, *ʿUyūn al-Akhbār*, II (Cairo, 1964), 146–147.

[62] Ibid. Cf. Balādhurī, *Ansāb*, V, 254; Tabarī, *Ta'rīkh*, II, 722.

the two armies met on the banks of the Khāzir River. 'Ubayd
Allāh's army was completely routed, and 'Ubayd Allāh himself
was killed.[63] This was the greatest and the last triumph of al-
Mukhtār. Mus'ab ibn al-Zubayr, the brother of the anti-caliph
'Abd Allāh, who held Basra in the name of the latter and who
was the commander of his forces in Iraq, took the decisive step
of moving against al-Mukhtār. He was at the head of an experienced army that had been augmented by those Arab notables
who had fled Kufa after their failure to overturn al-Mukhtār. Not
long after the Khāzir battle, the armies of Mus'ab and al-Mukhtār
met at the town of al-Madhār, four days' journey from Basra. Al-
Mukhtār's army was beaten.[64] Shortly after this Mus'ab inflicted a
crushing defeat upon al-Mukhtār at Harūra.[65] This was, in effect,
the end of the rebellion. Although al-Mukhtār escaped to Kufa
and managed to hold out for several months, his power was at
an end after the disaster at Harūra.

Before turning to the ideas of the Kaisāniyya, the religious
group that formed around al-Mukhtār, it is necessary to glance
briefly at the views that al-Mukhtār himself espoused. His major
claim was that the *Imāmate* (the spiritual and juridical leadership of the Muslim community) belonged rightfully to Muhammad ibn al-Hanafiyya.[66] He also referred to Ibn al-Hanafiyya as
the *Mahdī*.[67] The originality of his contribution in this respect
consisted in providing his followers with a leader of great religious and political significance – a messianic figure around whom
would cluster the hopes of the exploited and the oppressed. The

[63] Abū Hasan 'Alī ibn Husayn al-Mas'ūdī, *Kitāb Tanbīh wa al-Ishrāf* (Cairo, 1948),
270.
[64] Tabarī, *Ta'rīkh*, II, 720–723; Le Strange, *Lands*, 42–43.
[65] Tabarī, *Ta'rīkh*, II, 726–727.
[66] anon., *Ta'rīkh al-Khulafā'* (Moscow, 1967), 245b; Nawbakhtī, *Firaq*, 45 (trans.
Mashkūr), 201; Shahrastānī, *Milal*, I, 148.
[67] D. B. Macdonald, "Mahdī," in *Shorter Encyclopædia of Islam* (Ithaca, N.Y., 1965),
310.

followers of al-Mukhtār, as we have seen, were not the first Shī'ites to speak of the messiah, since Ibn Saba' had done so earlier. It is quite possible, however, that the Saba'iyya's view of 'Alī provided the basis for the messianic ideas of the Kaisāniyya. The Saba'iyya must still have been present in Kufa at the time of al-Mukhtār. Friedlaender maintains that there was a difference between the messianic concepts of the Kaisāniyya and Ibn Saba', in that the messiah of the former retains a more human aspect than that of Ibn Saba'.[68] This will be referred to in greater detail elsewhere.

Al-Mukhtār's exaltation of Ibn al-Hanafiyya was probably the most important aspect of his ideology. As for the attitude of Ibn al-Hanafiyya toward al-Mukhtār, it would seem that he neither acknowledged nor disavowed his self-appointed deputy.[69] It should be emphasized that Ibn al-Hanafiyya and, for that matter, later 'Alids in whose names groups formed played no role in these sects.

Al-Mukhtār is supposed to have claimed prophecy for himself or, at least, to have allowed it to be ascribed to him.[70] He seems to have declared that this revelation was brought to him by the angel Gabriel.[71] He also is said to have stated that the revelation was made in *saj'*, or rhymed prose.[72] At any rate, we do know that he himself was given to speaking and writing in *saj'*. The sources compare him to the pre-Islamic *Kāhins*, or soothsayers.[73] This manner of speaking no doubt lent an impressive

---

[68] Friedlaender, "'Abdallah b. Saba'," XXIV, 18.

[69] Tabarī, *Ta'rīkh*, II, 607.

[70] Mutahhār ibn Tāhir al-Maqdisī, *Kitāb al-Bad' wa al-Ta'rīkh*, V (Baghdad, 1916), 131; Abū Muzāffar Shahfūr ibn Tāhir al-Isfarā'īnī, *al-Tabsīr fī al-Dīn* (Cairo, 1940), 20.

[71] Balādhurī, *Ansāb*, V, 272.

[72] Muhammad ibn Yazīd al-Mubarrad, *Al-Kāmil*, III (Cairo, 1956), 264.

[73] 'Abd al-Qāhir ibn Tāhir ibn Muhammad al-Baghdādī, *Moslem Schisms and Sects (al Fark bain al-Firak)*, trans. K. C. Seelye (New York, 1919), 54; al-Mubarrad, *al-Kāmil*, III, 264.

bearing to the man and tended to corroborate his allegations of possessing special powers. One may compare him in this regard to the *prophetae* of medieval Europe, whose success seems to have been the result, in large measure, of their commanding presence and their eloquence.[74]

One of the more mysterious religious practices of al-Mukhtār concerns the supposed chair of ʿAlī. The details of this are presented in such a fashion as to discredit al-Mukhtār, but the accounts seem to be accurate in their essentials. According to one version, a native of Kufa named Ibn Tufayl had a neighbor, an oil merchant, who had in his possession an old, dilapidated chair. Ibn Tufayl decided to put it to good use. Having procured the chair from its owner, he cleaned it and then informed al-Mukhtār that he had a chair that contained a trace of (the spirit of) ʿAlī. Al-Mukhtār demanded the chair, and Ibn Tufayl handed it over to him, receiving a generous reward in the process.[75] Al-Mukhtār then summoned the people and, indicating the chair, likened it to the Ark of the Covenant of the Israelites.[76] He claimed that the chair would do for them what the Ark had done for the Israelites, that is, protect them against their enemies.[77] A number of South Arabian groups appear to have revered this chair, particularly the Shākir, Shibām, and the Khārif clans of the Banū Hamdān. The Banū Nahd also were known for their veneration of the chair. These groups are said to have covered the chair with a cloth of silk.[78] This last piece of information calls to mind the veil behind which the Israelites were enjoined to place the Ark.[79] The veneration paid the chair by the South Arabians is understandable if

[74] Norman Cohn, *The Pursuit of the Millenium* (2nd ed., New York, 1961), 70.

[75] Ibn al-Athīr, *al-Kāmil*, IV, 258.

[76] Tabarī, *Ta'rīkh*, II, 702.

[77] Ibn al-Athīr, *al-Kāmil*, IV, 259; Isaac Husik, "Ark of the Covenant," in *Jewish Encyclopædia*, II (New York, 1902), 105.

[78] Balādhurī, *Ansāb*, V, 242.

[79] Husik, "Ark of the Covenant," *J.E.*, II, 105.

one keeps in mind the strong Jewish influence in the homeland
of these groups, namely, the Yaman. One should also remember
that there is a possibility that at least some of the Banū Hamdān
had accepted Judaism in pre-Islamic days.[80]

It is of some interest to note that the followers of the chair are
referred to as Saba'iyya.[81] Friedlaender maintains that this does
not refer to followers of Ibn Saba', but rather to another name for
the South Arabians, who constituted the group paying homage
to the chair. As noted above, he denies a connection between
the followers of Ibn Saba' and the followers of al-Mukhtār on the
grounds that their messianic conceptions differ.[82] This difference should not be exaggerated, however. The essential aspect
of the messianic belief for both groups was the coming of a hero
who would establish righteousness and justice. This was undoubtedly of greater importance to these people than whether or not
the messiah was superhuman or merely a superior human being.
It is quite possible that the followers of Ibn Saba' simply substituted the *Mahdī* of the Kaisāniyya for their expected messiah and
supported al-Mukhtār actively. There is no way of proving this,
but it seems preferable to the rather uncertain interpretation
Friedlaender gives the word "*Saba'iyya*," a particularly hazardous
explanation if one notes that the historians usually refer to the
South Arabians as *Ahl al-Yaman*.

Al-Mukhtār is also reported to have claimed that angels aided
his followers in battle. This is said to have been suggested to
him by one Surāqa ibn Mirdās al-Bāriqi, who pretended to have
seen the angels fighting with al-Mukhtār's troops.[83] He appears
to have done this in order to save his life, as he had been among
the Arab notables attempting to overthrow al-Mukhtār when

---

[80] Schleifer and Watt, "Hamdān," in *E.I.*2, III, fasc. 41–42, 123.
[81] Tabarī, *Ta'rīkh*, II, 702; C. van Arendonk, "Kaisāniya," in *Shorter E.I.* (Ithaca,
N.Y., 1965), 208–209.
[82] Friedlaender, "'Abdallah b. Saba'," XXIV, 16–18.
[83] Balādhurī, *Ansāb*, V, 234.

captured. It is said that al-Mukhtār freed him for saying this.[84] There is no way of knowing the truth of the matter, because the incident seems intended to discredit al-Mukhtār.

A more significant contribution of al-Mukhtār was the concept of *Badā'*. This is the belief that, through the intervention of special circumstances, God changes his will.[85] It is probable that al-Mukhtār invented this concept, although the account in Tabarī states that it was the work of one 'Abd Allāh ibn Nawf.[86] Al-Mukhtār appears to have originated this doctrine in order to explain the defeat inflicted upon his forces by Mus'ab's army. He had claimed before the battle of Madhār that God had promised him victory.[87] This doctrine was to be of some importance in later Shī'ite thought. It would be found to be a convenient explanation for the failure of the Shī'a to secure power.

The religious group that formed around Mukhtār at the time of the rebellion bore the name Kaisāniyya, as indicated before. According to some sources, Kaisān was the nickname of al-Mukhtār.[88] In all probability, however, this appellation refers to the person who was the head of al-Mukhtār's bodyguard, Kaisān Abū 'Amr. This same Kaisān is supposed to have been the leader of the *Mawālī* contingent at the battle of Madhār.[89]

The basic belief of the Kaisāniyya was the same as that of al-Mukhtār, namely the *Imāmate* of Ibn al-Hanafiyya and the claim that he was the *Mahdī*.[90] According to Shahrastānī, they held the view that he was the master of all wisdom, having obtained from his brothers al-Hasan and al-Husayn mystical and esoteric

---

[84] al-Baghdādī, *Schisms* (trans. Seelye), 56.

[85] Ignaz Goldziher, "Bada'," in *Shorter E.I.* (Ithaca, N.Y., 1965), 53–54.

[86] Shahrastānī, *Milal*, I, 148; Tabarī, *Ta'rikh*, II, 732.

[87] Isfarā'īnī, *Tabsīr*, 20; Shahrastānī, *Milal*, I, 149.

[88] al-Baghdādī, *Schisms* (trans. Seelye), 48; al-Ash'arī, *Maqālāt*, I, 89–90.

[89] Balādhurī, *Ansāb*, 237–253.

[90] Abū Hasan 'Alī ibn Husayn al-Mas'ūdī, *Murūj al-Dhahab*, III (Beirut, 1965), 77; Maqdisī, *Bad'*, V, 131; Nawbakhtī, *Firaq*, 48 (trans. Mashkūr), 204.

knowledge, as well as knowledge of celestial spheres and souls.[91]
Opinion differed as to how he had come to be *Imām*. One group
claimed that 'Alī had specified him directly. Another felt that the
designation had come from al-Husayn.[92]

One group of the Kaisāniyya bore the name *Khashabiyya*, "club
bearers,"[93] which refers to the fact that many of the Kaisāniyya
appear to have used clubs as their battle weapons. This group is
especially noted for having traveled to Mecca in order to protect
Ibn al-Hanafiyya from Ibn al-Zubayr, who had threatened him
because he did not recognize the Zubayrid government. It is
said, in fact, that they used clubs on this occasion, refusing to
enter the holy area with swords.[94] According to one source, their
name comes from their use of clubs against the Umayyads at the
battle of the Khāzir.[95] It has been suggested that the club was the
customary weapon of the peasants in Mesopotamia, but it is quite
probable that the use of the clubs was influenced by the belief
that iron weapons should not be used until the coming of the
Mahdī.[96] In this regard it is interesting to note that the followers
of al-Mughīra and Abū Mansūr appear also to have avoided the
use of iron weapons. More will be said concerning this matter in
another section.

Upon the death of Ibn al-Hanafiyya, the Kaisāniyya split into
different groups. One major division claimed that the *Imāmate*
had passed to Abū Hāshim ibn Muhammad ibn al-Hanafiyya.
This group then differed concerning the leadership after Abū
Hāshim. One faction believed that Abū Hāshim had left it to
his brother, 'Alī ibn Muhammad ibn al-Hanafiyya.[97] Another
claimed that the heir of Abū Hāshim was 'Abd Allāh ibn 'Amr

---

[91] van Arendonk, "Kaisāniya," in *Shorter E.I.*, 208–209.
[92] al-Ash'arī, *Maqālāt*, I, 89. Cf. Tritton, *Theology*, 22.
[93] Mas'ūdi, *Tanbīh*, 270.
[94] Balādhurī, *Ansāb*, V, 231.
[95] Maqdisī, *Bad'*, V, 133.
[96] Tritton, *Theology*, 21.
[97] Nawbakhtī, *Firaq*, 52 (trans. Mashkūr), 209.

ibn Harb. They asserted that Ibn Harb was divine.[98] Still another group said that Abū Hāshim had left the leadership to Bayān ibn Sam'ān.[99] This is the Bayāniyya, which will be discussed at length in the following chapter.

Actually, as Moscati has convincingly demonstrated, Abū Hāshim entrusted the direction of his movement to the 'Abbā-sids. This transfer took place in the village of Humayma in Pales-tine, probably in the year 716. Apparently Abū Hāshim, journey-ing from the court of the caliph Sulaymān, had been poisoned on the orders of the latter. Stopping at Humayma, he bequeathed the leadership of his party to the 'Abbāsid Muhammad ibn 'Alī before his death. This testament seems to have involved a transfer of power, complete with the handing over of documents. Moscati points out that this information is confirmed by numerous reli-able sources, both pro-'Abbāsid and pro-'Alid. Further confirma-tion of this transfer may be seen in a fundamental historical fact. Prior to the coming of Abū Hāshim, the 'Abbāsids do not seem to have had any plans for the seizure of political power. They had no party of their own and had no contact with the Shī'a of Iraq. Immediately after the death of Abū Hāshim, however, the Iraqi Shī'a began to obey 'Abbāsid orders, and missionaries represent-ing the 'Abbāsids were dispatched to Khurasan and initiated a propaganda campaign on behalf of their masters. Thus one sees the 'Abbāsids gaining the leadership of a movement that was already well organized.[100]

One portion of the Kaisāniyya did not accept the death of Ibn al-Hanafiyya. This group, known as the Karibiyya (taking their name from one Abū Karib, their leader), believed that Ibn

---

[98] al-Baghdādī, *Schisms* (trans. Seelye), 49.

[99] Ibid.

[100] Bernard Lewis, "Abū Hashim," in *E.I.2*, I (Leiden, 1960), 125; Sabatino Moscati, "Il Testamento di Abū Hashim," *RSO*, XXVIII (1952), 40–44. Humayma was in the province of al-Shar'a, in the neighborhood of the dis-tricts of Amman; G. Le Strange, *Palestine under the Moslems* (Beirut, 1965), 455.

al-Hanafiyya had not died. They asserted that he had gone into concealment on Mount Radwa, seven days' journey from Medina. From there, they believed, he would emerge one day as *Mahdī* and fill the earth with righteousness and justice.[101] This is quite close to the belief of the Saba'iyya, as one may readily see, suggesting the influence of this group upon the Karibiyya. Among the most prominent members of this group were the poets Kuthayyir and al-Sayyid al-Himyari, both of whom were noted for their belief in *Raj'a* or "return." They are also said to have believed in *Tanāsūkh* (transmigration of souls), an idea of Buddhist or Hindu origin.[102] It appears, however, that they expected the return of Ibn al-Hanafiyya in his own body. For this reason it is improbable that they really entertained any doctrine of transmigration, although it is possible that there were those among the Karibiyya who held such a view. Because their primary doctrine, however, was the return of Ibn al-Hanafiyya as *Mahdī*, it is unlikely that they entertained any idea of his spirit transmigrating to another being. Also numbered among the Karibiyya is one Hamza ibn 'Umāra al-Barbarī. Bayān ibn Sam'ān is said to have been connected with him,[103] an issue to be discussed later.

Among other beliefs held by the Kaisāniyya and its subgroups, one finds the doctrine known as *Badā'*, which was examined above. The Kaisāniyya are also said to have taught that religion consists of obedience to a man. The commands of such men were felt to supersede the prescriptions of the law, these commands being based upon the allegorical interpretation of the law.[104] Hamza ibn 'Umāra is supposed to have declared that whoever

---

[101] Bernard Lewis, *Origins of Ismailism* (Cambridge, 1940), 27; van Arendonk, "Kaisāniya," in *Shorter E.I.*, 209.

[102] Abū al-Faraj 'Alī al-Isfahānī, *Kitāb al-Aghānī*, IX (Beirut, 1957), 4; Muhammad ibn Shākir al-Kutubī, *Fawāt al-Wafayāt*, I (Cairo, 1951), 34.

[103] Watt, "Umayyad Shī'ism," 167.

[104] Shahrastānī, *Milal*, I, 147.

knew the *Imām* could do as he liked.[105] The general effect of these ideas is to excuse members of the sect from the religious duties. Such a position is understandable if one keeps in mind that the normal religious rules were probably identified as the official Umayyad ideology, hence implicated with the regime of the "godless oppressors," as these sectarians tended to view the ruling house. It also seems to accord with the exaggerated veneration of Ibn al-Hanafiyya and his heirs. The mention of the allegorical interpretation of the law at this early date, however, sounds anticipatory. It would seem that such an idea does not appear among the Shī'ite sects until at least the time of Abū Mansūr al-'Ijli, if then. One should bear in mind that Shahrastānī, a late source, seems to be the only one who speaks of this allegorical interpretation of the religious duties.

The rebellion of al-Mukhtār and the movement growing out of it were of particular significance in the development of Shī'ism. One should also stress the new role of the *Mawālī* in Shī'ism. Prior to the rebellion, Shī'ism was primarily an Arab movement. As a result of the activities and teachings of al-Mukhtār, the *Mawālī* came to have an important role in Shī'ite sects. The new significance of the *Mawālī* is reflected, it would seem, in the probability that the Kaisāniyya, one of the most powerful Shī'ite elements in Umayyad times, owed their name to a member of the *Mawālī*, Kaisān Abū 'Amr. As will be seen, they are to be found in most subsequent Shī'ite sects, for example, those of Bayān and al-Mughīra.

It must be recalled, at the same time, that it was not only the *Mawālī* who supported al-Mukhtār. As indicated previously, at least some elements of certain Arab tribes also were strongly involved. Of special interest here is the presence of members of the same tribes among the followers of al-Mughīra ibn Sa'īd and Abū Mansūr, and possibly also those of Bayān.

[105] Nawbakhtī, *Firaq,* 50 (trans. Mashkūr), 207.

Another important feature of the al-Mukhtār-Kaisāniyya movement, one of particular significance for this study, is the emergence of Ibn al-Hanafiyya and Abū Hāshim as important figures in Shīʻite doctrine. Abū Hāshim figures prominently, for
instance, in the ideas of some of the groups forming the major
focus of this study. Bayān and ʻAbd Allāh ibn Jaʻfar claimed
to be his successors. On the basis of this, the movements of
Bayān and Ibn Jaʻfar may have been outgrowths of the
Kaisāniyya.

With the movement of al-Mukhtār the concept of *Mahdī*
appears to have become clearly defined. For the Kaisāniyya, the
Mahdī is plainly a messianic figure, a being whose function is to
establish the rule of justice and right religion. The importance
of this messianic figure in the ideology of the four sects to which
this study is devoted will be noted in the following chapters.

Al-Mukhtār, as suggested previouly, claimed prophecy or, at
any rate, allowed others to attribute it to him. He would appear
to have been the first Shīʻite leader to do so. Such pretensions
were to become a common feature of later extremist Shīʻite
teachings, of particular importance in those of Abū Mansūr al-
ʻIjli, for instance. This pretension was especially abhorrent to the
Umayyad government, whose ideological justification consisted
of their claim to be the guarantors of the message of the last and
greatest of God's prophets.

Al-Mukhtār's followers appear to have given added importance to the concept of the designation of the *Imām* by his predecessor. Such an idea was an earlier development. ʻAlī is supposed
to have appointed al-Hasan as his successor, and the latter is
said to have selected his brother al-Husayn. In the case of the
Kaisāniyya and its subgroups, the idea was associated primarily
with Abū Hāshim.

Finally, one notes with interest the Khashabiyya's use of
wooden weapons against their religious opponents. This seems to
indicate a possible parallel with the practices of strangulation and

stoning employed by the Mughīriyya and the Mansūriyya. The similarity rests upon the avoidance of the use of iron weapons. The probable reason for this is the belief that iron should not be used in a struggle until the advent of the *Mahdī*. There seems to be, again, a connection between the earlier and the later sects.

2

Bayān ibn Samʿān and the Bayāniyya

Among the various authors, early and modern, who have investigated the activities of the four sects under discussion, it is generally agreed that Bayān ibn Samʿān and his followers, the Bayāniyya, were the first of the extremist groups to surface in Iraq. For that reason, we propose looking initially at this group with a view to determining its nature and historical impact. The emphasis will be upon the ideas and tactics that seem to have been peculiar to this group.

Bayān b. Samʿān was of Arab extraction. Some sources refer to him as Bayān al-Tamīmī,[1] but there are strong indications that he did not in fact belong to this tribe. Rather it seems that he was a member of the Banū Nahd, one of the South Arabian tribes that had played an important role in the rebellion of al-Mukhtār in Kufa.[2] Since he was a native of Kufa,[3] where he is supposed to have earned his livelihood as a vendor of straw,[4] one may

---

[1] al-Ashʿarī, *Maqālāt*, I, 66.
[2] Nawbakhtī, *Firaq*, 49 (trans. Mashkūr), 206; Cf. Hodgson, "Early Shīʿa," 7, n.36.
[3] Maqdisī, *Badʾ*, V, 130; Abū ʿAlī Muhammad ibn Ismāʿīl al-Karbalāʾiʾ, *Muntahā al-Maqāl* (Teheran, 1885), 360.
[4] Nawbakhtī, *Firaq*, 50.

conjecture that he was by no means a member of the religious or political establishment of his city.

According to some accounts, Bayān was at one time a follower of an individual named Hamza b. 'Umāra, an adherent of the group known variously as the Karbiyya or Karibiyya. Hamza is said to have called Muhammad b. al-Hanafiyya (the individual to whom al-Mukhtār referred as *Imām* and *Mahdī*) God and himself a prophet.[5] Accused of having married his own daughter, he justified this action with the statement that whoever knew the *Imām* might do as he liked.[6] That Hamza venerated Ibn al-Hanafiyya is quite plausible. That he deified Ibn al-Hanafiyya and married his own daughter may, on the other hand, be examples of distorted information intended to discredit extremists. In any case, it is doubtful that Bayān was associated with Hamza because he, unlike Hamza and the Karibiyya, recognized the leadership of Abū Hāshim b. Muhammad b. al-Hanafiyya. Hamza's insistence that knowledge of the *Imām* freed one from ritual and legal obligations, which we shall see time and again with these extremist Shī'ite movements, may also be a reflection of the antinomianism to be found among certain gnostic and/or millenarian groups elsewhere.[7]

---

[5] Ibid., 49; see also Marshall G. S. Hodgson, "Bayān ibn Sim'ān al-Tamīmī," in *E.I.2*, I (Leiden, 1960), 1116.

[6] Nawbakhtī, *Firaq*, 50.

[7] With respect to antinomianism and gnosticism, see the provocative work of the late Ioan P. Couliano, *The Tree of Gnosis: Gnostic Mythology from Early Christianity to Modern Nihilism*, trans. H. S. Wiesner and the author (San Francisco, 1992), 153, 171, 179, 195, and 205. A very recent and even more controversial treatment of gnosticism also contains some useful remarks on antinomianism: Michael A. Williams, *Rethinking "Gnosticism": An Argument for Dismantling a Dubious Category* (Princeton, N.J., 1996), 172–174. An important and informative instance of antinomianism in millenarian movements is to be seen in the Joachimite Spirituals. Consult Norman Cohn, "Medieval Millenarism: Its Bearing on the Comparative Study of Millenarian Movements," *Millennial Dreams in Action: Essays in Comparative Study*, ed. Sylvia L. Thrupp (The Hague, 1962), 35–37.

According to Murtadā al-Rāzī, Bayān practiced magic.[8] While this information is not corroborated by other sources, it should not, for that reason, be dismissed, because Bayān is known to have engaged in speculation about the Greatest Name of God and the powers to be derived from knowledge of it, a common practice among magicians in the medieval Islamic world. What is more certain is that al-Mughīra b. Saʿīd, Bayān's co-conspirator against the Umayyads, was well known for his magical feats.

In A.D. 737 Bayān and al-Mughīra, after having joined forces, rose in revolt against the Umayyad governor of Iraq, Khālid b. ʿAbd Allāh al-Qasrī.[9] The rebellion was quickly put down, and the leaders as well as some of their followers were executed. Ibn Hazm relates that Bayān and al-Mughīra were executed on the same day.[10] On the contrary, the *Kitāb al-ʿUyūn wa al-Hadāʾiq fī Akhbār al-Haqāʾiq* indicates that Bayān's rebellion and death preceded the rising and execution of al-Mughīra.[11] Most of the primary materials clearly show, however, that Bayān and al-Mughīra shared the leadership of the insurrection and met their deaths on the same occasion. The slanderous verses recorded in Tabarī, purporting to show Khālid's terror at the news of the rebellion, are doubtless nothing more than an effort to make the great Umayyad governor the object of general ridicule.[12] It is a

---

[8] Murtadā ibn Dāʾī al-Rāzī, *Tabṣira al-ʿAwām fī Maʿrifa Maqālāt al-Anām* (Teheran, 1313 A.H.), 169.

[9] Abū Muhammad ʿAlī ibn Ahmad ibn Saʿīd ibn Hazm, "The Heterodoxies of the Shīʿites in the Presentation of Ibn Hazm," trans. Israel Friedlaender, *Journal of the American Oriental Society*, XXVIII (1907), 60; Abū al-Faraj ʿAbd al-Rahmān ibn al-Jawzī, *al-Muntāzam fī Taʾrīkh al-Mulūk wa al-Umām*, Aya Sofya Ms. 3095, fol. 62a. My thanks to the director and staff of the Suleymaniyye Kütübhanesi, Istanbul, for making this and other manuscripts available to me.

[10] Ibn Hazm, "Heterodoxies," *JAOS*, XXVIII (1907), 60.

[11] anon., *Kitāb al-ʿUyūn wa al-Hadāʾiq fī Akhbār al-Haqāʾiq*, ed. M. J. de Goeje, in *Fragmenta Historicum Arabicorum*, I (Leiden, 1871), 231.

[12] Tabarī, *Taʾrīkh*, II, 1621–1622.

reflection of the great hostility of the Iraqis toward Khālid
because of his faithful service to the despised Umayyads.[13]

Unfortunately, little is known about the composition of
Bayān's following. In all probability the *Mawālī* were involved,
as they were included in the group led by al-Mughīra. One may
assume that because Bayān and al-Mughīra collaborated in the
rising of 737, references to the rank and file rebels apply to the
followers of both men. There is no indication of the ethnic identity of the *Mawālī* involved. They may have been Persian, or,
considering the location, they may have belonged to the indigenous Aramaean population of Iraq.[14] Unfortunately, the source
materials do not provide a clue as to Arab participation in the
group recognizing the leadership of Bayān. Here again, one can
simply point out that Arabs from the Banū Kinda, Bajīla, and
'Ijl are known to have belonged to the sect forming around al-
Mughīra. It may then be conjectured that Bayān's group also
included members of these tribes as well as, perhaps, members
of Bayān's own tribe, the Banū Nahd. As noted above, however,
there is no evidence to confirm these speculations.

The nature of the source materials devoted to Islamic sects
makes the task of identifying them especially difficult. Aside from
problems of distortion and occasional outright fabrication, one
of the major defects of these sources is the failure of the authors
to indicate definitively which of the doctrines ascribed to a sect
were actually formulated by the leader of that sect. For example, some accounts attribute doctrines to a certain sect that were
introduced or developed after the death of its founder or leader.
The problem here stems from the fact that the heresiographers
do not indicate the evolution or modification of the beliefs of

[13] Francesco Gabrieli, "Il Califfato di Hishām," *Mémoires de la Société Archéologique d'Alexandrie*, VII (1935), 18.
[14] W. Montgomery Watt, *Islam and the Integration of Society* (Evanston, Ill., 1961), 109.

the sects. Ordinarily these works contain only a statement to the effect that the followers of a specific individual claim that he used to teach a particular doctrine. Obviously there is no certainty that the leader was in fact the originator or adherent of the belief mentioned. Given these limitations, it seems that the only feasible approach is to assume that the beliefs of the sect and the leader were identical, unless there is evidence to the contrary.

It is obvious from an examination of all relevant sources that the fundamental teaching of Bayān and the Bayāniyya was the *Imāmate* of Abū Hāshim, son of Muhammad b. al-Hanafiyya. This suggests some continuity between the movement of Bayān and the rebellion of al-Mukhtār, whose alleged recognition of Ibn al-Hanafiyya has been previously noted. The only source that links Bayān with any other descendant of ʿAlī reports that Bayān was a supporter of Muhammad b. ʿAbd Allāh b. Hasan b. Hasan (known in many instances as *al-Nafs al-Zakiyya*, "the Pure Soul") who, along with his brother, rose in rebellion against the second ʿAbbāsid caliph, Abū Jaʿfar al-Mansūr, and who was put to death by the latter in A.D. 762.[15] This obviously inaccurate information resulted in all probability from confusing Bayān with al-Mughīra, who was an advocate of the *Imāmate* of *al-Nafs al-Zakiyya.*[16]

There are conflicting opinions in the matter of how the Bayāniyya looked upon Abū Hāshim. Some authors maintain that the sect believed Abū Hāshim to be the Incarnate God, having, as it were, inherited this divine status from his father, Ibn al-Hanafiyya, who was also reported to have been the Incarnation.[17]

---

[15] anon., *ʿUyūn*, ed. de Goeje, in *F.H.A.*, I, 230.

[16] Saʿd ibn ʿAbd Allāh ibn Abī Khalaf al-Ashʿarī al-Qummī, *Kitāb al-Maqālāt wa al-Firaq* (Teheran, 1964), 37.

[17] Ibn al-Athīr, *al-Kāmil*, V, 209; Isfarāʾīnī, *Tabsīr*, 72. Cf. Muhammad ibn Rasūl al-Barzanjī, *al-Nawāfid li al-Rawāfid wa al-Nawāfid*, Bibliothèque Nationale, Ms. Arabes 1459, fol. 61b. I am grateful to the staff of the Bibliothèque Nationale, Paris, for their kind assistance. See also ʿAlī ibn Muhammad Jurjānī, *Kitāb al-Taʿrīfa* (Istanbul, 1883), 32; M. J. de Hammer, "Tableau Généalogique des soixante-treize sectes de l'Islam," *Journal Asiatique*, 1st Ser., VI (1825), 328.

Careful study of all the documents reveals that the Bayāniyya, in fact, did not entertain such an idea. It is conceivable, even probable, that they thought Abū Hāshim to contain a spark of the Divine Wisdom, or Divinity, which is not at all the same as the concept of successive Incarnations. The latter idea appeared in extreme Shī'ism only later among the followers of the anti-Umayyad rebel 'Abd Allāh b. Mu'āwiya (d. A.D. 747 or 748). There can be no doubt, furthermore, that the Bayāniyya believed Abū Hāshim to possess the gift of prophecy, with all of the implications that this phenomenon entailed in Islamic thought.

Nawbakhtī provides an extremely important piece of information concerning the claims of the Bayāniyya for Abū Hāshim. He states that they expected Abū Hāshim to return to the earth as the *Mahdī*, the "Rightly Guided," that is, the messiah.[18] Such a view appears reasonable, as messianic expectations had become an integral part of the religious ideas of the Shī'ite sects that appeared at the time of al-Mukhtār's revolt in Kufa, for example, the Kaisāniyya. For the Bayāniyya, as for the earlier groups, the *Mahdī* was the individual who would appear on earth in order to sweep away iniquity and tyranny. In this eradication of unrighteousness and false rule, the *Mahdī* was a prime example of the millenarian hero, who would inaugurate the new, pristine age.[19]

Aside from whatever claims Bayān may have made for Abū Hāshim, the heresiarch emphasized his own role in the movement. Bayān asserted that Abū Hāshim had designated him as successor to the *Imāmate*.[20] Such a claim was plainly fraudulent,

---

[18] Nawbakhtī, *Firaq*, 55.

[19] Examples of this phenomenon are common; at this juncture, we shall limit ourselves to two from very different geographical and cultural areas: Brazil and nineteenth-century Italy. For Brazil, see Alfred Metraux, "Les Messies des l'Amérique du Sud," *Archives de Sociologie des Religions*, IV (1957), 112. For Italy, consult Jean Seguy, "David Lazzaretti et la secte apocalyptique des Giurisdavidici," *Archives de Sociologie des Religions*, V (1958), 76–77.

[20] Abū Sa'īd Nashwān ibn al-Himyarī, *Kitāb al-Hūr al-'In wa Tanbīh al-Sami'īn* (Cairo, 1948), 161; al-Mahdī li Dīn Allāh Ahmad ibn Yahyā ibn al-Murtadā, *Al-Bahr al-Zakhkhār*, British Library Ms., Or. 4021, fol. 10b. For an interesting

if for no other reason than the fact that Abū Hāshim had bequeathed the leadership of his movement to the 'Abbāsids at
Humayma.[21] It is reported that Bayān's pretensions were not
confined to the *Imāmate*. He is also supposed to have claimed
to be a prophet, attributing his prophetic gift to Abū Hāshim.[22]
One amusing anecdote has it that Bayān invited the fifth *Imām*,
Muhammad al-Bāqir, to recognize his prophethood. Al-Bāqir
supposedly responded by having the messenger literally eat the
message.[23]

Bayān's prophetic claims implied a belief in and emphasis
upon the concept of the continuation of prophecy. This idea is
ultimately derived, it would seem, from an alteration or nullification of Islamic teachings. It is also interesting and perhaps
not coincidental to find a parallel teaching in other religions
present in the Near East at the time of Bayān and his followers. The Manichaeans, who are known to have been present in
Iraq during this period, held to the idea of prophetic succession.
Mani believed in a succession of prophets, claiming that he was
the last of these.[24] Prophetic succession also figured among the

---

later account see Abū Sa'īd Muhammad ibn al-Azdī al-Qalhātī, *Kitāb Kashf wa
al-Bayān*, British Library Ms., Or. 2606, fol. 218a. My thanks to the staff of the
British Library for their kind assistance.

[21] Moscati, "Il Testamento," 40–44; Humayma was located in the province of
al-Shar'a in the environs of Amman, according to Guy Le Strange, *Palestine*,
455.

[22] Ahmad ibn 'Abd al-Halīm ibn Taymiyya, *Minhāj al-Sunna wa al-Nabawiyya*, II
(Cairo, 1962), 401; Mīrza Muhammad al-Astarābādī, *Minhāj al-Maqāl fī 'Ilm
al-Rijāl* (Teheran, 1313 A.H.), 72. Cf. Muhsin Amīn, *A'yān al-Shī'a*, XIV (2nd
ed., Beirut, 1961), 113; 'Abbās Iqbāl, *Khāndāne Nawbakhtī* (Teheran, 1932),
252; Muhammad Taqī al-Tustarī, *Qāmus al-Rijāl*, II (Teheran, 1959/60), 246.

[23] al-Ash'arī al-Qummī, *Maqālāt wa al-Firaq*, 37; Cf. Muhammad Tayyib al-Najjār,
al-Mawālī fī al-'Asr al-Umawiyy (Cairo, 1949), 97.

[24] The most important recent study of Manichaeism is by Samuel N. C. Lieu,
Manichaeism in the Later Roman Empire and Medieval China: A Historical Survey
(Manchester, 1985), see 18–19. Other important studies by Lieu include a
series of essays published in Lieu, *Manichaeism in Mesopotamia and the Roman*

teachings of the Gnostics from whom, in fact, the Manichaeans may have derived the idea.[25] A Jewish sect of Persia, the ʾIsawites, named for their founder and leader Ishāq ben Yaʿqub Ubadia Abū ʾIsa al-Isfahānī, and active during the reign of the caliph ʾAbd al-Malik (A.D. 685–705), also believed in the continuation of prophecy. The records indicate that this sect awaited the coming of a messiah who was to be preceded by five messengers, their leader ʾIsa being the last of the five. Interestingly enough, Jesus and Muhammad figured among the prophets recognized by this group.[26]

Obviously then, the continuation of the prophecy idea was not unknown in Iraq and Iran at the time of Bayān. In all probability, Bayān acquired the idea not from any of the sources mentioned, but rather from the teachings of Islam itself. The Prophet Muhammad had spoken of the prophets and messengers sent to mankind prior to his own time. As is commonly known, the Qurʾān itself mentions some twenty-eight prophets.[27] A theory of prophetic continuation could easily be derived by simply modifying the Islamic teaching. After all, that is the crux of what happened with a more recent and significant millenarian movement, the Babi movement of nineteenth-century Iran.[28] This is in

East (Leiden, 1994); and, for China, idem., *The Religion of Light: An Introduction to the History of Manichaeism in China* (Hong Kong, 1979). Older accounts include those of F. C. Burkitt, *The Religion of the Manichees* (Cambridge, 1925), 38; L. J. R. Ort, *Mani: A Religio-Historical Description of his Personality* (Leiden, 1967), 121; and Henri-Charles Puech, *Le Manichéisme. Son Fondateur. Sa Doctrine* (Paris, 1949), 61.

[25] Hans Jonas, *The Gnostic Religion* (2nd ed. enlarged, Boston, 1963), 230; Kurt Rudolph, *Gnosis*, 207–210.

[26] Wasserstrom, *Muslim and Jew*, 68–70; still useful is the Max Schloessinger article, "Ishak ben Yaʾkub Obadiah Abu ʾIsa al-Isfahani," in *Jewish Encyclopædia*, VI (New York, 1904), 646.

[27] Hamilton A. R. Gibb, *Mohammedanism* (2nd ed., London and New York, 1953), 52–53.

[28] Abbas Amanat, *Resurrection and Renewal: The Making of the Babi Movement in Iran, 1844–1850* (Ithaca, N.Y., 1989), 205–206, 375–377.

all probability exactly what Bayān did, for rather obvious political considerations.

Several of the sources contain statements to the effect that Bayān pretended to be God or, at any rate, had such a claim made for him. According to al-Isfarā'īnī, as well as Maqrīzī, al-Ījī and others, the spirit of God passed into the prophets and *Imāms*, coming to 'Alī and being transmitted from him to Muhammad b. al-Hanafiyya, Abū Hāshim, and from the latter to Bayān.[29] 'Abd al-Wāhid b. Ahmad al-Kirmānī writes that the Bayāniyya believed that God descends into the form of a man.[30] On the other hand Ibn al-Athīr, who states in his history that Bayān believed in the divinity of 'Alī, Hasan, Husayn, Ibn al-Hanafiyya, and Abū Hāshim, makes no mention of Bayān ever having claimed divinity for himself. He confines himself to the statement that Bayān pretended to be a prophet.[31] Yet another version may be found in the works of Shahrastānī and al-Dhahabī, where one reads that a portion or particle of divinity came from Abū Hāshim to Bayān.[32]

How is one to reconcile the contradictory accounts? All indications are that Bayān, in reality, only claimed to be a prophet. Given the Islamic context, it is evident that such a claim would preclude any teaching of Incarnation. One bit of evidence that

[29] 'Abd al-Qāhir ibn Tāhir ibn Muhammad al-Baghdādī, *Usūl al-Dīn* (Istanbul, 1928), 331; 'Adūd al-Dīn 'Abd al-Rahmān ibn Ahmad al-Ījī, *Kitāb al-Mawāqif fī 'Ilm al-Kalam*, VIII (Cairo, 1909), 385; Taqi al-Din al-Maqrizi, *al-Mawa'iz wa al-I'tibar fi Dhikr al-Khitat wa al-Athār*, III, part I (Cairo, 1959), 302; 'Abd al-Karīm ibn Muhammad al-Sam'āni, *Kitāb al-Ansāb*, II (Hyderabad, 1963), 387; Mahmūd 'Alī Bishbishī, *al-Firaq al-Islāmiyya* (Cairo, 1932), 28; Hāshim ibn Ma'rūf al-Hasanī, *al-Shī'a bayna al-Ashā'ira wa al-Mu'tazila* (Beirut, 1964), 61.
[30] Abū al-Qāsim 'Abd al-Wāhid ibn Ahmad al-Kirmānī, "Ein Kommentar der Tradition über die 73 Sekten," Arabic text ed. Sven Dedering in *Le Monde Oriental*, XXV (1931), 40.
[31] Ibn al-Athīr, *al-Kāmil*, V, 209.
[32] Shahrastānī, *Milāl*, I, 184; Shams al-Dīn Muhammad ibn Ahmad al-Dhahabī, *Mizān al-I'tidāl fī Naqd al-Rijāl*, I (Cairo, 1325 A.H.), 166; A. C. Barbier de Meynard, "Le Seid Himyarite," *J.A.*, 7th Ser., IV (1874), 169–170.

supports the idea that Bayān opted for prophecy instead of divinity is the interpretation he gave to S. 3:132. The verse in question reads: "This is a manifestation (*bayān*) to the people." Bayān insisted that the word *bayān* in the verse was a reference to him.[33] His intention here was to buttress his claim to prophecy. Of further interest here is the method of Qur'ānic interpretation employed by the sectarian leader. Should this method of exegesis be considered literalist or symbolic? It appears that it might be best understood as a rather rudimentary form of symbolic interpretation. This method, albeit in a gradually more sophisticated manner, was to be an important part of extremist Shī'ite religious ideas and practices. Perhaps the most fully developed system of symbolic Qur'ānic interpretation would be that of the later Ismā'īlīs, whose system was infinitely more sophisticated and complex than that of Bayān and the early sectaries.[34]

One of the most famous teachings associated with Bayān was the idea that God is in the form of a man who will ultimately disappear entirely except for his face.[35] It is further reported that he taught that God is in the form of a man of light,[36] but this

---

[33] Abū al-Fadl 'Abbās ibn Mansūr ibn 'Abbās al-Burayhī al-Saksakī al-Hānbalī, *Kitāb al-Burhān fī Ma'rifa Aqā'id al-Adyān*, Nuri Osmaniye Kütübhanesi Ms. 4919, fol. 138b. Microfilm copy available in the Library of Indiana University, Bloomington, Ind.

[34] W. Ivanow, "Ismā'īliya," in *Shorter E.I.* (Ithaca, N.Y., 1965), 179–183.

[35] 'Abd al-Qādir al-Jīlānī, *al-Ghunya li Tālib Tarīq al-Haqq* (Cairo, 1322 A.H.), 99; Fakhr al-Dīn al-Rāzī, *I'tiqādāt Firaq al-Muslimīn wa al-Mushrikīn* (Cairo, 1949), 57. For a later account see anon., *al-Sawā'iq al-Muhriqa li-Ikhwān al-Shayātīn wa al-Dalāl wa al-Zandaqa*, Library of the India Office Ms. 2167, Delhi 916, fol. 16a. This is one of several India Office manuscripts devoted to Islamic sects. My thanks to the staff of the India Office Library in London for their aid in my research. See also Muhammad A'lā ibn 'Alī al-Tahānawī, *Kashshaf Istilāhāt al-Funūn*, I (Cairo, 1963), 219; Sylvestre de Sacy, *Exposé de la Religion des Druzes*, I (Paris, 1964), xlvi.

[36] Nāshi' al-Akbar, *Kitāb Usūl al-Nihal*, in *Frühe Mu'tazilitische Häresiographie: zwei Werke des Nāshi' al-Akbar*, (Gest 293 H.), text edited by Josef van Ess (Beirut, 1971), 40 of the Arabic text. One may also consult here the fascinating

statement cannot be accepted with certainty. The fact is that the concept of God as a man of light is attributed more convincingly to al-Mughīra b. Sa'īd. The sources including this idea among Bayān's teachings mention it only very briefly and do not develop it or place it within a meaningful context, as is the case with the sections devoted to al-Mughīra and his followers. As a result, it may be argued that the man-of-light idea is wrongly attributed to Bayān, stemming from a confusion of his teachings with those of al-Mughīra.

The belief that God would disappear entirely save for his face was apparently suggested to Bayān by certain Qur'ānic passages: for example, S. 28:88 ("Everything perishes but His face") and S. 55:26–27 ("Everyone on it must pass away and the face of your Lord will endure forever"),[37] Here again one encounters speculation upon Qur'ānic passages, clearly in this case of a more literal nature.

Another unusual doctrine attributed to Bayān is the belief that there are two gods, one in Heaven and one on earth. He maintained that the one in Heaven was greater than the one on earth.[38] Presumably, the source for such a belief must be sought outside of Islam. One scholar has stated that this idea had its origins in the Gnostic distinction between God and the Logos emanating from him.[39] A similar belief is credited to the Gnostic thinker, Marcion of Sinope. Marcion taught that there are two gods, one of whom is superior; the other, identified with the

---

new heresiography published by Wilferd Madelung and Paul Walker, *Abū Tammām's An Ismaili Heresiography: The "Bāb al-Shaytān" from Abū Tammām's Kitab al-Shajara* (Leiden, 1998), 68–69. See also al-Baghdādī, *Usūl*, 73.

[37] al-Baghdādī, *Schisms* (trans. Halkin), 47.

[38] Abū 'Amr Muhammad ibn 'Umar ibn 'Abd al-Azīz Kashshī, *Rijāl al-Kashshī-Ma'rifa* (Karbala, 1963), 257; Hājj Shaykh 'Abd Allāh al-Mamaqānī, *Tanqīh al-Maqāl fī Ahwāl al-Rijāl*, I (Najaf[?], 1349), 183; Muhammad Abū Zāhra, *Ta'rīkh al-Madhāhab al-Islāmiyya*, II (Cairo, 1963[?]), 49.

[39] Friedlaender, "Ibn Hazm: Commentary," 88.

Creator God of the Old Testament, he deemed inferior.[40] In his opinion, the superior god was to be looked upon as the redeemer of mankind.[41]

Was Bayān acquainted with the teachings of Marcion? It is impossible to say, given the silence of the sources on this point. Certainly, however, the doctrines of Marcion were widespread in the East (mainly in pre-Islamic times), especially in Arabia, Syria, Armenia, and Persia. Although these teachings were proscribed by Constantine the Great, they continued to exist, having a role of some significance in certain sectors of Eastern Christendom.[42] Furthermore, Ibn al-Nadīm attests to the existence of Marcionites in Khurasan presumably in his own day, that is, the tenth century.[43] The matter must rest here, but it is no exaggeration to say that belief in two gods, one superior and the other inferior, is hardly a feature of Islamic belief.

Yet another of Bayān's teachings that may have come from a non-Islamic source is his claim to know the "Greatest Name" of God and thus have supernatural powers. Bayān professed that by means of his knowledge of the Greatest Name, he was able to call to the planet Venus and elicit a response.[44] There are a number of parallels or possible sources for the importance of a great name. Alfred Guillaume has pointed out, for example, that the belief of gaining special powers through the knowledge and use of a secret or great name has been present in the Near East for thousands of years. The idea inherent in such a teaching is

---

[40] Couliano, *Tree of Gnosis*, 151. According to Kurt Rudolph, Marcion's concept involved an antithesis between the "God of law" and the "God of salvation." Rudolph, *Gnosis*, 314–315. Similar information is forthcoming from older accounts. See E. C. Blackman, *Marcion and his Influence* (London, 1948), 74; Eugène de Faye, *Gnostiques et Gnosticisme* (2nd ed. aug., Paris, 1925), 154–155.

[41] Blackman, *Marcion*, 70.

[42] N. McLean, "Marcionism," in *Hastings Encyclopædia of Religion and Ethics*, VIII (New York, 1961), 409.

[43] Muhammad ibn Ishāq ibn al-Nadīm, *Kitāb al-Fihrist* (Beirut, 1966), 339.

[44] al-Ash'arī, *Maqālāt*, I, 66; Murtadā al-Rāzī, *Tabsīra al-'Awām*, 169.

that whoever knows a person's name thereby has power over that individual.[45] An indication of the great antiquity of the concept may be seen in the content of an ancient Egyptian tale, according to which Isis is said to have gained power over the sun god, Ra, after having learned his secret "great name."[46]

A great-name belief can also be found in Judaism. The Jewish equivalent of the Greatest Name is the *Shem ha-Mephorash*, "ineffable Name,"[47] which was the subject of magical speculation. It was thought to have supernatural power and was, therefore, used as a magic formula.[48] Speculation about the Greatest Name was a key feature of Jewish Merkaba mysticism. In this connection there was a rite by which the magician assumed special power by impregnating himself with the Greatest Name, namely, by clothing himself with a special garment into which the name had been woven.[49]

The Mazdakian sectarians of Sasanid Persian are said to have involved themselves in theorizing about the power of the Greatest Name. Shahrastānī, in his study of Islamic and non-Islamic sects, reports that the Mazdakians believed that whoever knows the Greatest Name comes to know the "Greatest Secret" (Ultimate Secrets?).[50] It is possible that Bayān could have learned of the Mazdakian teaching, as this sect continued to exist in Persia, Iraq's neighboring province, until as late as the tenth to twelfth

[45] Alfred Guillaume, *Prophecy and Divination among the Hebrews and Other Semites* (London, 1938), 20.

[46] James G. Frazer, *The Golden Bough, III: Taboo and the Perils of the Soul* (New York, 1935), 387–389.

[47] Friedlaender, "Ibn Hazm: Commentary," 82.

[48] Wilhelm Bacher, "Shem ha-Mephorash," in *Jewish Encyclopædia*, XI (New York, 1905), 263–264.

[49] Gershom Scholem, *Major Trends in Jewish Mysticism* (2nd ed. rev., New York, 1946), 77.

[50] Christensen, *L'Iran*, 342. Important information about the Mazdakian concept of the Great Name is available in the old but still definitive study by Otakar Klima, *Mazdak* (new ed., New York, 1979), 191.

centuries,[51] although such a connection cannot be proved. What is certain is that manipulation of the Greatest Name of God was from ancient times until at least the last century a common feature of Near Eastern magic.[52] As noted before, Bayān may well have engaged in the practice of magic. Certainly his associate al-Mughīra b. Saʿīd was particularly noted for his magical knowledge and feats and could have initiated Bayān into magical use of the Greatest Name.

The famous medieval author Ibn Qutayba, who lived during the early ʿAbbāsid period, states that Bayān b. Samʿān was the first person to speak of the Qurʾān being created.[53] This charge, absent in all of the other sources, appears to have been a fabrication of the author. As those familiar with Islamic history are aware, the idea of the Qurʾān being created was a cardinal tenet of the Muʿtazilite theologians.[54] Muʿtazilite theology had been the officially sanctioned ideology of the ʿAbbāsid state from the reign of al-Maʾmūn (beginning in 813) until the accession of the caliph al-Mutawwakil (847). Ibn Qutayba, who was a Sunni Muslim, had come into favor with al-Mutawwakil, who had devoted himself to restoring Sunni predominance in the Islamic realm. The caliph appears to have used Ibn Qutayba's literary talents in his religious campaign.[55] For this reason, one strongly suspects that Ibn Qutayba's purpose in ascribing the origin of a Muʿtazilite doctrine to Bayān was an attempt to establish a connection between the Muʿtazilites and the Shīʿite heresiarch and thus to discredit the former.

A few of the sources contain erroneous information about the teachings of Bayān and the Bayāniyya. Shahrastānī contends,

[51] Bertold Spuler, *Iran in Früh-Islamischer Zeit (633 bis 1055)* (Wiesbaden, 1952), 206.
[52] E. W. Lane, *Arabian Society in the Middle Ages* (London, 1883), 81.
[53] Ibn Qutayba, *ʿUyūn*, II, 148.
[54] H. S. Nyberg, "Muʿtazila," in *Shorter E.I.* (Ithaca, N.Y., 1965), 426.
[55] Gerard Lecomte, "Ibn Kutayba," in *E.I.2*, III (Leiden, 1971), 845–846.

for instance, that Bayān taught that ʿAlī was in the clouds and that the thunder was his voice.[56] This is clearly a confusion of the Bayāniyya doctrines with those of another, earlier sect, the Sabaʾiyya, followers of ʿAbd Allāh b. Sabaʾ.[57] Shahrastānī further reports that Bayān spoke of the *Rajʿa*, or return from death or concealment, of the *Imām* ʿAlī.[58] As we have seen, however, the Bayāniyya in fact expected the return of Abū Hāshim as messiah. In view of the well-documented importance of Abū Hāshim for Bayān and his followers, it is quite likely that Shahrastānī's reference to ʿAlī is an error. In this respect it should be pointed out that most extremist Shīʿite groups, such as the Mansūriyya, Janāhiyya, Khattābiyya, and Rāwandiyya, considered their expected messiah to be someone other than ʿAlī.[59]

In assessing the impact of Bayān and his followers upon Islamic thought and history, a point of primary significance is that Bayān was the first non-ʿAlid, non-Hāshimite to lay claim to the *Imāmate*. His allegation that an ʿAlid had designated him to be *Imām* established an important precedent. Later Shīʿite heresiarchs having no relation to ʿAlī or his descendants made similar claims, justifying in many cases their roles in leading sociopolitical opposition movements.

Bayān, furthermore, appears to have been the first extremist sectarian leader to make speculation about the nature of God an important component of the religious ideology. No doubt this question was of considerable importance to the broad masses of Muslims, for whom incipient Sunnism, with its transcendental Deity, had no satisfying answers. One may view such speculation as an attempt to establish some sort of personalized relationship with God. That such a relationship fulfilled an important

---

[56] Shahrastānī, *Milal*, I, 152.
[57] Hodgson, "Ibn Sabaʾ," *E.I.*2, I, 51.
[58] Shahrastānī, *Milal*, I, 152.
[59] Tritton, *Theology*, 23–29.

need was demonstrated by the later popular success of Sufism. In addition, the insight presumably generated by these conjectures about the nature of God served to heighten the charismatic status of leaders such as Bayān.

With the possible exception of the Hāshimiyya, Bayān and his followers appear to have been the first Shī'ite extremists to engage in a form of symbolic Qur'ānic exegesis. Qur'ānic interpretation of this variety developed into a significant feature of subsequent Shī'ite thought, although it would become much more sophisticated in the hands of later Shī'ite activists and thinkers. Qur'ānic exegesis would be of particular importance in Ismā'īlī Shī'ism, which, according to the late Marshall Hodgson, received it via the Khattābiyya sect.[60]

Although there is some uncertainty, the Bayāniyya appear to have believed that their leader contained within himself a divine particle and in so doing originated an idea of fundamental importance in moderate Shī'ism. According to this concept, the *Imām* remains a mortal being, but a part of the divine becomes embodied within him by means of what may be called a partial incarnation.[61] Possibly, the idea one encounters here with Bayān and some of the others is the belief examined recently by Amīr-Moezzi of the pre-existent light of the Prophet, Fatima, and the *Imāms*.[62] There is an important distinction to be drawn between this idea and the doctrine of complete incarnation, the state in which the individual is thought to be an embodiment of God.

The belief in a transmission of prophetic power appeared for the first time in Shī'ite dogmatics with Bayān and his group. Whereas Hamza b. 'Umāra and al-Mukhtār are also supposed to have claimed prophetic status, there is no indication that they thought in terms of a succession of prophecy based upon

---

[60] Marshall G. S. Hodgson, "Bātiniyya," in *E.I.2*, I (Leiden, 1960), 1098–1099.
[61] Rudolf Strothmann, "Shi'a," in *Shorter E.I.* (Ithaca, N.Y., 1965), 536.
[62] Amir-Moezzi, *The Divine Guide*, 30–33.

designation by a predecessor, as did Bayān and the Bayāniyya. A more explicit and better-defined doctrine of prophetic continuation appeared, as we shall see presently, later with Abū Mansūr al-ʿIjli and the sect acknowledging his leadership. Transmission and continuation of prophecy was a particularly serious crime from the Umayyad point of view, because it suggested the nullification or displacement of Muhammad's revelation and status as seal of the prophets, upon which the Islamic state and, consequently, Umayyad rule rested. Whatever the religiosity of individual rulers, and whatever their possible claims to be legislator-caliphs/*Imāms*, the fact remains that Muhammad's prophetic mission lay at the foundation of Islamic, and thus Umayyad, government. Whether or not one accepts Patricia Crone's and Martin Hinds' argument that Umayyad caliphs saw themselves as having the function of God's agents and thereby possessing powers similar to those of a prophet, the fact remains that they had no intention of allowing such a prerogative to any dissenting group, be it primarily religious or political in nature.[63] Any attempt by such a dissenting group or political pretender to alter or add to what was emerging as the officially sanctioned version of the revelation threatened the very foundations of dynastic rule.

As other scholars have noted, Bayān and the Bayāniyya may have introduced certain non-Islamic ideas into extremist Shīʿite thought. Although it is difficult, if not impossible, to ascertain the degree to which such borrowing occurred, the belief in two gods was without question a doctrine of non-Islamic provenance. It is apparent, however, that many, perhaps most, of the teachings of this group have their roots ultimately in Islam.

In the final analysis, the activities of Bayān and the Bayāniyya, as well as of other extremist Shīʿites of the Umayyad period, were significant because of their impact upon the power of the Syrian

[63] Patricia Crone and Martin Hinds, *God's Caliph: Religious Authority in the First Centuries of Islam* (Cambridge, 1986), 27–30.

dynasty. It would be preposterous to argue that any one of these rebellious groups taken separately constituted a grave threat to Umayyad power. One may suggest, however, that the recurring uprisings or antigovernment violence indulged in by these sects kept the province of Iraq and, occasionally, the area of Iran in a state of turmoil and agitation. In the long run, such continual unrest could only weaken the power of the Umayyad government. Extremist Shī'ite rebels, among them Bayān and his followers, constituted a persistent irritant to the Umayyad body politic.

3

Al-Mughīra ibn Saʿīd and the Mughīriyya

As indicated in the previous chapter, Bayān was aided in his seditious activities by a man named al-Mughīra ibn Saʿīd and a group
known as the Mughīriyya. Aside from their role in Umayyad history and their contributions to extremist Shīʿite doctrine, the
Mughīriyya deserve attention because of the curious manner in
which they combined, in action and idea, a form of gnosticism
(with its connotations of extreme spiritualism) coupled with a
militance and exclusiveness ultimately manifested in violence
and terrorism. With the Mughīriyya we see not only important
doctrinal contributions, but also significant developments in tactics and actions.

Although information concerning the life and doctrines of
al-Mughīra ibn Saʿīd is more complete than that for many Shīʿite
heresiarchs, it still leaves much to be desired, particularly in
respect to his social and economic position. The sources generally agree on at least one point, namely that he was blind. Ibn
Qutayba records a poem in which al-Mughīra is called *al-Aʿma*,
("the blind one").[1] Another work describes him as having been
both old and blind.[2] But little agreement exists regarding other

---

[1] Ibn Qutayba, *ʿUyūn*, II, 146.
[2] Abū ʿUthmān, Amr ibn Bahr al-Jāhiz, *Kitāb al-Bayān wa al-Tabyīn*, I, part II
(Cairo, 1949), 267.

data on al-Mughīra. Even his ethnic identity is in dispute. The best indication of this uncertainty is to be seen in the work of Shahrastānī who, in one place, calls al-Mughīra, al-ʿIjli (member of the Banū ʿIjl) but then proceeds to refer to him as *Mawlā* (client) of Khālid ibn ʿAbd Allāh, the famous governor of Iraq who belonged to the Banū Bajīla.³ Other authorities generally avoid the contradiction by designating him either as al-ʿIjli or as *Mawlā*. A possible solution to the dilemma is suggested by the fact that al-Mughīra's grammar was poor. One may hazard a guess that he was, in fact, a *Mawlā*, since, as Goldziher pointed out, the Arabs were quick to ridicule the *Mawālī* for linguistic errors.⁴

Al-Mughīra appears to have been a sort of magician or, at least, familiar with the occult sciences.⁵ Tabarī, for example, calls him a wizard⁶ and records a story to the effect that al-Mughīra visited cemeteries, murmuring some sort of incantations over the graves.⁷ Tabarī's story, however, is somewhat suspicious, and the entire episode may well be a hostile fabrication. Kashshī reports that al-Mughīra learned magic from a Jewish woman.⁸ It should be pointed out that there is no reason to doubt altogether that al-Mughīra dabbled in some form of magic. Wizards and diviners

---

3 Shahrastānī, *Milal,* I, 176. Cf. Astarābādī, *Minhāj,* 340.
4 Ignaz Goldziher, *Muslim Studies,* trans. C. R. Barber and S. M. Stern, I (Chicago, 1967), 115. For al-Mughīra's grammar cf. Ibn Qutayba, *Kitāb al-Maʿārif* (Cairo, 1883), 206; Dhahabī, *Mīzān al-Iʿtidāl fī Naqd al-Rijāl,* IV (Cairo, 1963), 161.
5 Shams al-Dīn Sibt Ibn al-Jawzī, *Mirʾāt al-Zamān fī Taʾrīkh al-Aʿyān,* Bodleian Library, Oxford University, Ms. Pococke 371, fol. 139a. My appreciation to the administration and staff of Oxford University, particularly the Bodleian Library, for making available to me photostatic copies of the relevant pages. Cf. Shihāb al-Dīn ibn Hajar al-ʿAsqalānī, *Lisān al-Mīzān,* VI (Hyderabad, 1331 H.), 76; ʿAbd al-Hamīd ibn Abī al-Hadīd, *Sharh Nāhj al-Balgha,* VIII (Cairo, 1960), 121.
6 Tabarī, *Taʾrīkh,* II, 1620. Cf. Salāh al-Dīn Muhammad ibn Shākir al-Kutubī, *ʿUyūn al-Tawārīkh,* Bibliothèque Nationale Ms., Arabes 1587, fol. 163a. My thanks to the administration and staff of the Bibliothèque Nationale for their kind assistance in my research.
7 Tabarī, *Taʾrīkh,* II, 1619.
8 Kashshī, *Rijāl,* 196.

appear to have been accepted in al-Mughīra's time and region as a part of the natural order.[9] Al-Mughīra's skill in matters of the occult or magic, furthermore, may have been an important factor in attracting followers to him. Indeed, the magic and even sinister powers imputed to al-Mughīra indicate the sort of charismatic hold he appears to have had over his followers, the sort of control analogous to that of such millenarian leaders as the so-called Drummer of Niklashausen, Thomas Müntzer, and John of Leiden, all sectarian commanders in late fifteenth-century Germany and Holland.[10]

Al-Mughīra, according to some accounts, engaged in the fabrication of *Hadīth*, although one individual is supposed to have stated that he did not know of a single sound *Hadīth* from al-Mughīra.[11] Elsewhere one reads that Ja'far al-Sādiq accused al-Mughīra of forging *Hadīth* in the name of Muhammad al-Bāqir (the fifth *Imām* and father of Ja'far).[12] Although these reports are undoubtedly exaggerated, there is no reason to discount their essential accuracy. Clearly al-Mughīra did transmit spurious *Hadīth*.

Al-Mughīra and Bayān ibn Sam'ān (the extremist Shī'ite leader) joined forces in 737 and rose in rebellion against Khālid ibn 'Abd Allāh al-Qasrī, the Umayyad governor in Iraq.[13] Khālid is said to have been so surprised at the news of the revolt that he

---

[9] Guillaume, *Prophecy and Divination*, 188.

[10] Norman Cohn, *The Pursuit of the Millennium* (rev. and exp. ed., New York, 1970), 223–251, 261–280.

[11] al-Dhahabī, *Mīzān*, IV, 162.

[12] Kashshī, *Rijāl*, 196. Similar accounts may be found in the following: Mīr Mustafā al-Husaynī al-Tafrīshī, *Naqd al-Rijāl*, British Library Ms., Or. 3640, fol. 206b. Muhammad ibn ('Abd al-) Rasūl al-Sharīf al-Husaynī al-Musāwī, *al-Nawāqid li al-Rawāfid wa al-Nawāfid*, Library of the India Office Ms., Delhi 971, fol. 23b. As this note should indicate, I believe it to be important to examine differing, even conflicting, perspectives on these issues.

[13] Prince Leone Caetani, *Chronographia Islamica*, V (Paris, 1922), 1481; Gerlof van Vloten, *De Opkomst der Abbasiden in Chorosan* (Leiden, 1890), 66.

exclaimed: "Give me water to eat [sic]!"[14] This account comes from the satirical poem of Ibn Nawfal, which, directed against Khālid, purports to show his terror in the face of this minor *emeute.*[15] This is clearly an attempt to discredit Khālid because of his loyalty to the Umayyads (widely hated in Iraq). Al-Mubarrad states that Khālid had previously given al-Mughīra an amnesty, but, as Francesco Gabrieli has shown, this information is erroneous. The amnesty mentioned probably was given to another, earlier, rebel named Rāzin.[16]

It is difficult, in fact nearly impossible, to determine how many individuals took part in the revolt. Tabarī, followed by Ibn Kathīr, gives the number as only seven.[17] Al-Mubarrad, on the other hand, sets the figure at twenty.[18] Both estimates are probably too low, and in any case, Mughīra and Bayān had followers who survived them.

It is of particular interest to note that al-Mughīra's group included both Arabs and *Mawālī.* We know that *Mawālī* of some sort participated in the rebellion.[19] Wellhausen claims that they were Persian, but this is uncertain.[20] They may, on the other hand, have belonged to the indigenous Aramaean population of Iraq. The Arabs involved in the Mughīriyya were elements of Bajīla, Kinda, and 'Ijl.[21] Interestingly enough, the same tribes

---

[14] Abū al-Faraj al-Isfahānī, *Kitāb al-Aghānī,* XXII (Beirut, 1960), 20.
[15] al-Jāhiz, *Bayān,* I, part II, 266–267.
[16] Gabrieli, "Hishām," 18, n.1.
[17] Tabarī, *Ta'rīkh,* II, 1621; 'Imād al-Dīn Abū al-Fidā Ismā'īl ibn 'Umar ibn Kathīr, *al-Bidāya wa al-Nihāya fī al-Ta'rīkh,* IX (Cairo, 1932), 323.
[18] Muhammad ibn Yazīd al-Mubarrad, *al-Kāmil fī al-Lugha wa al-Adab* (Cairo, n.d.), 20.
[19] Tabarī, *Ta'rīkh,* II, 1622.
[20] Wellhausen, *Arab Kingdom,* 327.
[21] A'sha Hamdān, untitled poem, in *Diwan al-A'sha: Gedichte von Abu Bashir Maimun ibn Qais al-A'sha nebst Sammlungen von Stücken Anderer Dichter des Gleichen Beinamens und von al-Musayyab ibn A'las,* Gibb Memorial Series, N. Ser., VI (London, 1928), 336, no. 33.

were involved in the rebellion of al-Mukhtār in Iraq and in the terrorist sect led by Abū Mansūr al-ʿIjli.[22]

There are indications that al-Mughīra taught his followers to look upon themselves as an elite whose mission was to spread his teachings.[23] They appear, for example, to have been given a special name: *al-wusafā*, "the servants."[24] This name suggests that al-Mughīra imbued his supporters with a spirit of service and missionary dedication and zeal. The implication takes on added significance when one considers al-Malatī's report that the Mughīriyya believed in freedom of behavior for those who exerted themselves or suffered injury on behalf of the ʿAlids.[25] The emphasis here upon devotion to and suffering for a special cause indicates the cultivation of a sense of exclusiveness, that is, elitism. A further sign of elitist feeling may be seen in the fact that the Mughīriyya, after al-Mughīra's death in all probability, began to resort to the assassination of opponents (religious and/or social-political opposition).[26] It is evident that they believed themselves to be God's chosen ones, whose duty it was to eliminate the "sons of darkness." In this respect, the Mughīriyya most closely resemble the militant and violent Taborite movement in fifteenth-century Bohemia.[27]

After the death of al-Mughīra the leadership of the movement went to an individual named Jābir al-Juʿfī.[28] In turn, Jābir's

---

[22] Balādhurī, *Ansāb*, V, 248, 254; Ibn Qutayba, *ʿUyūn*, II, 147; al-Jāhiz, *Kitāb al-Hayawān*, II (2nd ed., Cairo, 1965), 146.

[23] Muhammad Jābir ʿAbd al-ʿĀl, *Harakāt al-Shīʿa al-Mutatarrifīn* (Cairo, 1954), 41.

[24] Tabarī, *Taʾrīkh*, II, 1621.

[25] Abū al-Husayn Muhammad ibn Ahmad al-Malatī, *Kitāb al-Tanbīh wa al-Radd ʿalā Ahl al-Ahwāʾ wa al-Bidāʾ* (Istanbul, 1936), 122.

[26] al-Jāhiz, *Hayawān*, II, 267; Gerlof van Vloten, "Worgers in Iraq," in *Feestbundel van Taal-Letter-, Geschied-an Aardrijkskundige Bijdragen van zign Tachtigsten Geboortedag aan Dr. P. J. Veth* (Leiden, 1894), 62; Charles Pellat, *Le Milieu Basrien et la Formation de Djahiz* (Paris, 1953), 199.

[27] Cohn, *Pursuit* (rev. ed., 1970), 205–214.

[28] al-Ashʿarī, *Maqālāt*, I, 73.

successor was a certain Bakr al-A'war al-Hajari,[29] of whom nothing is known. Jābir al-Ju'fī was a person of some stature. A strong
'Alid supporter, he was a traditionist whose *Hadīth* were accepted
by the *Imāmite* Shī'ites.[30] There are indications that he believed
in the doctrine of *Raj'a*, return from occultation or, possibly, from
the dead. He died in 128 or 132 H.[31]

Al-Mughīra ibn Sa'īd is said to have preached the *Imāmate* of
Muhammad al-Bāqir (fifth Shī'ite *Imām*).[32] One authority states
that al-Mughīra insisted that al-Bāqir was the *Mahdī-Qa'im*.[33]
Numerous other sources indicate, however, that al-Mughīra was a
partisan not of al-Bāqir, but rather of Muhammad ibn 'Abd Allāh,
known as *al-Nafs al-Zakiyya* (the Pure Soul), who, along with his
brother, rebelled against the 'Abbāsid al-Mansūr and was put to
death.[34] Al-Mughīra apparently believed al-Nafs al-Zakiyya to be
the *Mahdī*.[35] What emerges from the two accounts is that al-
Mughīra recognized al-Bāqir at first, but after the latter's death
or disavowal he turned his attention and allegiance to al-Nafs al
Zakiyya.[36] Clearly, the account in the *Kitāb al-Aghānī*, according
to which al-Mughīra and Bayān rose on behalf of Ja'far al-Sādiq,
is incorrect.[37]

[29] Ibid.
[30] al-Ash'arī al-Qummī, *Maqālāt wa al-Firaq*, 183, editor's note.
[31] al-Baghdādī, *Schisms* (trans. Halkin), 55, n. 1.
[32] al-Himyarī, *Hūr*, 168. Cf. Moscati, "Antica Sī'a," 260.
[33] al-Ash'arī al-Qummī, *Maqālāt wa al-Firaq*, 76.
[34] Isfarā'īnī, *Tabsīr*, 73; Nawbakhtī, *Firaq*, 80. For an account of the rising
of Muhammad and Ibrahim, see the chapter entitled "Caliph Mansur" in
Theodore Nöldeke, *Sketches from Eastern History*, trans. J. S. Black (Beirut,
1963), 107–145.
[35] Isfarā'īnī, *Tabsīr*, 73; Muhammad Ridā al-Shabībī, *Mua'rrikh al-'Irāq ibn al-
Fuwātī*, I, part 1 (Baghdad, 1950), 85; 'Ārif al-Tāmir, *al-Imāma fī al-Islām* (Beirut,
n.d.), 81.
[36] Wilferd Madelung, *Der Imām al-Qāsim ibn Ibrahīm und die Glaubenslehre der
Zaiditen* (Berlin, 1965), 46; Claude Cahen, "Points du vue sur la Révolution
'Abbaside," *Revue Historique*, CCVII (1963), 315.
[37] Abū al-Faraj al-Isfahānī, *Kitāb al-Aghānī*, XVI (Beirut, 1959), 342–343.

Following the death of Muhammad al-Nafs al-Zakiyya in 762, the Mughīriyya split into factions. One group refused to believe that he had died, arguing that a devil had been killed in his place (an idea strongly reminiscent of the mysterious 'Abd Allāh ibn Saba'). This faction asserted that al-Nafs al-Zakiyya had gone into concealment in Mount Hajir, from which place he would some day reappear as the messiah.[38] This belief reflects, perhaps, the impact of the Karibiyya (or Karbiyya), who taught that Muhammad ibn al-Hanafiyya had secluded himself in Mount Radwa. The idea of a devil being killed instead of al-Nafs al-Zakiyya is a further manifestation of Docetism, an important concept not only among certain Shī'ite extremists but also with the Gnostics and early Christians.[39] In the sources, this branch of the Mughīriyya is called the Muhammadiyya. In addition to the teachings already mentioned, they insisted that, when al-Nafs al-Zakiyya returned in his messianic role, he would receive the people's allegiance between the Rukn and the Maqām in Mecca. He would then, they taught, bring to life seventeen men, each of whom would be given one of the letters of the Greatest Name of God. By means of this power, they would defeat armies and establish the messianic reign on earth,[40] a clear instance of the impact of millenarian ideas in medieval Islam. This is precisely the sort of militant rhetoric one encounters with the Anabaptist prophets John

---

[38] Nawbakhtī, *Firaq*, 84; Ghulam H. Sadighi, *Les Mouvements Religieux Iraniens au IIe et au IIIe Siècles de l'Hégire* (Paris, 1938), 141. Mt. Hājir is said to be one of the mountains of Radwā in Arabia; Shāh 'Abd al-'Azīz Ghulām al-Hākim al-Dahlawī, *Mukhtasār Tuhfa al-'Ithnā 'Ashariyya* (Cairo, 1387 A.H.), 11.

[39] anon., "Docetism," in *The Oxford Dictionary of the Christian Church* (London, 1958), 409; Adolph Harnack, *History of Dogma*, trans. from German 3rd ed. by Neil Buchanan, I (Boston, 1905), 259–260; G. Bareille, "Docétisme," in *Dictionnaire de Théologie Catholique*, IV, part II (Paris, 1939), cols. 1490–1491.

[40] Shihāb al-Dīn Ibrahīm ibn Abī al-Dām, *Dhikr Jama'ā min Ahl al-Milal wa al-Nihal*, Fatih Kūtūbhanesi, Ms. 3153, fol. 17b. My sincere appreciation goes to the former director, H. Dener, and the staff of the Suleymaniye Kūtūbhanesi for making available to me a microfilm copy of this manuscript in 1970.

of Leiden and the man called Dusentschur in early sixteenth-century Holland.[41]

Another faction of the Mughīriyya accepted the death of al-Nafs al-Zakiyya, and, as a result, they found themselves lacking an *Imām*. They did not recognize the *Imāmate* of anyone else after the death of al-Nafs al-Zakiyya.[42] Still another party repudiated al-Mughīra's ideas after the death of al-Nafs al-Zakiyya, arguing then that al-Mughīra had lied when he referred to al-Nafs al-Zakiyya as the *Mahdī*. The latter was not the *Mahdī*, for he had died without ruling the earth "or a tenth of it."[43] Obviously, these groups encountered problems common to millenarians when the new order fails to appear. The sort of disillusionment associated with the failure of a millenarian leader or program can either turn sect members away or can lead to significantly modified expectations and *goal displacement*, in other words, drastically moderated behavior.[44]

Some of the Mughīriyya are said to have recognized the *Imāmate* of al-Mughīra himself. They believed that he had become *Imām* after having been designated such by Muhammad al-Bāqir, and they maintained that he would continue to be *Imām* until the appearance of the *Mahdī*, al-Nafs al-Zakiyya.[45] Al-Mughīra no doubt did nothing to discourage such a belief. One reads, in fact, that he claimed to be a prophet.[46] Such a claim is quite plausible. His references to al-Bāqir and al-Nafs al-Zakiyya may

---

[41] Cohn, *Pursuit* (rev. ed., 1970), 271–280.

[42] Nawbakhtī, *Firaq*, 80.

[43] al-Ashʿarī, *Maqālāt*, I, 73.

[44] Robert W. Balch, John Domitrovich, Barbara Lynn Mahnke, and Vanessa Morrison, "Fifteen Years of Failed Prophecy: Coping with Cognitive Dissonance in a Bahaʾi Sect," *Millennium, Messiahs, and Mayhem: Contemporary Apocalyptic Movements*, ed. Thomas Robbins and Susan J. Palmer (New York and London, 1997), 87–88.

[45] Nawbakhtī, *Firaq*, 83. Cf. al-Kirmānī, "Ein Kommentar," 41.

[46] al-Jilānī, *Ghunya*, 99; al-Saksakī al-Hānbalī, *Kitāb al-Burhān*, fol. 139a; for a later account see al-Qalhātī, *Kāshf*, fol. 222a.

have been attempts to legitimize his own position by establishing links with 'Alids. It is instructive to note that al-Mukhtār ibn Abī 'Ubayd, the earlier Shī'ite leader of Kufa, pretended to be a prophet, while referring to Muhammad ibn al-Hanafiyya as the *Mahdī*. Al-Mughīra's pretensions to supernatural powers add plausibility to the reports of his prophetic claim.

One of the most distinctive features of al-Mughīra's teachings was his description of God. He stated that God is a man of light, with a crown of light on his head,[47] a concept strikingly similar to the Mandaean idea of the Deity. The Mandaeans referred to God as the "King of Light."[48] This Light Deity was in fact identified with the life principle itself.[49] The Mandaeans considered him to be the source of all good, the ruler of all worlds and kings, and the creator of forms and beauty.[50] Al-Mughīra's reference to the crown of light is reminiscent of the *Tāj* (crown) worn on the sleeve by the Mandaean priest.[51]

Without proof of any direct influences or contacts between al-Mughīra and the Mandaeans, one still must note the striking parallels in their teachings. The Mandaeans, after all, were numerous in Iraq in the time of al-Mughīra. It is said that by the time of the 'Abbāsids they had some four hundred churches and their leader resided in Baghdad.[52] Their physical proximity added to the noticable similarity in ideas strongly implies linkages between al-Mughīra and this venerable Baptist sect.

---

[47] anon., *al-Sawā'iq*, Library of the India Office Ms., Delhi 916, fol. 16a; Cf. Khayr al-Dīn Ziriklī, *al-A'lām Qāmus Tarājim li 'Ashhar al-Rijāl wa al-Nisā' min al-'Arab wa al-Musta'riba*, VIII (2nd ed., Cairo, 1956), 199.

[48] E. S. Drower, trans., *The Thousand and Twelve Questions* (Berlin, 1960), 13, 114; Mark Lidzbarski, trans., *Mandäische Liturgien* (Berlin, 1920), 171; Idem., *Das Johannesbuch der Mandäer* (Berlin, 1966), 90.

[49] Kurt Rudolph, *Die Mandäer*, II (Göttingen, 1960), 122.

[50] W. Brandt, "Mandaeans," in *Hastings Encyclopædia of Religion and Ethics*, VIII (New York, 1961), 383; Kurt Rudolph, *Theogonie, Kosmogonie, und Anthropogonie in den Mandäischen Schriften* (Göttingen, 1965), 77.

[51] Friedlaender, "Ibn Hazm: Commentary," 83.

[52] Ibid.

Among al-Mughīra's other speculations was his teaching that God has limbs that correspond to the letters of the Arabic alphabet.[53] His foot, for example, was likened to the letter *alif*, whereas his eyes were compared with the *'ayn*.[54] Once more, a non-Muslim parallel suggests itself. Marcos the Gnostic maintained that the body of the Supreme Wisdom (*Aleutheria*) was made up of the letters of the Greek alphabet.[55] The head was represented by the *alpha* and *omega*, the back by the *delta* and *tau*.[56] The basis of Marcos' idea was apparently the assumption that universal forces were revealed in the form of letters.[57] The letters of the Arabic alphabet came to be viewed in extremist Shī'ite circles as being endowed with occult properties.[58] From the time of Abū al-Khattāb (d. ca. 762–764 A.D.), the equivalent numerical values replaced the actual letters of the alphabet.[59] Such a practice also occurred in Sufism.[60] And, as is well known, alphabet speculation and mysticism came to be the most distinctive feature of the teachings of the Hurūfiyya in fifteenth-century Iran.[61]

---

53 Ibn al-Murtadā, *al-Bahr al-Zakhkhār*, Or. 4021, fol. 10b. Cf. al-Himyarī, *Hūr*, 259; Isfarā'inī, *Tabsīr*, 70.

54 al-Baghdadi, *Schisms* (trans. Halkin), 50.

55 Henri Corbin, *Histoire de la Philosophie Islamique*, I (Paris, 1964), 112, 204.

56 Irenaeus, *Irenaeus against Heresies*, text in *The Ante-Nicene Fathers*, I, ed., Alexander Roberts and James Donaldson (Buffalo, 1887), book I, chapter XIV, 337.

57 de Fay, *Gnosticisme*, 340.

58 T. Fahd, "Djafr," in *E.I.2*, II (Leiden, 1954), 376.

59 Louis Massignon, "Karmatians," in *Shorter E.I.* (Ithaca, N.Y., 1965), 221.

60 Fahd, *Djafr*, in *E.I.2*, 376.

61 Alessandro Bausani, "Hurūfiyya," in *E.I.2*, III (Leiden, 1971), 601; Edward G. Browne, "Some Notes on the Literature and Doctrines of the Hurūfī Sect," *Journal of the Royal Asiatic Society* (1898), 82–86. An older but still useful account is to be found in the essay by Dr. Riza Tevfiq, "Étude sur la Religion des Houroufis," in *Textes persans relatifs a la secte des houroufis*, ed. and trans. M. Clement Huart (Leiden and London, 1909), 296–303. The important sociological discussion of the Hurūfī sect is to be found in Said Arjomand's *Shadow of God*, 72–74. One of the clearest statements of the Hurūfī doctrines and literature is an unpublished seminar paper from UCLA, Vahid Rafati, "The Hurūfis: Their Main Doctrines and Works," Winter 1976. My profound thanks to Dr. Rafati

Al-Mughīra is undoubtedly best known for his elaborate theory of the creation of the world and mankind. According to him, when God wished to create the world, he first spoke the Greatest Name. This flew up to his head and became a crown ($T\bar{a}j$),[62] a concept that, as Israel Friedlaender pointed out many years ago, is similar to that of Marcos the Gnostic, who said that God opened his mouth and sent forth the "Word" (obviously the *Logos* concept) when he wished to create.[63] Al-Mughīra's inspiration for the idea of the Greatest Name becoming a crown was the Qur'ān verse (87:1): "Glorify the Name of your Lord most high."[64] This is a prime example of the allegorical interpretation of the Qur'ān, a practice that appears to have originated within the offshoots of the movement led by al-Mukhtār ibn Abī 'Ubayd. The remainder of al-Mughīra's complicated and even contradictory creation epic is given here in translation. The most precise and coherent account is that of al-Ash'arī, who wrote:

He then wrote with his finger on His palm men's deeds of obedience and disobedience, and he was angered by the [deeds of] disobedience and he sweated, and two seas were formed from His sweat, one salt and dark and the other sweet and bright. He then gazed into the sea and saw His shadow. And he went forth to seize it, but it flew away. He then plucked out the eye of His shadow and from it created the sun. He then annihilated the shadow and said: "There should not be another God besides me." He then created all creation from the two seas. He created the unbeliever from the salt, dark sea and the believers from the bright, sweet sea. And He created the shadows of men. The First shadow he created was that of Muhammad, may God's prayers and peace be upon him. He said, and that is His saying [i.e., in the Qur'ān], "say: 'If the merciful had a son, then I am the first of the worshippers'" (Qur'ān, 34:81).

and my friend and colleague Professor Michael Morony for granting me access to this paper. Most recently, see Shahzad Bashir, *Fazlāllah Astarabadi and the Hurufis* (Oxford, 2005).

[62] Murtadā al-Rāzī, *Tabsīra al-'Awām*, 170.

[63] Friedlaender, "Ibn Hazm: Commentary," 82.

[64] al-Ash'arī, *Maqālāt*, I, 72.

He then sent Muhammad who was [still] a shadow to all mankind. He then proposed to the heavens to protect 'Alī ibn Abī Ṭālib, may God's approval be upon him, and they refused. He then proposed to the earth and the mountains [to protect 'Alī], and they refused. And then he proposed to all men [to protect 'Alī], and 'Umar ibn al-Khattāb went to Abū Bakr and ordered him to undertake his ['Alī's] protection and to betray him. And Abū Bakr did so. And this is [the meaning of] His saying, "[w]e proposed the trust to the heavens and to the earth and to the mountains" (Qur'ān 33:72). He [al-Mughīra] stated: And 'Umar said, "I shall assist you against 'Alī provided you arrange to give the Caliphate to me after you." This is [the meaning of] His saying "Like unto Satan when he says to a man, 'Be an infidel'." The devil according to him [al-Mughīra] is 'Umar.[65]

The first striking element in this story is the clear-cut dichotomy between dark and light, which is reminiscent of Manichaean teachings. The opposition between light, deemed synonymous with good, and dark, identified with evil, is the basic tenet of the Manichaean religion.[66] For al-Mughīra, too, light and dark represent good and evil, as is clear from the context of the creation story, especially the comment about unbelievers coming from the dark sea.[67]

Al-Mughīra is reputed to have forbidden the use of water from the Euphrates because of its impurities. He also banned utilization of any other water into which anything unclean had been thrown.[68] This is another instance of the emphasis on spiritual aspects, particularly ritual purity, which seems to run through al-Mughīra's teachings. A parallel belief exists in the Mandaean system, in which one sees great importance attached to "pure"

[65] Ibid., 72–73.
[66] Roman Ghirshman, *L'Iran des Origines à l'Islam* (Paris, 1951), 284; R. McLean Wilson, "Mani and Manichaeism," in *Encyclopædia of Philosophy*, V (New York, 1967), 149; Burkitt, *Manichees*, 39.
[67] Ibn al-Athīr, *al-Kāmil*, V, 208; 'Ïjī, *Mawāqif*, 385; Louis Massignon, "Die Ursprunge und die Bedeutung des Gnostizismus im Islam," in *Opera Minora*, I (Beirut, 1963), 501.
[68] Ibn Hajar al-'Asqalānī, *Lisān*, VI, 76.

water. The Mandaeans believed water to be a purification, as well as a life-giving substance. Individual purification, involving an infusion of (spiritual) life, was to be attained through immersion.[69] Because the Mandaeans always considered the Euphrates to be a sanctified body of water,[70] the parallel between them and al-Mughīra breaks down at this point.

Yet another intriguing aspect of the story is the idea of two seas,[71] which also has a parallel in the Mandaean faith. A prominent part of the Mandaean system is the concept of *Maye Hiware* and *Maye Siyawe*, or "light waters" and "dark waters."[72] The dark or black water is believed to have covered the surface of the earth before creation. The King of Darkness (Great Devil) is supposed to have dwelt in the dark water, to which in fact he is presumed to have owed his creation.[73] According to one prominent authority, the dark or black water is symbolic of chaos.[74] The light or white water, on the other hand, was understood to symbolize life itself, being referred to as the "living water,"[75] or as "pure water." It was thought to encircle or traverse the realm of the "higher beings."[76] This Mandaean idea was ultimately derived from the ancient belief that the earth was created from water, an idea associated with the Sumerians, who, interestingly enough, appear to have distinguished in their religion between salt and sweet waters.[77]

That part of the story that relates how God looked down and saw his shadow also has a Mandaean counterpart. According to

---

[69] E. S. Drower, *The Mandaeans of Iraq and Iran* (2nd ed., Leiden, 1962), 100.

[70] Ibid., 101.

[71] Shahrastānī, *Milal*, I, 177.

[72] Friedlaender, "Ibn Hazm: Commentary," 84.

[73] Rudolph, *Theogonie*, 340.

[74] Rudolph, *Die Mandäer*, II (Göttingen, 1961), 63.

[75] Justin, "Baruch by Justin," trans. R. M. Grant, *Gnosticism. A Source Book of Heretical Writings from the Early Christian Period* (New York, 1961), 94.

[76] Brandt, "Mandaeans," in *E.R.E.*, VIII, 382.

[77] S. G. F. Brandon, *Creation Legends of the Ancient Near East* (London, 1963), 72.

the Mandaean tale, *Abatur,* a creative power, looked down into the black water of chaos. He saw the reflection of his image, and at that moment the demiurge *Ptahil* was born.[78] *Ptahil* created the earth and its inhabitants. One sees here another instance of the demiurge as Creator of the World, so important and common in gnostic thought.[79]

There is yet another aspect of al-Mughīra's creation legend that has a non-Islamic counterpart. As noted previously, al-Mughīra asserted that God created both good and bad men.[80] One encounters a similar idea in the teachings of a Gnostic named Saturninus, who believed that the angels responsible for the creation of mankind created both good men and bad men.[81] It is impossible to speak, at least with any certainty, of "influences," but doctrinal similarities should not be overlooked. It is worth noting that Gnostic groups had existed in Mesopotamia and lower Iraq,[82] and their ideas had been preserved in the beliefs of the Mandaeans, who are in fact themselves a form of Gnostic sect.

According to al-Ashʿarī's account, al-Mughīra claimed that Muhammad was the first person whom God created. Shahrastānī's treatment differs in saying that al-Mughīra believed that Muhammad and ʿAlī were created first.[83] This latter version may very well be the correct one, since it coincides in part with a concept called *Tafwīd,* which is often associated with the extremist Shīʿites.[84] Essentially, the idea involved in *Tafwīd* is that God

---

[78] G. Bardy, "Mandéens," in *Dictionnaire de Théologie Catholique,* IX, part II (Paris, 1927), col. 1819.
[79] Couliano, *Tree of Gnosis,* 96–98, 120–121, and passim.
[80] al-Maqrīzī, *Khitat,* III, 303.
[81] R. M. Grant, *Gnosticism and Early Christianity* (New York, 1966), 102; Rudolph, *Gnosis,* 185–186.
[82] Christensen, *L'Iran,* 43.
[83] Shahrastān, *Milal,* I, 177.
[84] Friedlaender, "Ibn Hazm: Commentary," 90–91.

created Muhammad and ʿAlī first, entrusting these two with the task of creating the rest of the world.[85] The term *"Tafwīd"* refers to God's "entrusting" of creation to Muhammad and ʿAlī, an idea that may reflect the influence of the Gnostic demiurge. Moreover, the statement that shadows were created prior to bodies calls to mind the antique identity of the shadow and soul.[86]

The allegorical interpretation of Qurʾānic passages was still another important element in the creation legend. For example, al-Mughīra interpreted Qurʾān 59:16 ("Like unto Satan when he says to a man 'Be an Infidel'") symbolically.[87] In this instance, Satan is considered to be a reference to ʿUmar, whose evil consisted in causing Abū Bakr to "betray" ʿAlī, that is, usurp the caliphal office. Al-Mughīra's symbolic Qurʾānic interpretation is another indication of the importance of this practice for extremist Shīʿism.

Al-Mughīra's belief that Abū Bakr and ʿUmar betrayed ʿAlī has been the source of considerable dispute. Ibn Hajar al-ʿAsqalānī claimed that al-Mughīra cursed the first two caliphs,[88] whereas Nawbakhtī records, in contrast, that the followers of Ibn Sabaʾ were the first to curse the first three caliphs.[89] Nawbakhtī's view appears more plausible: in the first place, Nawbakhtī lived about three centuries earlier than al-ʿAsqalānī and was thus much closer to the events in question; furthermore Nawbakhtī, as well as the other early heresiographers and historians, are agreed that the followers of Ibn Sabaʾ were the first individuals to undertake widespread agitation against the Caliph ʿUthmān, insisting that he had usurped ʿAlī's rightful authority.

[85] The most important work dealing with *Tafwīd* concept extant is the work of Hossein Modarressi, *Crisis and Consolidation*, passim.
[86] H. B. Alexander, "Soul (Primitive)," in *Hastings Encyclopædia of Religion and Ethics*, XI (New York, 1961), 727.
[87] *Qurʾān* 59:16.
[88] Ibn Hajar al-ʿAsqalānī, *Lisān*, VI, 76.
[89] Nawbakhtī, *Firaq*, 44.

With regard to other aspects of al-Mughīra's teachings, the heresiarch claimed, like Bayān Sam'ān,[90] to know the Greatest Name of God. He pretended that this knowledge enabled him to raise the dead.[91] Some sources say that he assigned this power to 'Alī rather than himself.[92] One author maintains that al-Mughīra attributed the power to Muhammad ibn al-Hanafiyya,[93] a statement not confirmed by any other source. The possible origins of the Greatest Name belief among extremist Shī'ites have been discussed elsewhere, and the essential point here is that the concept is not unique to extremist Shī'ite sects. The magic use of the Greatest Name and the power derived therefrom may, however, be considered an element in the attraction of some individuals to these Shī'ite groups.

Al-Mughīra is said to have engaged in the excessive exaltation of 'Alī ibn Abī Tālib. Indeed, some sources report that he even elevated 'Alī above all of the prophets recognized by Islam. Those who credit al-Mughīra with saying that 'Alī was better than Muhammad himself[94] appear to have exaggerated. Most authorities do not attribute such a belief to him. This idea is in fact much more compatible with the teachings of the Ghurābiyya, who held that Gabriel's revelation was intended for 'Alī rather than Muhammad.[95]

One of the most significant practices of the Mughīriyya was their use of violence and terrorism against opponents. They came to be known especially for their practice of strangulation.[96] According to the account in the *Shārh Nāhj al-Balāgha*, al-Mughīra

---

90 William Tucker, "Bayān ibn Sam'ān and the Bayāniyya: Shī'ite Extremists of Umayyad Iraq," *Muslim World*, LXV, 4 (1975).

91 al-Ash'arī, *Maqālāt*, I, 72; Tabarī, *Ta'rīkh*, II, 1916.

92 Ibn al-Jawzī, *al-Muntāzam*, Aya Sofya Ms. 3095, fol. 62a.

93 Maqdisī, *Bad'*, V, 130.

94 al-Saksakī al-Hānbalī, *Kitāb al-Burhān*, fol. 139a.

95 anon., *al-Sawā'iq*, fol. 16b.

96 al-Jāhiz, *Hayawān*, II, 267.

68   *Mahdis and Millenarians*

gave his followers permission to strangle or to poison their opponents, justifying such tactics by his assertion that al-Nafs al-Zakiyya had authorized him to employ practices of this sort.[97] No other source duplicates this story, and its authenticity is suspect. It seems unlikely that al-Mughīra himself advocated or encouraged terrorism. The use of terror by the Mughīriyya probably dates from a period subsequent to the death of al-Mughīra. It is likely that members of the Mughīriyya later associated themselves with the movement led by Abu Mansūr al-'Ijli and engaged in the violent practices for which this extremist was so infamous. The information is not altogether clear, but, aside from any doctrinal consideration, one wonders about the social implications of this terrorism. Was it perhaps a way of getting rid of wealthy or prosperous individuals and expropriating their goods? There is reason to believe so, yet, as in so many instances, the source materials do not afford indisputable proof. On the other hand, one may simply see here the self-assured violence perpetrated by millenarians against those they deemed their enemies, as, for example, with the various Anabaptist and Hussite groups in fifteenth- and sixteenth-century Holland and Germany.[98]

Finally, in several sources, al-Mughīra is said to have been a member of the Saba'iyya – a rather odd statement at first glance. Such information appears in the *'Iqd al-Farīd*, as well as in the geography of Ibn Rusta and the *Kitāb al-Ma'ārif* of Ibn Qutayba.[99] If these authors are using Saba'iyya as a generic term for extremist Shī'ite, then one may readily accept their statements. If, on the other hand, they mean to suggest that al-Mughīra's religious beliefs were identical with or even very similar to those of 'Abd Allāh ibn Saba', this view cannot be sustained. Another apparent

---

[97] Ibn Abī al-Hadīd, *Nāhj*, VIII, 121.

[98] Cohn, *Pursuit* (rev. ed., 1970), 205–280.

[99] Ibn Qutayba, *Ma'ārif*, 206; Ahmad ibn 'Umar ibn Rusta, *Kitāb al-A'lāq al-Nāfisa*, *BGA*, VII (2nd ed., Leiden, 1967), 218. Ibn 'Abd al-Rabbīhī, *'Iqd*, I, 266.

error is to be found in the work of al-Kirmānī, where one reads
that al-Mughīra taught that God descends into every being and
every inanimate object.[100] Such information, not found in any
other source, is clearly anachronistic.

By way of assessing the significance of al-Mughīra and the
group derived from him, one notes first the unusual nature (in
the Islamic context) of some of the beliefs and doctrines taught.
Is it possible to see here an infusion of non-Islamic ideas into
extremist Shīʿite thought? Obviously, positing "influences" in
doctrine is difficult, if not dangerous, especially in view of the
nature of the sources. It is, nevertheless, instructive to note
the similarities between the thought of al-Mughīra and those of
the Mandaeans, other Gnostics, and, to a lesser extent, the Manichaeans. In any case, what is clear and worthy of note is the impact
that al-Mughīra's ideas were to have on subsequent Shīʿite sects.
A specific example of this influence, which was noted previously,
is the speculation about the letters of the Arabic alphabet, which
later Shīʿite groups, including the Ismāʿīlīs, would include among
their beliefs.

Of much greater impact, the origins of religious elitism among
extremist Shīʿites can be traced to al-Mughīra and his followers.
The real importance of al-Mughīra lies in the sense of exclusiveness that he inculcated among his followers. Such particularism
or special status was indispensable for anyone seriously attempting to take control of the state, because it obviously required
the discipline and organization necessary for such an effort. By
its very nature, also, elitist feeling created a sense of militance
and hostility toward those outside the group. In fact, religious
elitism was the psychological foundation of the sort of terrorism that manifested itself later in extremist Shīʿism, with Abū
Mansūr al-ʿIjli and his followers, and that, in the case of millenarian movements elsewhere, has already been noted. One may see

[100] al-Kirmānī, "Ein Kommentar," 40.

in al-Mughīra's teaching, furthermore, the germ of revolutionary violence later associated with the terrorist wing of the *Nizārīs*
("Assassins," as they are known in the West).

   Al-Mughīra and his followers were the first to generate support
for the descendants of al-Hasan ibn 'Alī. The Hasanid involved
was Muhammad al-Nafs al-Zakiyya. In a sense one may consider
al-Mughīra the founder of the movement that later supported al-
Nafs al-Zakiyya and his brother in their abortive rebellion against
Abū Ja'far al-Mansūr. Probably this insurrection had little significance for al-Mughīra. Judging from his pretensions to prophecy,
it is unlikely that he was deeply committed to the Hasanid cause.
For al-Mughīra, as for most of the other heresiarchs, claims to
support the 'Alids were primarily attempts to legitimize their own
political activities and ideologies and became signifiers of their
status as revolutionary millenarian leaders. For their followers, by
contrast, the 'Alids were of special significance, as they had come
to be seen as the guarantors of right belief and, more importantly,
as the sources of justice and goodness on earth. This explains the
great veneration of the Mughīriyya for al-Nafs al-Zakiyya, the central feature of their religious beliefs after the death of al-Mughīra.
Al-Nafs al-Zakiyya was the obvious source of al-Mughīra's charismatic status. Here, again, the millenarian leader surfaced in the
medieval Islamic world.

4

Abū Mansūr al-ʿIjlī and the Mansūriyya

Because we live in an age plagued by religious/political violence and calculated atrocity or intimidation of the "Other" (e.g., "ethnic cleansing"), it is well to remember that neither phenomenon is of recent origin. Although the motivating factors have, to a certain extent, changed over the centuries, some of the causes advanced for the contemporary use of violence are not altogether novel to the historian of Europe or the East. Students of medieval Islam, for example, will immediately recall the violent tactics of the *Azāriqa* Kharijites and the terrorism practiced by the *Nizārī* Ismāʿīlīs. Among other terrorist groups in the medieval Near East was the less well-known sect the Mansūriyya, which consisted of the followers of Abū Mansūr al-ʿIjli, whose actions and ideas assume particular significance when considered within the contexts of Shīʿism and medieval Islamic history in general.

Abū Mansūr al-ʿIjli was a native of the *Sawād al-Kufa*.[1] As his name indicates,[2] he was probably a member of the Banū ʿIjl, although Nawbakhtī and al-Ashʿarī al-Qummī claim that he belonged to the ʿAbd al-Qays.[3] These two writers are the only

---

[1] al-Ashʿarī al-Qummī, *al-Maqālāt wal al-Firaq*, 66.
[2] al-Ashʿarī, *Maqālāt*, I, 74.
[3] Nawbakhtī, *Firaq*, 59.

ones to attribute his origins to the 'Abd al-Qays, and it seems more likely that he was indeed an 'Ijlite. Apparently his childhood was spent in the desert, for we are informed that he was raised there.[4] He is said to have owned a house in Kufa,[5] the same authority noting that he was illiterate.[6] There is an extremely remote possibility that Abū Mansūr had been familiar with Christianity, because he claimed that God had spoken to him in Syriac, referring to him as "my son,"[7] a Christian expression characterizing the relationship between God and man. The evidence here is inconclusive, although it should be noted that a portion of the Banū 'Ijl was Christian.[8] Abū Mansūr's religious and political activism finally led to his death at the hands of Yūsuf ibn 'Umar al-Thaqafī, Umayyad governor of Iraq from 738 to 744.[9] Professor Claude Cahen gives 740 as the year of Abū Mansūr's death,[10] but because his source is not apparent, one can only say with certainty that it occurred between 738 and 744.

Abū Mansūr's followers, the Mansūriyya, included both Arabs and *Mawālī*. Most of the Arabs involved were members of the 'Ijl, Kinda, and Bajīla tribes. Shahrastānī states, for example, that individuals from the Kinda were members of the Mansūriyya.[11] Ibn Qutayba repeats this information but adds that the Bajīla were also present.[12] According to a verse attributed to A'sha Hamdān, the 'Ijl were likewise numbered among the followers of Abū Mansūr.[13] It is interesting to note that the Kinda and Bajīla

---

[4] al-Ash'arī al-Qummī, *Maqālāt wa al-Firaq*, 46.

[5] Nawbakhtī, *Firaq*, 59.

[6] Ibid.

[7] Ibid.

[8] Moscati, "Antica Sī'a," 267.

[9] al-Ash'arī, *Maqālāt*, I, 75; Gabrieli, "Hishām," 27–33.

[10] Cahen, "La Révolution 'Abbaside," 315.

[11] Shahrastānī, *Milal*, 178.

[12] Ibn Qutayba, *'Uyūn*, II, 147.

[13] al-Jāhiz, *Hayawān*, II, 147; Cf. Ibn Qutayba, *'Uyūn*, II, 146.

were associated at some point with the movement of al-Mughīra ibn Saʿīd.[14] From the backgrounds of these tribes, one may possibly discern reasons for their involvement with Abū Manṣūr. The Banū ʿIjl were members of the Lahāzim group of the Bakr ibn Wāʾil confederation.[15] They produced a number of noted leaders in both pre-Islamic and Islamic times. Among the pre-Islamic notables were Bujayr ibn ʿĀʾidh, a great military leader, and Hānzala ibn Thaʿlaba ibn Sayyār, who led the ʿIjl at the battle of Dhū Qār. In early Muslim times, one Madhʿūr ibn ʿAdī participated in the conquests of Syria and Egypt. Two ʿIjlites, ʿUtayba ibn al-Nahhās ibn Hānzala and Hajjār ibn Abjār ibn Bujayr, were members of the Rabīʿa aristocracy in Kufa.[16] At some point, as noted previously, a part of the ʿIjl are reported to have adopted Christianity.[17] It has also been suggested that certain elements of the tribe had become Persianized, supposedly as a result of the alliance between the ʿIjl of Bahrayn and Persian settlers who had come into the area from Istakhr.[18]

The Kinda tribe had been the head of a powerful confederation in Central Arabia prior to the coming of Islam.[19] Having

[14] William Tucker, "Rebels and Gnostics: al-Mugīra ibn Saʿīd and the Mugīriyya," *Arabica*, XXII (1975), 36.

[15] Important details concerning the background of the Bakr ibn Wāʾil tribes are to be found in Fred M. Donner, "The Bakr b. Wāʾil Tribes and Politics in Northwestern Arabia on the Eve of Islam," *Studia Islamica*, 51 (1980), 5–38.

[16] I am most grateful for this information to my late teacher and adviser, Professor Wadie Jwaideh, formerly Professor of History and Chairman, Department of Near Eastern Languages and Literatures, Indiana University, Bloomington, Ind.

[17] Moscati, "Antica Sīʿa," 267.

[18] Ignaz Goldziher, "Islamisme et Parsisme," *Revue de l'histoire des Religions*, XLIII (1901), 23; Idem., *Muslim Studies*, trans. C. R. Barber and S. M. Stern, I (Chicago, 1967), 100.

[19] I. Shahid, "Kinda," in *E.I.2*, 5 (Leiden, 1979), 118–120. For an older account, still useful especially because of its references, see Hitti, *Arabs*, 85; sources cited therein.

accepted Islam from the Prophet Muhammad, they turned
against the Muslim state at the time of the *Ridda* wars. Al-Ash'ath
ibn Qays and other notables led the futile struggle against the
Islamic forces.[20] Certain elements of the Kinda aligned themselves with the 'Alids at the beginning of the Umayyad period.
The first Shī'ite conspiracy to erupt under the Umayyads, in fact,
was the work of a Kindite, Hujr ibn 'Adī, who was then put to death
on the orders of Mu'āwiya ibn Abī Sufyān.[21] Later, when Muslim
ibn 'Aqīl attempted to win Kufa for al-Husayn ibn 'Alī, a member
of the Kinda sheltered him (ibn 'Aqīl) in his home.[22] Members
of the Kinda also played a role in the subsequent rebellion of
al-Mukhtār ibn Abī 'Ubayd in Kufa.[23] Finally, the Kinda took
part in the anti-Umayyad insurrections of 'Abd al-Rahmān ibn
al-Ash'ath and Yazīd ibn al-Muhallab.[24] The anti-Umayyad activities here enumerated were probably the results of Iraqi regional
feeling or the Qays-Yamani dispute. One wonders if the Arabism-
versus-assimilation argument of Professor M. A. Shaban might
not be applicable here.[25] Unfortunately, the sources provide no
corroboration in this instance.

Although the Bajīla were a relatively small tribe, they played a
very important role in early Muslim history. At the time of the conquest of Iraq, 'Umar ibn al-Khattāb is said to have entered into an
agreement with the Bajīla, whereby one-fourth of the whole booty
obtained from that country would be assigned to this tribe upon the successful conclusion of the campaign.[26] The Bajīla were

---

[20] Ahmad ibn Yahyā al-Balādhurī, *Kitāb Futūh al-Buldān*, trans. Hitti as *The Origins of the Islamic State* (2nd ed., Beirut, 1966), 154.
[21] Abū al-'Abbās Ahmad ibn Abī Ya'qūb al-Ya'qūbi, *Ta'rīkh*, II (Beirut, 1960), 230; Dīnawārī, *Akhbār*, 223.
[22] Tabarī, *Ta'rīkh*, II, 275.
[23] Balādhurī, *Ansāb*, V, 248; Tabarī, *Ta'rīkh*, II, 644.
[24] Tabarī, *Ta'rīkh*, III (Leiden, 1964), 1397.
[25] Shaban, *Islamic History*, 120–124.
[26] Balādhurī, *Futūh*, trans. Hitti, 424–425.

also supporters of al-Mukhtār during the latter's serious rebellion in Kufa and served in his army at the disastrous battle of Madhār.[27] Evidence for the presence of the *Mawālī* among the Mansūriyya is much less clear. From the time of al-Mukhtār the *Mawālī* are known to have taken an active part in Shī'ite movements, particularly those of an extremist cast. In this instance there is a strong indication that elements of the Mughīriyya joined Abū Mansūr after their own leader's death, which probably meant that those *Mawālī* among the Mughīriyya became a part of the Mansūriyya.

The Mansūriyya owe their place in Islamic history primarily to their indulgence in acts of terror (in other words, not random, but calculated violence). Al-Baghdādī records that they regarded the murder of opponents as a lawful act.[28] Indeed, they seem to have considered it not only a permissible but a meritorious act. Similar utilization of violence can be seen in other millenarian movements, especially the Taborites of fourteenth-century Bohemia.[29] The Mansūriyya were especially identified with the practice of strangulation.[30] Jāhiz has given an intriguing account of their tactics and methods. He informs us, for instance, that they not only always traveled together, but also resided on particular streets. Each member of their households possessed drums, tambourines, and dogs, which were essential ingredients in their terrorist tactics. Whenever a victim entered their streets, they alerted one another by striking the instruments and causing the dogs to bark, a practice that served also to drown out the cries of victims. Aside from strangulation, the Mansūriyya also adopted the practice of stoning those unfortunates who fell into their

[27] Tabarī, *Ta'rīkh*, II, 722.
[28] al-Baghdādī *Usūl*, 331.
[29] Paul Boyer, *When Time Shall Be No More: Prophecy Belief in Modern American Culture* (Cambridge, Mass., 1992), 54–55.
[30] Ibn Rusta, *A'lāq*, 218; Jāhiz, *Hayawān*, II, 267.

hands.[31] The impression given by all of this information is that the followers of Abū Mansūr were merely common criminals. Such a conclusion, although tempting, seems on further reflection to be unwarranted, because the Mansūriyya actually used violence as a religious-political tactic. The appropriation of the victims' goods may be seen as an indication of social bitterness and hatred or simply a fringe benefit.

After the death of Abū Mansūr, the Mansūriyya apparently recognized his son al-Husayn ibn Abī Mansūr, who purportedly claimed the gift of prophecy for himself and gained a large following. He was put to death by the 'Abbāsid caliph al-Mahdī.[32] According to al-Ash'arī, the Mansūriyya split after the death of Abū Mansūr. This author states that a second group, rather than recognizing Abū Mansūr's son, turned to Muhammad al-Nafs al Zakiyya, who was killed in a rebellion against the Caliph Abū Ja'far al-Mansūr. They asserted that Muhammad al-Bāqir (the fifth *Imām*) had passed the *Imāmate* on to Abū Mansūr; after his death it went to al-Nafs al-Zakiyya, whom they believed to be the *Mahdī*.[33] Probably, this group is to be identified with the remnants of the Mughīriyya, at least some of whom joined Abū Mansūr. There is no indication that Abū Mansūr himself ever recognized al-Nafs al-Zakiyya.

In the brief work of al-Kirmānī, it is stated that the group recognizing al-Nafs al-Zakiyya after Abū Mansūr's death claimed that the former had bequeathed the *Imāmate* to Abū Mansūr.[34] Al-Kirmānī is evidently in error here. The correct version is to be found in the work of al-Ash'arī, who states that the group recognizing al-Nafs as-Zakiyya after Abū Mansūr believed that Muhammad al-Bāqir had left the *Imāmate* to Abū Mansūr.[35]

---

[31] Jāhiz, *Hayawān*, II, 264–267.
[32] al-Kirmānī, "Ein Kommentar," 41; Nawbakhtī, *Firaq*, 60.
[33] al-Ash'arī, *Maqālāt*, I, 97.
[34] al-Kirmānī, "Ein Kommentar," 41.
[35] al-Ash'arī, *Maqālāt*, I, 97.

Al-Kirmānī's version is incorrect for the simple reason that al-Nafs al-Zakiyya, who was killed in 762, could hardly have bequeathed the *Imāmate* to Abū Mansūr, who died between 738 and 744. Al-Bāqir, who died in 735, could, on the other hand, very easily have done so.

At one point, Abū Mansūr appears to have acknowledged the *Imāmate* of al-Bāqir. The latter, however, is reported to have disavowed Abū Mansūr.[36] After the death of al-Bāqir, Abū Mansūr proclaimed himself *Imām*, pretending that he had been so designated by al-Bāqir.[37] There can be little doubt that his recognition of al-Bāqir was meant to lend legitimacy to his personal ambitions.

Abū Mansūr's most extreme claim was his assertion that he had been in the presence of God. He stated that God had raised him to Heaven, had touched him with his hand and then told him to go preach.[38] In Nawbakhtī's account, Abū Mansūr is made to say that God spoke to him in Syriac.[39] Kashshī, on the other hand, says that God had spoken in Persian.[40] Nawbakhtī's account is preferable, as Syriac (Aramaic) was the language of many of the indigenous inhabitants of Iraq, regardless of religion. After Abū Mansūr's audience with God, he returned to the earth. He claimed that the Qur'ānic verse: "If they see a fragment

[36] al-Qalhātī, *Kashf,* fol. 222b. Cf. Zayn al-ʿAbidīn Yūsuf ibn Muhammad al-Kūrānī, *al-Yamāniyya al-Maslūla ʿalā Rawāfid al-Makhdhūla,* Bibliothèque Nationale Ms., Arabes 1462, fol. 19b.

[37] Abū al-Faraj ʿAbd al-Rahmān ibn ʿAlī ibn al-Jawzī, *Naqd al-ʿIlm wa al-ʿUlamāʾ = Talbīs Iblīs* (Cairo, 1966), 95; Iqbāl, *Khāndāne,* 261. It should be noted that Iqbāl refers to the Mansūriyya as *Kisfiyya,* a reference to the fact that Abū Mansūr called himself the *kisf* (fragment) fallen from the sky.

[38] [Abū Muhammad?], *Milal wa al-Nihal,* Atif Effendi Kütübhanesi, Istanbul, Ms. 1373, fol. 75a. A microfilm copy of this work is available in the library of Indiana University, Bloomington, Ind.; Cf. Isfarāʾīnī, *Tabsīr,* 70; Ibn Dāʿī al-Rāzī, *Tabsīra,* 170.

[39] Nawbakhtī, *Firaq,* 59.

[40] Kashshī, *Rijāl,* 256.

fallen from the sky, they will say it is piled up clouds," referred
to his descent back to earth.[41] Another authority says that Abū
Mansūr maintained that "'Alī ibn Abī Tālib was the 'fragment
fallen from the sky.'"[42] This latter account, however, is no doubt
incorrect, because it does not fit the general context in which
Abū Mansūr's statement was made. Interestingly enough, one
sees here again an example of the allegorical interpretation of
the Qur'ān, a practice frequent in extremist Shī'ite circles.[43] One
finds, incidentally, other examples of millenarian prophets or
leaders claiming to have been in Paradise, for example, among
cult movements in Fiji in the 1940s.[44]

Abū Mansūr's tale of his ascent to Heaven was probably
intended to buttress the heresiarch's claim to prophecy. In addition to proclaiming himself a prophet, he taught that prophecy
does not cease, but rather that God continues to send prophets
to mankind.[45] Abū Mansūr is reported to have announced that
six of his sons would be prophets after him, the last of them
also being the *Mahdī*.[46] In al-Himyarī's version, he believed that
al-Nafs al-Zakiyya was the *Mahdī*.[47] Al-Himyarī's account does
not appear in any of the other sources and is probably not correct, because, as already noted, Abū Mansūr is usually linked
with Muhammad al-Bāqir. An extremely interesting, if somewhat

---

[41] *Qur'ān* 52:44. Abū Muhammad 'Abdallāh ibn Muslim ibn Qutayba, *Kitāb Ta'wīl*
Mukhtalif al-Hadīth, trans. Gerard Lecomte (Damascus, 1962), 81; Maqdisī,
Bad', V, 131.

[42] 'Īji, *Mawāqif*, 386.

[43] Tucker, "Rebels and Gnostics," 44. Cf. Tucker, "Bayān ibn Sam'ān," 247.

[44] Jean Guiart, "Institutions religieuses traditionelles et messianismes modernes
à Fiji," *Archives de Sociologie des Religions*, IV (1957), 26–28.

[45] Friedlaender, "Ibn Hazm: Commentary," 62; al-Jīlānī, *Ghunya*, 99; Josef van
Ess, "Dirār ibn 'Amr und die 'Cahmiye.' Biographie einer vergessenen Schule,"
Der Islam, XLIV (1968), 19; Ignaz Goldziher, "Neuplatonische und Gnostische
Elemente im Hadit," *Zeitschrift für Assyriologie*, XXII (1909), 339, n.4.

[46] al-Ash'arī, *Maqālāt*, 47.

[47] al-Himyarī, *Hūr*, 169.

cryptic, reference to Abū Mansūr's ideas about prophecy is to be found in the geographical work of Ibn al-Faqīh al-Hamadhānī, where one reads that Abū Mansūr accepted seven prophets from the Banū 'Ijl and seven from the Banū Quraysh.[48] One may explain this statement in the following manner: Abū Mansūr is supposed to have asserted that 'Alī, al-Hasan, al-Husayn, 'Alī ibn Husayn (*Zayn al-'Abidīn*), and Muhammad ibn 'Alī al-Bāqir were prophets.[49] As indicated above, he also believed that he and six of his descendants possessed the gift of prophecy. It will be noted that 'Alī and the four *Imāms* mentioned add up to five Qurayshite prophets. If one adds to these the prophet Muhammad, the result is six. The seventh prophet could be Muhammad ibn al-Hanafiyya, Abū Hāshim, and so on. The seven prophets of the Banū 'Ijl are, of course, Abū Mansūr and his six descendants.

Abū Mansūr's theory of the continuation of prophecy is the most developed expression of that idea that had appeared among the extremist Shī'ites up to that time. Al-Mukhtār and Hamza ibn 'Umāra had called themselves prophets, but they had not stressed the unceasing nature of prophecy in specific terms. Bayān ibn Sam'ān had claimed prophecy on the basis of its having been transmitted to him from Abū Hāshim ibn Muhammad ibn al-Hanafiyya. Here again, however, there is no sign of a theory of prophetic continuation as explicit as that of Abū Mansūr. It is perhaps worth noting the presence of this same idea in Gnostic, Manichaean, and Islamic thought prior to Abū Mansūr or other Shī'ite extremists.

Abū Mansūr is said to have asserted that Jesus was the first person whom God created, the second being 'Alī.[50] Al-Mughīra

---

[48] Abū Bakr Ahmad ibn Muhammad ibn al-Faqīh al-Hamadhānī, *Mukhtasār Kitāb al-Buldān*, B. G. A., V (Leiden, 1885), 185.

[49] al-Ash'arī, *Maqālāt*, 47.

[50] al-Ash'arī, *Maqālāt*, I, 74.

ibn Saʿīd had made a similar claim, maintaining, however, that Muhammad was the first to be created.[51] Abū Mansūr may have derived this idea from Mughīra, simply substituting Jesus for Muhammad. Once more one wonders about possible Christian influences. Though he was not himself of Christian origin, Abū Mansūr may well have assimilated some Christian ideas. In contrast to the above figures, al-Himyarī reports that Abū Mansūr believed Moses to have been the first to be created.[52] This information is not duplicated in any other source and seems extremely implausible.

According to some authorities, Abū Mansūr preached that Paradise and Hell were men.[53] He is supposed to have asserted that Paradise referred to a man whom the Shīʿa were to serve, that is, the *Imām* of the time. Hell was a reference to the adversaries of the *Imām*, for example, Abū Bakr, ʿUmar, ʿUthmān, Muʿāwiya.[54] In the version given by al-Baghdādī, the Mansūriyya interpreted Heaven as the pleasure obtained in this world and Hell as the world's misfortunes.[55] The concept of an anthropomorphic Heaven and Hell is also to be seen as an important part of the teachings, later, of Abū al-Khattāb al-Asʿadī and his followers, the Khattābiyya, who argued that such knowledge freed them from religious prohibitions.[56] In spite of contradictions, what clearly emerges here is that Heaven and Hell were simply symbolic designations in the religious thought of Abū Mansūr and his followers. With regard to both Abū Mansūr and Abū al-Khattāb, this concept borders on the antinomianism of the

---

[51] Tucker, "Rebels and Gnostics," 43.
[52] al-Himyarī, *Hūr*, 159.
[53] al-Ashʿarī, *Maqālāt*, I, 74.
[54] Shahrastānī, *Milal*, I, 179.
[55] al-Baghdādī, *Schisms* (trans. Halkin), 57.
[56] Abū Hanīfa Qādī al-Nuʿmān b. Muhammad, *The Book of Faith from the Daʿāʾim al-Islām (Pillars of Islam) of al-Qādī al-Nuʿmān b. Muhammad al-Tamīmī*, trans. A. A. A. Fyzee (Bombay, 1974), 58.

adepts of the Free Spirit, a view that came to be very important in late medieval Europe.[57] Abū Mansūr and the Mansūriyya viewed the religious duties and prohibitions in much the same way that they did Heaven and Hell. They professed to believe that the written prohibitions referred to men whom the Shīʿa were to treat as enemies, whereas the religious duties represented those to be served.[58] One author has it that the forbidden things were really people whom the Shīʿa were to love, for example, ʿAlī, Fatima, and their sons.[59] Given the context of the statement, the author seems to have confused his information. The prohibition would more logically refer to those whom one should despise. Shahrastānī reports that the Mansūriyya assigned the names of men to the religious prescriptions. The reason for this, he continues, was that whoever was able to gain ascendancy over one of these men became exempt from the duty represented by that individual.[60] As Goldziher has rightly indicated, this is another example of allegorical interpretation,[61] a practice that would be of major importance later in the Ismāʿīlī system.

Abū Mansūr appears to have introduced into extremist Shīʿite thought an idea of fundamental importance with regard to the position of the Qurʾān. He claimed that Muhammad had been given the revelation, while he (Abū Mansūr) had been chosen to interpret this same revelation.[62] All of his allegorical interpretations rested, without doubt, upon this basic concept. The importance of the idea lies in the suggestion that the function

---

[57] Cohn, "Medieval Millenarism," *Millennial Dreams*, ed. Thrupp, 36–37.

[58] Shahrastānī, *Milal*, I, 179.

[59] Abū Muhammad ʿUthmān ibn ʿAbdallāh ibn al-Hasan al-ʿIrāqī al-Hanafī, *al-Firaq al-Muftariqa bayna Ahlī al-Zaygh wa al-Zandaqa*, Ankara Universitesi Ilahiyat Fakultesi Publication no. XXXII (Ankara, 1961), 41.

[60] Shahrastānī, *Milal*, I, 179.

[61] Goldziher, "Gnostische Elemente," 339, n.4.

[62] al-Ashʿarī, *Maqālāt*, 47.

of religious interpretation belonged to someone other than Muhammad. One can see here probably the most explicit attempt to justify allegorical interpretation of the Qur'ān and the precepts of Islam.

The Mansūriyya's techniques of assassination are of special interest, because it is quite likely that they had a theological significance. The use of stones and rope was probably dictated by the belief that steel weapons should not be employed until the advent of the *Mahdī* (that is, the coming of the Millennium).[63] As Ibn Hazm noted parenthetically in his examination of the movement of Abū Mansūr, the Khashabiyya of Mukhtār's following carefully avoided steel weapons, hence their name (the "wood bearers").[64] As Ibn Hazm seems to suggest, the Mansūriyya may have copied the Khashabiyya in their choice of weapons.

All of the sources appear to be in agreement that Abū Mansūr enjoined his supporters to kill those not of their religious persuasion.[65] This would seem to reflect the millenarian dynamic formulated by Cohn in his study of medieval millenarianism. In his discussion of the way in which millenarian revolts formed around some prophet or prophetic figure, he states the following:

On the strength of supernatural revelations, the social conflict of the moment was presented as essentially different from other struggles known to history, a cataclysm from which the world was to emerge totally transformed and redeemed. A movement fighting such a battle under a divinely inspired leader inevitably regarded itself as an elite set infinitely above the rest of mankind, infallible and incapable of sin. Avowedly concerned to purify the world of sin in preparation for the coming of the Millennium, these movements commonly showed themselves very bloodthirsty indeed.[66]

---

[63] Lewis, *Assassins*, 128.

[64] Friedlaender, "Ibn Hazm: Commentary," 62–63; Cf. anon., *Risāla fī Bayān Firaq al-Azilla*, Istanbul Universitesi Merkez Kūtūbhanesi, Arabic Ms. 5295, fol. 3a. My thanks to the staff of this library for their gracious and kind aid to me.

[65] Ibn Qutayba, '*Uyūn*, II, 147; Nawbakhtī, *Firaq*, 60.

[66] Cohn, "Medieval Millenarism," *Millennial Dreams*, ed. Thrupp, 38.

Isfarā'īnī states that the Mansūriyya "deemed it permissible" to strangle opponents.[67] It is clear, however, that they considered such action not only permissible but, in fact, praiseworthy. According to some accounts, Abū Mansūr preached that whoever killed forty of his opponents was assured of attaining Paradise.[68] Others report that Abū Mansūr and his son permitted their followers to strangle opponents and seize their wealth.[69] Terrorism and assassination were not new phenomena in the Muslim world. Out of the first four leaders of the Islamic state, three had met death at the hands of assassins. Certain elements of the Kharijites, as is well known, had slain those who did not accept their teachings. Abū Mansūr and his followers, then, were not the first terrorists in Muslim history. They were, however, innovators in a very important sense: They seem to have been responsible for the *institutionalization* of violence and terror, which came to be a matter of policy, an integral part of a religious-political program. One sees here not murder as the result of passion or even crude religious fanaticism, but instead murder as a rationalized method or technique. The Mansūriyya's use of terror, it may be argued, anticipates that of the later terrorist wing of the *Nizārī* Ismā'īlīs. Goldziher, in fact, suggested some years ago that the activity of the Mansūriyya provided the precedent for such *Nizārī* terrorism.[70]

The Mansūriyya are said to have taken oaths in an interesting manner. The sources indicate that they used to swear as follows: "No, by the Word (*Kalima*)."[71] It seems likely that the concept involved here is traceable to the Qur'ān. In such passages as Qur'ān 3:45 and 4:171 (Cairo edition), Jesus is referred to as the

---

[67] Isfarā'īnī, *Tabsīr*, 73.

[68] Attributed to Ahmad ibn Hānbal by Abū al-Husayn Muhammad ibn Muhammad ibn Abī Ya'lā, *Tabaqāt al-Hanābila*, I (Cairo, 1952), 33.

[69] al-Ash'arī, *Maqālāt*, 47.

[70] Ignaz Goldziher, *Zeitschrift des Ghazali gegen die Batinijje-Sekte* (2nd ed., Leiden, 1956), 4.

[71] al-Ash'arī, *Maqālāt*, I, 74.

Kalima (Word) of God, suggesting an idea similar to the Christian *Logos*. It is possible, although less likely, that Abū Mansūr derived the *Kalima* idea from Christianity.

Abū Mansūr and the Mansūriyya characterized the relationship between the *Imām* and his supporters in an unusual fashion. The family of the prophet Muhammad, they believed, was Heaven; the Shī'a were the earth.[72] W. Montgomery Watt has asserted that this belief is similar to one held by the ancient Mesopotamians.[73] Although Watt does not specify the Mesopotamian parallel, he may have in mind the following idea: in the religious lore of ancient Mesopotamia, the god of the sky, *Anu*, who was held to be the source of majesty and authority, was believed to be the prototype of all fathers and gods. He was responsible for lifting the universe out of chaos and for the establishment of order.[74] This belief corresponds quite closely, it would seem, to Abū Mansūr's view of Muhammad's family, whose members he considered to be the source of religious-political authority and the guarantors of the universe. His estimation of the role of the Shī'a, on the other hand, calls to mind the Mesopotamian *Ensi*, the earthly representative of one of the gods. The task of the *Ensi* was to uphold the order of the city-state, the manor of the gods.[75] The *Ensi* had, then, essentially two roles: as earthly images of the gods, they were the depositaries of the divine law, while they also acted as intermediaries between man and the gods.[76] This is in fact a fair description of the role and functions that Abū Mansūr and other heresiarchs arrogated to themselves.

---

[72] al-Himyarī, *Hūr*, 169.

[73] Watt, "Umayyad Shī'ism," 168.

[74] Henri Frankfort et al., *Before Philosophy. The Intellectual Adventure of Ancient Man* (4th ed., Baltimore, Md., 1961), 151–152.

[75] Ibid., 203.

[76] Francis Dvornik, *Early Christian and Byzantine Political Philosophy*, I (Washington, D.C., 1966), 36–37.

Certain sources offer erroneous information about Abū
Mansūr and his followers. Malatī, for example, seems to con-
fuse the Mansūriyya with the Sabaʾiyya, followers of the enigmatic
ʿAbd Allāh ibn Sabaʾ. He asserts that the Mansūriyya believed that
ʿAlī had not died but was concealed in the clouds, from which
he and his followers would return prior to the resurrection.[77]
These ideas are to be associated with the Sabaʾiyya and certainly
not the Mansūriyya. Not one of the other sources attributes any
such teachings to Abū Mansūr or his followers.

Al-Kirmānī reports that the Mansūriyya claimed that God had
appeared in the persons of Christ and ʿAlī.[78] The only possible
basis for such a statement is offered by Shahrastānī, who credited
Abū Mansūr with saying that ʿAlī was the fragment fallen from
the sky, mentioned in the Qurʾān. He then goes on to say that
Abū Mansūr claimed that God himself was the fragment. Finally,
in a third statement, Abū Mansūr is made to declare that he himself is the fragment.[79] It is clear that the last statement is the
correct one. Al-Kirmānī's information is not directly supported
by other early sources, particularly those of al-Ashʿarī and Nawbakhtī, whose accounts of the Mansūriyya seem to be the most
detailed and balanced.[80]

ʿAbd al-Qādir al-Jīlānī's work also betrays some confusion or
inaccuracy with regard to the Mansūriyya. He writes that the
Mansūriyya believed Gabriel to have made an error in the deliv-
ery of God's revelation.[81] This information is clearly mistaken,
as the concept mentioned was the major tenet of the group
known as the Ghurābiyya. The Ghurābiyya argued that God had
destined the revelation for ʿAlī, but Gabriel had been confused

[77] Malatī, *Tanbīh*, 120.
[78] al-Kirmānī, "Ein Kommentar," 40.
[79] Shahrastānī, *Milal*, I, 179.
[80] al-Ashʿarī, *Maqālāt*, I, 96; Nawbakhtī, *Firaq*, 60.
[81] al-Jīlānī, *Ghunya*, 99.

because Muhammad and ʿAlī looked as much alike "as two crows" (*Ghurāb* means "crow," hence the name of the sect).[82]

In terms of evaluating the role of Abū Mansūr and his followers in medieval Islam, one sees in them the development and introduction of certain concepts, some of them significant in Shīʿite (at least extremist) thought. His claim of ascension to Paradise and an audience with God was unique to Abū Mansūr. His teaching that Heaven and Hell were individuals also appears to have been an original contribution, one that was to reappear in certain Shīʿite circles. Abū Mansūr's allegorical interpretation of the Qurʾān and religious duties was not peculiar to him, but he and his followers did further develop the practice. It may in fact be argued that their application of allegorical interpretation to ritual and dietary practices was one of their significant contributions. Abū Mansūr's idea regarding the continuation of prophecy was probably the most developed expression of that concept by an extremist Shīʿite thinker of the Umayyad period.

The theory about the family of Muhammad and the Shīʿa being equal to Heaven and earth, respectively, seems to have been another of Abū Mansūr's original contributions, although its role in Shīʿism subsequently is uncertain. Similarly Abū Mansūr's reference to Jesus is another feature not associated with other Shīʿite groups. Certainly one of the most important ideas originating with this Iraqi sectarian was his teaching that he was the interpreter of the revelation that Muhammad had transmitted. This is not simply a question of delusions of grandeur. Such an idea in fact is important in that it furnishes the fundamental sanction for the Shīʿite practice of symbolic or allegorical interpretation of Islamic teachings. It also can be seen as providing prophetic justification for Abū Mansūr, just as, in modern South Africa,

---

[82] Muhammad ibn Ahmad ibn Jubayr, *The Travels of Ibn Jubayr*, trans. R. J. C. Broadhurst (London, 1952), 291; for a later account of the Ghurābiyya see anon., *al-Sawāʾiq*, Library of the India Office Ms. 2167, Delhi 916, fol. 16b.

Bantu prophets claim to have the power of prophecy and revelation of God's will, and to, in fact, be a revelation of the living
God.[83]

In the final analysis, however, Abū Mansūr and his followers
were most important for the way in which they practiced terrorism. They did not originate terroristic methods, but they took the
significant step of institutionalizing and rationalizing them. As
pointed out previously, such institutionalized assassination would
later be the trademark of certain *Nizārī* Ismāʿīlīs.[84]

[83] Jacqueline Eberhardt, "Messianisme en Afrique du Sud," *Archives de Sociologie des Religions*, IV (1957), 53–56.
[84] Hodgson, *Assassins*, 83–84.

5

'Abd Allāh ibn Mu'āwiya and the Janāhiyya

In the various treatments of late Umayyad history available to the student of the Islamic societies, little attention is given to the rebellion and ideology of the fourth group examined in the present monograph, that of 'Abd Allāh ibn Mu'āwiya ibn 'Abd Allāh and his core followers, usually known as the Janāhiyya, who were the bulwark of his revolutionary movement and who were partisans of an extremist Shī'ite ideology focusing on the person of Ibn Mu'āwiya. The obvious reason for such an omission is, of course, that *in the event* it was a rebellion led by the famous Abū Muslim al-Khurasānī, *not* Ibn Mu'āwiya, that overturned the Damascene dynasty, thereby ushering in a new order as well as a new ruling family. Whereas history as the study of victors rather than losers may be readily understandable and perhaps even justifiable, one may nevertheless question in this instance the validity of ignoring an "also-ran." An examination of Ibn Mu'āwiya and his adherents touches upon three important issues. First, an investigation of the rising shows the nature and extent of opposition to the rulers in Damascus by the middle 740s. Second, a close look at the composition of Ibn Mu'āwiya's movement may suggest why Abū Muslim and not Ibn Mu'āwiya attained the victor's laurels. Finally, an analysis of the teachings of the Janāhiyya, the extremist Shī'ites who made up the core of the revolutionary movement, sheds further light upon the evolution of extremist Shī'ite thought in the late Umayyad and early 'Abbasid periods. The purpose of this chapter, then, is to elucidate as far as possible the activities and ideas of Ibn Mu'āwiya and those who followed him within the framework of the three themes just enunciated.

'Abd Allāh ibn Mu'āwiya ibn 'Abd Allāh ibn Ja'far ibn Abī Tālib was, as the name indicates, a descendant of 'Alī's brother Ja'far ibn Abī Tālib.[1] The historical information about Ibn Mu'āwiya is much more complete than the data we have for the other Shī'ite heresiarchs Bayān ibn Sam'ān, al-Mughīra ibn Sa'īd, or Abū Mansūr al-'Ijli, upon whom we have focused up to this point.[2] Ibn Mu'āwiya is reported to have been an eloquent and generous person.[3] He was also known for his poetic talent.[4] At the same time, however, the majority of sources accuse him of religious heterodoxy.[5] This charge is probably more readily applicable to his followers, since he himself was more interested in politics than in dogma, but there are no indications that he disavowed their religious ideas. In addition to indicating the more positive

---

[1] Fakhr al-Dīn Muhammad ibn 'Alī ibn al-Tiqtaqa, *al-Fakhrī fī al-Adab al-Sultāniyya*, trans. Emile Amar, *Archives Marocaines*, XVI (Paris, 1910), 219; Tritton, *Theology*, 23; Laoust, *Schismes*, 35.

[2] Tucker, "Bayān ibn Sam'ān," 241–253; Idem., "al-Mugīra and the Mugīriyya," 33–47; Idem., "Abū Mansūr al-'Ijli and the Mansūriyya: A Study in Medieval Terrorism," *Islam*, 54 (1977), 66–76.

[3] Jamāl al-Dīn Muhammad ibn Muhammad ibn Nubāta al-Misrī, *Sarh al-'Uyūn fī Sharh Risāla ibn Zaydān* (Cairo, 1964), 347; Ahmad ibn Muhammad ibn Sa'īd al-Hamdānī=ibn 'Uqda, *Dhikr al-Nabī*, trans. Nabia Abbott, *Studies in Arabic Literary Papyri*, I, *Historical Texts*, University of Chicago Oriental Institute Publications, LXXV (Chicago, 1957), 102.

[4] Julius Wellhausen, *Die Religiös-politischen Oppositionsparteien im Alten Islam*, Arabic trans. 'Abd al-Rahmān Badawī (Cairo, 1957), 264. For examples of Ibn Mu'āwiya's verse, consult Abū Mansūr 'Abd al-Malik ibn Muhammad ibn Ismā'īl al-Tha'ālibī, *Thimār al-Qulūb fī al-Mudaf wa al-Mansūb* (Cairo, 1965), 326–327, 688.

[5] Abū Muhammad 'Alī ibn Ahmad ibn Sa'īd ibn Hazm, *Jamhārat Ansāb al-'Arab* (Cairo, 1962), 68; Abū al-Faraj al-Isfahānī, *Maqātil al-Tālibiīn* (Cairo, 1949), 162.

aspects of Ibn Muʿāwiya's personality, a number of the sources also level charges of cruelty and violence at him. Al-Isfahānī says that Ibn Muʿāwiya used to have servants who aroused his anger beaten to death.[6] This may be a fabrication, on the one hand, or may point, significantly, to his determination and will to power. Detailed information about Ibn Muʿāwiya begins with his arrival in Kufa some time prior to the autumn of 744. He and his brothers appeared in this city and sought the favor of the Umayyad governor, ʿAbd Allāh ibn ʿUmar ibn ʿAbd al-ʿAzīz, a son of the pious Umayyad caliph. Ibn ʿUmar received Ibn Muʿāwiya and his brothers with generosity, granting them an allowance of substantial proportions.[7] In September 744 Yazīd III, the reigning caliph, died, and his brother Ibrahim ibn Walid I became the new ruler.[8] At this time Marwān ibn Muhammad, grandson of Marwān ibn al-Hakam and a veteran of the Caucasus campaigns, entered into rebellion against the new caliph. Ibn ʿUmar assumed an attitude of hostility toward the rebel Marwān. This fluctuating political situation caused Ibn ʿUmar to consign Ibn Muʿāwiya to prison. At the same time, however, he appears to have increased Ibn Muʿāwiya's stipend.[9] Ibn ʿUmar then arranged to pay allegiance to his prisoner in the event that Marwān gained the caliphal power. His purpose in doing so was to use Ibn Muʿāwiya against Marwān.[10] Ibn ʿUmar, however, quickly lost control of events.

[6] al-Isfahānī, *Kitāb al-Aghānī*, XII (Beirut, 1958), 231; Idem., *Maqātil*, 163.
[7] Tabarī, *Taʾrīkh*, II, 1881; Yazīd ibn Muhammad al-Azdī, *Taʾrīkh al-Mawsil* (Cairo, 1968), 66.
[8] Wellhausen, *Arab Kingdom*, 369. For a more recent account of Umayyad history, see Hawting, *First Dynasty*.
[9] Abū Zayd ʿAbd al-Rahmān ibn Khaldūn, *al-ʿIbar wa Diwān al-Mubtadāʾ wa al-Khabar fī Ayyām al-ʿArab wa al-ʿAjam wa al-Barbar wa man ʿAsārahum min Dhawī al-Sultān al-Akbār-Taʾrīkh*, III (Beirut, 1957), 247.
[10] Ibn al-Athīr, *al-Kāmil*, V, 325; Tabarī, *Taʾrīkh*, II, 1881. For a modern Arab account, see ʿAlī Hūsnī al-Kharbūtlī, *Taʾrīkh al-ʿIrāq fī Zill al-Hukm al-Umawī* (Cairo, 1959), 221–223.

During or just prior to the occurrences mentioned previously, Ibn 'Umar had been awarding stipends to Mudar and Rabī'a, the North Arabian groups. In distributing this booty, however, he had neglected two important members of the Rabī'a. These individuals had proceeded to incite their fellow tribesmen against him. In order to resolve this affair, Ibn 'Umar had resorted to paying off the disaffected parties.[11] The settlement of this problem, however, did not lead to the reestablishment of peace and order. Ibn 'Umar's actions had caused the Shī'ites of Kufa to perceive the instability and weakness of his position. This party now urged Ibn Mu'āwiya to move against Ibn 'Umar. It is said that they encouraged him to call the people to pay allegiance to him instead, since "the Banū Hāshim were more worthy of the caliphate" than the Umayyads.[12] Ibn Mu'āwiya's rebellion began in October 744.

Information concerning the nature of his claims is contradictory. According to one version he referred to himself as the representative of the House of Muhammad, that is, as an agent of the Banū Hāshim.[13] It is reported that he began to advance his personal agenda only upon his establishment later in Persia.[14] The other account has it that he worked on his own behalf from the beginning of his revolt.[15] Whatever the case, there is no doubt that Ibn Mu'āwiya had personal goals in mind.

When the time for fighting arrived, the Kufans, not surprisingly, proved to be generally unreliable. One author goes so far

---

[11] Ibn al-Athīr, al-Kāmil, V, 325; Tabarī, Ta'rīkh, II, 1882–1883; see also Muhammad ibn Khvānd Shāh ibn Mahmūd-Mīr Khvānd, Rawda al-Safā fī Sīra al-Anbiyā' wa al-Mulūk wa al-Khulafā', III (Teheran, 1959–1965), 359.

[12] anon., Ta'rīkh al-Khulafā' (Moscow, 1967), 239b.

[13] al-Isfahānī, Kitāb al-Aghānī, XII, 227; Ibn Nubāta, Sarh al-'Uyūn, 347; Cahen, "La Révolution Abbaside," 317. See also the modern Arabic work of Thābit al-Rāwī, 'Iraq in the Umayyad Period (Baghdad, 1965), 220.

[14] Ibn Nubāta, Sarh al-'Uyūn, 347; al-Rāwī, Iraq, 220.

[15] al-Isfahānī, al-Aghānī, XII, 227.

as to say that some Kufans had not even bothered to pay allegiance to Ibn Mu'āwiya. They had informed him that they were not in a position to help him, having already lost too many people on behalf of the 'Alid cause. The same authority further states that, on the advice of these individuals, Ibn Mu'āwiya decided to go to the east without fighting Ibn 'Umar.[16] Whereas no doubt some Kufans refused to fight for Ibn Mu'āwiya, it seems that the Hāshimite rebel did combat Ibn 'Umar before proceeding to the Persian provinces. The major battle took place in the outskirts of Kufa.[17] According to one source, a member of Ibn Mu'āwiya's army, having been won over by Ibn 'Umar, fled at a crucial moment, thereby causing the rest of Ibn Mu'āwiya's troops to abandon the field.[18] Another account, perhaps more accurate, relays the information that the Yamanites in Ibn Mu'āwiya's force left the field when the battle was joined. The only groups that held firm for him appear to have been the remnants of the Zaydiyya and the Rabī'a. The latter were, in fact, the last to leave the field.[19] Finally, however, Ibn Mu'āwiya, the Zaydiyya, and Rabī'a had to retreat to within Kufa itself, where they shut themselves up in the citadel. After holding out against the forces of Ibn 'Umar for a time, they were given a safe-conduct (*amān*) and allowed to leave the city unharmed.[20]

At this point Ibn Mu'āwiya and his supporters moved into the Persian provinces, where they began to gain control. Ibn

---

[16] *Ibid.*

[17] al-Isfahānī, *Maqātil,* 166.

[18] Tabarī, *Ta'rīkh,* II, 1880.

[19] Ibn al-Athīr, *al-Kāmil,* V, 326; Tabarī, *Ta'rīkh,* II, 1884–1885.

[20] Tabarī, *Ta'rīkh,* II, 1887; Ibn Khaldūn, *Ta'rīkh,* III, 248; al-Azdī, *Mawsil,* 67; Richard N. Frye, "The 'Abbasid Conspiracy' and Modern Revolutionary Theory," *Indo-Iranica,* 5iii (1952–1953), 12; Ghiyāth al-Dīn Muhammad ibn Khvāja Hamām (Khvāndamīr), *Ta'rīkh Habīb al-Siyar fī Akhbār Afrād Bashāra,* II (Teheran, 1444), 191.

Mu'āwiya first settled in Isfahan. He then entered Istakhr in the province of Fars, following the fall of that region to his forces. Among the cities that submitted to him were Qumm, Shiraz, and Qumis. His holdings in Persia included at least parts of the provinces of Jibal, Fars, Kirman, Khuzistan, and Qumis.[21] During his stay in these areas he gained the support of numerous disaffected elements. These included *Mawālī*, escaped slaves, Kharijites, members of the Banū 'Abbas, and even some Umayyads.[22] Such a diverse following is most surprising at first glance, but it points to the fundamental reason underlying his *brief* success. This was his readiness to accept the aid of anyone hostile to the Umayyad rulers. As al-Isfahānī informs us, he welcomed equally those who followed him out of loyalty and those who joined him because he happened to be the enemy of their enemies.[23] As a result, Ibn Mu'āwiya was able, as one author has affirmed, to form in Persia a solid, although *provisional*, state.[24] He even issued his own coins.[25]

Meanwhile, however, Marwān ibn Muhammad had succeeded in seizing the reins of government. By the year 129 (746/747) or 130 (747/748) Marwān had turned his attention to the eastern

[21] Jamāl al-Dīn Ahmad ibn 'Alī ibn 'Ināba, *'Umda al-Tālib fī Ansāb Āl Abī Tālib* (Beirut, 1963), 34; al-Mas'ūdi, *Murūj*, III, 242; Yāqūt ibn 'Abd Allāh al-Rūmī, *Mu'jām al-Buldān*, II (Leipzig, 1867), 3. See also the following: Muhsin 'Azizi, *La Domination Arabe et l'Épanouissement du Sentiment National en Iran* (Paris, 1938), 26, n.1; Paul Schwarz, *Iran im Mittelälter nach den Arabischen Geographen*, fasc. 5 (Leipzig, 1925), 561; V. V. Ivanov, "Early Shi'ite Movements," *Journal of the Bombay Branch of the Royal Asiatic Society*, N. Ser. XVII (1941), 8; Gerlof van Vloten, "Über einige bis jetzt nicht erkannte Münzen aus der letzten Omeijadenzeit," *Zeitschrift der Deutschen Morgenländischen Gesellschaft*, XLVI (1892), 554.
[22] Ibn al-Athīr, *al-Kāmil*, V, 327, 371–372; al-Isfahānī, *Maqātil*, 167; Tabarī, *Ta'rīkh*, II, 1880–1881. See further, Sadighi, *Mouvements*, 39.
[23] al-Isfahānī, *Kitāb al-Aghānī*, XII, 227.
[24] 'Azizi, *Domination*, 26, n.1.
[25] van Vloten, "Münzen," 443.

provinces. At this time, he sent the general ʿAmīr ibn Dubāra against Ibn Muʿāwiya. In the ensuing hostilities the latter was defeated and forced to flee.[26] He subsequently made his way to Khurasan and, on his way to this province, he stopped in Sistan. Encountering no notable success there, he passed into Khurasan.[27] It was in the latter province that he met his death.

The date of his death was probably 129 (746/747) or 130 (747/748).[28] One author gives the year as 131, but this is unlikely.[29] Ibn ʿInāba's statement that Ibn Muʿāwiyia was imprisoned until 133 is incorrect, because it is well known that his death occurred before the ʿAbbāsid accession to power (132 H.).[30] He was put to death on the orders of Abū Muslim al-Khurasānī, the architect of ʿAbbāsid victory. Ibn Muʿāwiya had sought the aid of the latter upon his (Ibn Muʿāwiya's) entry into Khurasan, the scene of Abū Muslim's activity on behalf of the ʿAbbāsids.

There are two versions of the events leading to Ibn Muʿāwiya's death. According to the first, he went to the city of Herat, which was governed by one Abū Nasr Malik ibn al-Haytham al-Khuzāʿī, a representative of Abū Muslim. Abū Nasr demanded of Ibn Muʿāwiya the reason for his coming to that region. The latter replied that he had arrived to aid in the struggle on behalf of the descendants of the Prophet. Abū Nasr then questioned him about his genealogy. Upon hearing his reply, Abū Nasr is reported to have said that the names Jaʿfar and ʿAbd Allāh were to be found among the names of Muhammad's family, but not

[26] Abū Nuʿaym Ahmad ibn ʿAbd Allāh al-Isbahānī, *Kitāb Dhikr Akhbār Isbahān*, II (Leiden, 1934), 42; Tabarī, *Taʾrīkh*, II, 1978; C. E. Bosworth, *Sistan under the Arabs, from the Islamic Conquest to the Rise of the Saffārids. (30–250/651/864)* (Rome, 1968), 77.
[27] anon., *Taʾrīkh-i-Sīstān* (Teheran, 1935), 133; Bosworth, *Sistan*, 77.
[28] Abū al-Mahāsin Yūsuf ibn Taghrī-Birdī, *al-Nujūm al-Zāhira fī Mulūk Misr wa al-Qāhira*, I (Cairo, 1959), 310; Ibn al-Athīr, *al-Kāmil*, V, 372–373.
[29] Abū Nuʿaym, *Isbahān*, II, 42.
[30] Ibn ʿInāba, *ʿUmda*, 34.

the name Mu`āwiya. He then informed Abū Muslim of what had taken place. On the orders of the latter, Abū Nasr imprisoned Ibn Mu`āwiya and then put him to death.[31] Moscati reproduces this account from Ibn al-Athīr, but for some reason he states that Malik also denied the presence of `Abd Allāh and Ja`far among the family names of the Hāshimites.[32] This is either a mistake in the text of Moscati's article or a misreading of Ibn al-Athīr's account.

In the second account of Ibn Mu`āwiya's death, it is said that he approached Abū Muslim with a view to obtaining his aid. Abū Muslim is reported to have cast him into prison. At the same time he put a spy in with Ibn Mu`āwiya in order to learn what the prisoner said and did. Ibn Mu`āwiya berated the Khurasanians for their blind faith in Abū Muslim. Furthermore he wrote a letter to Abū Muslim. This epistle was in essence an admonition to Abū Muslim that he seek the salvation of his soul rather than greatness in this world. Upon receiving this letter, Abū Muslim exclaimed that Ibn Mu`āwiya was a danger to the `Abbāsids even while being confined in their prison. In order to be rid of such a menace, Abū Muslim had poison administered to his prisoner, who in this fashion met his death.[33]

One authority reports that Abū Muslim did not himself execute Ibn Mu`āwiya, but turned him over to `Amīr ibn Dubāra, who had him killed.[34] This may indeed have been the case, since such an action would be a clever maneuver on the part of Abū Muslim to have a dangerous rival liquidated by the common enemy, the Umayyads. In the episode of Ibn Mu`āwiya's death, we have further evidence of the speed and efficiency with which

---

[31] Ibn al-Athīr, al-Kāmil, V, 372–373.
[32] Sabatino Moscati, "Studi di Abu Muslim. II. Propaganda e politica religiosa di Abu Muslim," Atti della Accademia Nazionale dei Lincei, Ser. VIII, vol. IV (1949), 484–485.
[33] Ibn Nubāta, Sarh al-`Uyūn, 349; Moscati, "Abu Muslim," 169.
[34] al-Isfahānī, Maqātil, 169.

Abū Muslim disposed of individuals deemed compromising to the revolutionary movement in Khurasan.

Ibn Muʿāwiya was a serious threat to the movement that Abū Muslim had painstakingly formed over a period of time. Theodor Nöldeke aptly summarized the situation in an essay written early in the last century.

He (Ibn Muʿāwiya) had served his turn, so far as he had thrown the empire into wilder confusion, and called the attention of the people to the family of the Prophet; now as a rival he might prove inconvenient. Abū Moslim therefore first cast him into prison, and afterwards took his life.[35]

One might simply add that by increasing the "confusion" Ibn Muʿāwiya had helped to further weaken the Umayyads, thus doing the ʿAbbāsid cause a service for which he was ill compensated.

Ibn Muʿāwiya's following, as indicated previously, was composed of heterogeneous elements. The bond that united them was their opposition to Marwān ibn Muhammad. The immediate entourage of Ibn Muʿāwiya was reputed to be composed of heretics and atheists. One of his assistants was known as *al-Baqli*, the "herb" or the "green." He was given this name because he used to say that human beings were similar to greens or herbs; after their deaths they do not return.[36] In other words, he denied the resurrection. Ibn Muʿāwiya is also said to have had a secretary named ʿUmāra ibn Hamza, who was a *zindīq*, the term here denoting atheist or heretic. The chief of police, Qays, was also accused of heresy or schism.[37] If one may view these people as belonging to the Janāhiyya, to be discussed, it is probable that the charges of heresy are true. It should be emphasized, however, that these individuals are not mentioned in accounts devoted specifically

35 Nöldeke, "Caliph Mansur," in *Sketches*, 112.
36 Ibn Nubāta, *Sarh al-ʿUyūn*, 347.
37 al-Isfahānī, *al-Aghānī*, XII, 230; Idem., *Maqātil*, 162.

to the Janāhiyya or other sects recognizing Ibn Mu`āwiya. The
manner in which they are discussed, in particular the application to them of the pejorative *zindīq*, casts some doubt upon the
absolute reliability of the information about them.

The most reliable support for Ibn Mu`āwiya, in the early stages
at least, came from the Zaydiyya and the Rabī`a. The Zaydiyya
were the adherents of Zayd ibn `Alī (grandson of al-Husayn), who
had risen against the Umayyads and been killed in 740.[38] Those
who had survived the revolt were among the people who joined
Ibn Mu`āwiya. The Rabī`a of Kufa also entered his ranks. They
and the Zaydiyya were the last to leave the field in the battle with
Ibn `Umar. They had then stubbornly defended the citadel until
forced to accept a safe-conduct.[39] The presence of the Zaydiyya
among the forces of Ibn Mu`āwiya is another indication of the
fact that opposition to the Umayyads was of more importance to
him than was religious ideology, since the religious views of the
Zaydiyya and the Janāhiyya were poles apart.

Ibn Mu`āwiya also gained the support of many *Mawālī* and
escaped slaves. As Ibn Athīr and Tabarī note, the slaves of Kufa
flocked to his ranks.[40] It is likely that these *Mawālī* were largely
Persian. One modern authority maintains that a great many
Persians took part.[41] In view of the activities and successes of Ibn
Mu`āwiya in the Persian provinces, there is no reason to dispute
this statement. It is probably from among the slaves and clients
that the Janāhiyya found many of its members. Social and political considerations were no doubt the motive forces here. The
phenomenon of the disinherited and those feeling themselves
to have pariah status joining a millenarian prophet, as is the case

---

[38] Rudolph Strothmann, "al-Zaidiya," in *Shorter E.I.* (Ithaca, N.Y., 1965), 651–
652.

[39] Tabarī, *Ta'rīkh*, II, 1885.

[40] Ibid., 1880–1881. See also Ibn al-Athīr, *al-Kāmil*, V, 327.

[41] Sadighi, *Mouvements*, 39.

here, can be readily seen in other cultures as well, for example, in Brazilian messianic movements of the nineteenth and twentieth centuries.[42]

One also notes with interest that prominent members of the 'Abbāsid family supported Ibn Mu'āwiya. Among those reported to have joined him, one finds the names of al-Saffāh, Abū Ja'far al-Mansūr, and 'Isa ibn 'Alī, their cousin.[43] With these individuals, as well as with others who supported him, Ibn Mu'āwiya appears to have been generous in the awarding of favors or offices.[44] Jahshiyārī reports that he made al-Mansūr the *'Āmil*, that is, director of finance in charge of revenue collection, for Idhāj, the chief town of Great Lur in Khuzistan.[45] 'Abbāsid support for Ibn Mu'āwiya no doubt resulted from a belief that this pretender might attain some success that they could exploit for their own ends. If nothing else he was useful in further damaging the rule of the Damascene dynasty.

Ibn Mu'āwiya attracted two other even more surprising elements – Kharijites and Umayyads. The Kharijite leader Shaybān ibn 'Abd al-'Azīz joined Ibn Mu'āwiya in Persia.[46] This seems to have taken place after Marwān II had driven Shaybān and his followers out of the Mosul area.[47] The Kharijites, having been unable to defeat Marwān alone, adhered to Ibn Mu'āwiya, without doubt, in the belief that he might be strong enough to overthrow the Umayyads, yet weak enough to have power wrested, in turn, from him.

[42] Roger Bastide, *The African Religions of Brazil: Toward a Sociology of the Interpenetration of Civilizations*, trans. Helen Sebba (Baltimore, Md., 1978), 356–364.

[43] Ibn al-Athīr, *al-Kāmil*, V, 371; Ibn Nubāta, *Sarh al-'Uyūn*, 348; Moscati, "Abu Muslim," 484.

[44] Ibn Nubāta, *Sarh al-'Uyūn*, 348.

[45] Abū 'Abd Allāh Muhammad ibn 'Abdūs al-Jahshiyārī, *Kitāb al-Wuzarā' wa al-Kuttāb* (Cairo, 1938), 98. For the location of Idhāj, consult Le Strange, *Lands*, 245.

[46] Ibn al-Athīr, *al-Kāmil*, V, 371.

[47] Wellhausen, *Oppositionsparteien*, Badawī, 263.

Prominent Umayyads were also to be found among his supporters.[48] Among them were ʿUmar ibn Suhayl ibn ʿAbd al-
ʿAzīz ibn Marwān and Sulaymān ibn Hishām ibn ʿAbd al-Malik.[49]
These individuals had gravitated to the cause of Ibn Muʿāwiya by
reason of their intense opposition to Marwān ibn Muhammad. As
Wellhausen suggests, this was probably a struggle of the Syrian
Kalb against Marwān and his Qaysite supporters.[50] In the case
of Sulaymān, personal ambition for the caliphal throne was also
involved. After the anti-Marwān efforts in Syria and Mesopotamia
had failed, the disgruntled elements had little choice but to move
farther east. Without doubt, they had cast their lot with Ibn
Muʿāwiya because his success in the Persian regions suggested
that he might be able to cope with the forces of Marwān. Here
again, then, we see an example of a marriage of expediency. In
this instance the enmity was directed not against the dynasty, but
rather against the particular ruler and, apparently, the tribal element that constituted his power base.

There is also the possibility that the forces of Ibn Muʿāwiya
included members of a Persian group known as the Khurramdīniyya (also known as Khurramiyya). This sect adhered to
such beliefs as the transmigration of souls and the abandonment
of certain doctrinal constraints, ideas similar to those held by the
Janāhiyya.[51] As G. H. Sadighi has pointed out, Shahrastānī's assertion that Ibn Muʿāwiya was the founder of the Khurramdīniyya
is incorrect, because the Khurramdīniyya and Mazdakians, who
appear to be identical, were in existence long before the time of
Ibn Muʿāwiya.[52]

Some authorities seek the origins of the extremist groups clus-
tering about Ibn Muʿāwiya in a party known as the Harbiyya. The

---

[48] Frye, "'Abbasid Conspiracy,'" 12.
[49] al-Isfahānī, *Maqātil*, 167; Kharbūtlī, *Ta'rīkh*, 222.
[50] Wellhausen, *Arab Kingdom*, 378. For a different perspective on the Qays-Yaman
dispute, see Shaban, *Islamic History*.
[51] Mohamed Rekaya, "Khurramites," 20–57.
[52] Sadighi, *Mouvements*, 182.

name of this group comes from the person who is said to have been its leader, 'Abd Allāh ibn 'Amr ibn Harb al-Kindī. The heresiographers inform us that this group believed that Abū Hāshim had designated their leader *Imām* after himself.[53] They also declared that the spirit of Abū Hāshim had become indwelling in Ibn Harb through the transmigration of souls (*Tanāsūkh*).[54] It is also reported that they claimed that whoever knew the *Imām* could do as he liked.[55] Hamza ibn 'Umāra, it will be recalled, is supposed to have entertained a similar idea.[56]

The heresiographers provide the following information about the relationship of the Harbiyya with Ibn Mu'āwiya. For some reason the followers of Ibn Harb became disenchanted with him and set out to find a new leader.[57] Ibn Hazm maintains that Ibn Harb had renounced his own extremist views, alienating his supporters in the process.[58] Al-Ash'arī al-Qummī, on the other hand, suggests that the Harbiyya abandoned their leader because they believed him to be too unintelligent to possess the powers he claimed for himself.[59] Whatever the reason, the Harbiyya are said to have sought out a new *Imām*. They are supposed to have met Ibn Mu'āwiya in the city of Medina. Accepting his invitation to follow him, they recognized him as their new leader.[60] The validity of all this information is impossible to establish. If there was such a group, it probably did support Ibn Mu'āwiya, although it is doubtful that he shared their religious views.

Al-Baghdādī's account of the Harbiyya is very curious. He states that, after the death of al-Nafs al-Zakiyya, the section of

---

[53] al-Ash'arī, *Maqālāt*, 95; al-Himyarī, *Hūr*, 160.
[54] Emin Sadreddin al-Shirwani, untitled treatise on the sects of Islam, Nuri Osmaniye Kūtūbhanesi Ms. 2144, fol. 11a.
[55] al-Ash'arī al-Qummī, *Maqālāt wa al-Firaq*, 40–41.
[56] Nawbakhtī, *Firaq*, 49.
[57] Shahrastānī, *Milal*, 151.
[58] Friedlaender, "Ibn Hazm: Commentary," 73.
[59] al-Ash'arī al-Qummī, *Maqālāt wa al-Firaq*, 40–41.
[60] al-Ash'arī, *Maqālāt*, I, 95.

the Mughīriyya that had turned away from al-Mughīra went to Medina seeking a new *Imām*. They met Ibn Mu`āwiya and gave allegiance to him.[61] This report is obviously inaccurate. Ibn Mu`āwiya died long before al-Nafs al-Zakiyya, who was put to death by the `Abbāsid al-Mansūr in 762.[62] It is difficult to determine the reason for al-Baghdādī's mistake. His chapter about the Harbiyya seems to be accurate in other respects, as does his discussion of the Mughīriyya. One should note that there is no mention of this change of allegiance to Ibn Mu`āwiya in his information about al-Mughīra ibn Sa'id and his followers. In the *Hūr al-`Īn* of al-Himyarī, the Harbiyya are called the *Hizbiyya*.[63] This is probably simply a copyist's mistake.

The extremist faction most frequently identified with Ibn Mu`āwiya was the group called the Janāhiyya (sometimes called the Tayyariyya). The name was apparently derived from the nickname given Ja`far ibn Abī Tālib, Ibn Mu`āwiya's great-grandfather. The name, *Dhū al-Janāhayn* (possessor of wings), is said to have been given to Ja`far by the Prophet. The story has it that this occurred after the death of Ja`far at the battle of Mut`a. Muhammad is reported to have said that he saw Ja`far with wings, flying about in Heaven.[64] Friedlaender's suggestion that the name was that of Ibn Mu`āwiya's father rather than his great-grandfather is an error.[65] Ja`far was also called Tayyār, hence the occasional appearance of the name Tayyariyya rather than Janāhiyya.[66]

It is impossible to determine exactly Ibn Mu`āwiya's attitude toward the ideas of the Janāhiyya. Probably he did not share their extremist doctrines, some of which may have appeared only after his death. There is no doubt, on the other hand, that he tolerated

---

[61] al-Baghdādī, *Schisms* (trans. Halkin), 59.
[62] Tucker, "Rebels and Gnostics," 37.
[63] al-Himyarī, *Hūr*, 160–161.
[64] al-Baghdādī, *Schisms* (trans. Halkin), 59, n.1.
[65] Ibid.
[66] Laoust, *Schismes*, 35.

such views among his followers. As indicated by the nature of his supporters, Ibn Mu'āwiya, the ultimate pragmatist, was more concerned with wresting political power from the Umayyads than with the theological peculiarities of his followers. That some of the sources should ascribe these ideas to Ibn Mu'āwiya is not surprising. No doubt the Janāhiyya convinced themselves that their leader originated and shared their doctrines.

Among those doctrines, the one for which they are perhaps best known was that of *Hulūl*, the incarnation of God in their leader. They asserted that the spirit of God had become indwelling in Adam. It had then passed to the prophets and *Imāms*, including 'Alī, Muhammad ibn al-Hanafiyya, and Abū Hāshim. From the latter it had been transferred to Ibn Mu'āwiya.[67] This successive incarnation idea was to be of considerable importance in later extremist groups. As al-Ash'arī clearly indicates, then, the Janāhiyya actually worshipped Ibn Mu'āwiya.[68]

The Janāhiyya are said to have denied the resurrection.[69] This is the corollary of *Tanāsūkh*, the transmigration of souls, through which Ibn Mu'āwiya had become divine.[70] Their concept of transmigration had another interesting facet, as al-Ash'arī al-Qummī informs us that they taught that the spirits of the *Sahāba*, companions of Muhammad, had come to reside in them through transmigration. For this reason they called themselves by the name of the companions. Al-Ash'arī al-Qummī goes on to say that they claimed the ability to commune with those who had formerly

---

[67] anon., *al-Sawā'iq*, fol. 16a. Among published accounts, see the following: Ibn al-Jawzī, *Naqd*, 95; 'Īji, *Mawāqif*, 386; al-Kirmānī, "Ein Kommentar," 40; Omar A. Farrukh, *Islam and the Arabs in the Eastern Mediterranean Down to the Fall of the Umayyad Caliphate (132 A.H./750 C.E.)*, in Arabic (2nd ed., Beirut, 1966), 131; Mustafā Ghurābī, *Ta'rīkh al-Firak al-Islāmiyya wa Nashā' 'Ilm al-Kalām 'ind al-Muslimīn* (Cairo, n.d.), 299.

[68] al-Ash'arī, *Maqālāt*, I, 67.

[69] al-Kūrānī, *Yamāniyya*, fol. 19a. See also al-Sam'ānī, *Kitāb al-Ansāb*, II, 338.

[70] al-Ash'arī, *Maqālāt*, I, 67; 'Īji, *Mawāqif*, VIII, 386.

occupied the bodies into which they had passed.[71] Al-Jilānī also
provides an interesting account of their transmigration theory.
According to him they declared that after death the spirit passed
into a camel. From there it descended through ever lower and
lower states. The souls of sinners, they claimed, passed into iron,
clay, and pottery. As a result they were tortured by smelting, ham-
mering, and so on.[72] It is clear from all of this information that
the Janāhiyya were probably the first to formulate such an elaborate and comprehensive theory of transmigration of souls. The
idea of transmigration, incidentally, may have come to the Arabs
and Persians from Hinduism, Buddhism, or Greek ideas. By the
time of Ibn Mu`āwiya's movement, the Muslims, as is well known,
had come into contact with Hinduism and Buddhism in Central
Asia and northern India.

The Janāhiyya are said to have permitted those things prohibited by the Qur'ān.[73] Al-Baghdādī states, for example, that they
eliminated the religious observances.[74] Their reason for doing
so is similar to that of Abū Mansūr and the Mansūriyya. The prohibitions, they argued, referred to men whom one must hate,
for example, Abū Bakr and `Umar.[75] This doctrine is the same
as that held by the Mansūriyya.[76] Shahrastānī and Fakhr al-Dīn
al-Rāzī declare that the Janāhiyya believed that whoever knows
the *Imām* can do as he chooses.[77] This millenarian, antinomian
idea is one that the Mansūriyya shared.[78]

[71] al-Ash`arī al-Qummī, *Maqālāt wa al-Firaq*, 48.
[72] al-Jilānī, *Ghunya*, 99.
[73] Ibn al-Murtadā, *al-Bahr al-Zakhkhār*, Or. 4021, fol. 10b. Among published
sources, see al-Isfarā'īnī, *Tabsīr*, 73.
[74] al-Baghdādī, *Usūl*, 331.
[75] Ibid., 233; al-Maqrīzī, *Khitat*, III, 303; Abd al-Razzāq al-Ras`ānī, *Mukhtasar
al-Fark bayn al-Firaq* (Cairo, 1924), 154.
[76] al-Ash`arī, *Maqālāt*, 95; see also my article, "Abū Mansūr," 72.
[77] al-Rāzī, *I`tiqādāt*, 59; Shahrastānī, *Milal*, I, 152.
[78] See my article, "Abū Mansūr," 72.

The Janāhiyya, it is said, claimed that Ibn Mu'āwiya used to say that learning sprouted "in his heart like truffles and green grass."[79] It is perfectly reasonable that Ibn Mu'āwiya should have made such a statement, as there is nothing particularly extreme about it. There is no reason, furthermore, to doubt the assertion that the Janāhiyya believed Ibn Mu'āwiya to have received the *Imāmate* from Abū Hāshim.[80] There is ample evidence to show that the Janāhiyya considered Ibn Mu'āwiya to be the successor to Ibn al-Hanafiyya and Abū Hāshim.

After the death of Ibn Mu'āwiya, his partisans split into several groups. One of these insisted that he had not died. He had, instead, withdrawn into the mountains of Isfahan. Some day he would reappear and establish the reign of justice on earth, for he was the awaited *Mahdī*.[81] Another group is said to have claimed that Ibn Mu'āwiya would return from the mountains of Isfahan in order to install the Banū Hāshim.[82] It is intriguing to note the similarity here with another millenarian leader said to have gone into a mountain from which he would return. The relevant story is to be found in Cohn:

In southern Italy and Sicily, where Frederick [the Emperor Frederick II] had spent most of his life, a cryptic Sibylline phrase was heard: "Vivit et non vivit" and a monk saw the Emperor enter into the bowels of Etna while a fiery army of knights descended into the hissing sea. If to the monk this meant that Frederick had gone down to hell, many Sicilians put another construction on the matter. Etna had long been regarded as an abode of departed heroes, including King Arthur himself; when Frederick took his place among these he became a Sleeping Emperor who would one day return as saviour. And when the critical time arrived he did in fact reappear: for a couple of years after 1260 an impostor dwelling on the slopes of Etna was able to attract a numerous following.[83]

---

[79] al-Baghdādī, *Schisms* (trans. Halkin), 152.
[80] al-Ash'arī al-Qummī, *Maqālāt wa al-Firaq*, 41.
[81] al-Baghdādī, *Schisms* (trans. Halkin), 61; Friedlaender, "Ibn Hazm: Commentary," 45.
[82] al-Ash'arī, *Maqālāt*, I, 95; Nawbakhtī, *Firaq*, 57.
[83] Cohn, *Pursuit*, 113.

Still another party professed that Ibn Mu`āwiya had died without naming a successor. They recognized no *Imām* after him.[84] In addition to the Janāhiyya or, in some instances, instead of this sect, some of the sources mention a group of Ibn Mu`āwiya partisans known as the Hārithiyya. The person for whom this sect was designated appears under different names. Shahrastānī calls him Ishāq ibn Zayd ibn Hārith al-`Ansārī.[85] In Nawbakhtī, the name given is `Abd Allāh ibn al-Hārith.[86] The beliefs of this group are essentially the same as those of the Janāhiyya. They maintained, for example, that Ibn Mu`āwiya had received the *Imāmate* from Abū Hāshim. The only point of difference is that an individual named Salih ibn Mudrik held the *Imāmate* for Ibn Mu`āwiya until the latter came of age.[87] They, like the Janāhiyya, are said to have believed in transmigration of souls.[88] They are also alleged to have allowed those things prohibited by religious law.[89]

It is possible that the Hārithiyya were another branch of the Janāhiyya to appear after Ibn Mu`āwiya's death. Shahrastānī, in fact, notes that they sprang up after the death of the Hāshimite.[90] Nawbakhtī indicated the same thing, adding that `Abd Allāh Ibn al-Hārith introduced all of the extremist views associated with Ibn Mu`āwiya.[91] This last information is unlikely, because, as we have seen, such ideas were in circulation long before the death of Ibn Mu`āwiya.

There is also the chance that the Hārithiyya are simply the Janāhiyya under another name. Their founder may be a fiction or perhaps the result of confusion with `Abd Allāh ibn Harb of

---

[84] al-Himyarī, *Hūr*, 161; Nawbakhtī, *Firaq*, 57.

[85] Shahrastānī, *Milal*, I, 152.

[86] Nawbakhtī, *Firaq*, 53.

[87] A. S. Tritton, "A Theological Miscellany," *Bulletin of the School of Oriental and African Studies*, IX (1937–1939), 925.

[88] Nawbakhtī, *Firaq*, 56.

[89] Shahrastānī, *Milal*, I, 152.

[90] Ibid.

[91] Nawbakhtī, *Firaq*, 56.

the Harbiyya. As we have noted, the doctrines of the Hārithiyya are the same as those of the Janāhiyya. If the Hārithiyya sect was distinct from that of the Janāhiyya, it unquestionably grew out of the latter and made no new doctrinal contributions.

A number of conclusions emerge from an examination of Ibn Muʿāwiya and the Janāhiyya. In the first place, there can be no doubt that the leader of the Janāhiyya was concerned with political power rather than religious ideology. This is illustrated by the fact that his followers represented almost every religious current to be found in the Muslim world at that time. As in the case of the Janāhiyya, some of these ideas were radical, allowing even for the exaggeration of hostile sources. There is no record, nevertheless, of Ibn Muʿāwiya having spoken out against these views or having repudiated those who adhered to them. In all probability, however, he did not personally subscribe to such doctrines, but they were, after all, useful, therefore eliciting no protest from him.

The heterogeneity of his following constitutes the primary cause for the success that Ibn Muʿāwiya achieved. The presence of the different groups is an indication of the hatred of the majority of Muslims at the time for the Umayyads or, at any rate, for Marwān ibn Muhammad. Thus one finds among the supporters of Ibn Muʿāwiya Shīʿites, ʿAbbasids, Kharijites, members of the Rabīʿa, *Mawālī*, escaped slaves, and even some individuals from the Umayyad family. This ability to attract diverse elements was something of a mixed blessing. If this diversity enabled Ibn Muʿāwiya to thus increase his following, it is also true that his following's varied composition prevented it from being welded into an effective revolutionary fighting force. There can be no doubt that the various groups had joined Ibn Muʿāwiya in the hope of advancing their own causes. As a result, Ibn Muʿāwiya could expect the support of each party to the extent and in the manner deemed beneficial to its own interests and goals. The reader should bear in mind, after all, that the groups examined here were part of a political context.

The major and crucial difference between Ibn Muʿāwiya and Abū Muslim with regard to the diversity of their followings seems to have lain in the ability of Abū Muslim to convince various groups that their goals and desires would be achieved when victory came. Ibn Muʿāwiya was apparently unable to maintain among his disparate supporters the feeling that their ambitions would be realized when his were.

In spite of the uncertain nature of his following, Ibn Muʿāwiya might yet have overturned the reigning dynasty and established himself at least temporarily. He encountered, however, an obstacle too great to be overcome: the ʿAbbāsid movement under the leadership of the ingenious Abū Muslim, a charismatic leader also playing on messianic/millenarian expectations. As an Arab historian of our own time pointed out some years ago, the ʿAbbāsids had no intention of allowing Ibn Muʿāwiya to jeopardize an effort developed over the course of a number of years.[92] As long as Ibn Muʿāwiya weakened Umayyad rule and helped to focus attention upon the family of the Prophet, they tolerated, indeed even openly supported, his activities. When he became a threat to the movement in Khurasan, however, he had clearly outlived his usefulness.

The Janāhiyya appear to have been the first group to have formulated a developed doctrine of transmigration of souls. They believed that the divinity of the *Imāms* was transmitted in this way, and furthermore, that the souls of ordinary men passed into other bodies or into objects after death. Although certain members of the Kaisāniyya are sometimes said to have been the first Shīʿites to accept this doctrine, it is much more likely that the Janāhiyya were the first Muslim group to adopt it, because after all most sources do not include it among Kaisāniyya beliefs.

The succession-of-incarnations concept may also be the contribution of the Janāhiyya. The Bayāniyya are sometimes said to

---

[92] Kharbūtlī, *Taʾrīkh*, 224.

have been the first *Ghulāt* group to believe this. As indicated
in my previously published study of this group, however, it is
doubtful that they did so.[93] They may have thought that a divine
particle passed to the *Imāms*. This is not the same as the incarnation concept to which the Janāhiyya subscribed. This doctrine
was to be of some significance in the systems of later extremist
Shī'ite groups, for example, the Rāwandiyya.[94] It was also to figure prominently in the teachings of the Druzes, the Ahl i-Haqq
(among whom, interestingly enough, the Divinity is said to
become manifest seven successive times, accompanied each time
by four or five angels), and the Nusayris ('Alawites), who also
argue for the manifestation of God in seven periods.[95]

[93] Tucker, "Bayān ibn Sam'ān," 241

[94] Salih, "Mahdiism in Islam," 267–269.

[95] For the Druze, see Josef van Ess's insightful study, *Chiliastische Erwartungen
und die Versuchung der Göttlichkeit: Der Kalif al-Hākim (386–411 H.)* (Heidelberg, 1977), 74–76. The important information and bibliography for the Ahl-i
Haqq is still to be found in the article by Vladimir Minorsky, "Ahl-i Hakk,"
in *E.I.2*, I (Leiden, 1960), 260–263, especially 260. See more recently Matti
Moosa, *Extremist Shiites: The Ghulat Sects* (Syracuse, N.Y., 1988), 186–193. For
the Nusayris, see Halm, *Islamische Gnosis*, 300–306; and Moosa, *Extremist Shiites*,
311–317.

6

Influence and Significance of the Four Sects

In the concluding paragraphs of each of the preceding chapters, I have attempted to specify the particular contribution of each group, and, in this manner, the doctrinal evolution of the *Ghulāt* has been demonstrated. Among the major themes that have been delineated are: continuation of prophecy, allegorical interpretation of the Qur'ān and religious norms, speculation about the nature of God, the magic use of esoteric knowledge (the Greatest Name), religious elitism, terrorism against opponents, transmigration of souls, and successive incarnations of God.

I have also attempted to suggest the possible sources of the religious doctrines of the four groups. A number of these, it will be recalled, seem to have stemmed from the theological ideas of Manichaeism, Gnosticism, and Mandaeism. Others give the impression of having had a Christian or Jewish origin. The primary influence, of course, was the Islamic, especially Qur'ānic, one. The ideology of the four groups was, therefore, a synthesis of non-Islamic and Islamic ideas. This was one of the strengths of these parties, no doubt, as it accounted, at least in part, for the attraction that they held for the *Mawālī*.

The influence of the ideas of the four groups upon later religious movements has also been noted. I have indicated, for example, the possibility of a doctrinal connection with the Ismā'īlīs. Particular doctrines involved here seem to have been those of allegorical Qur'ānic interpretation and speculation about the mystical properties of the letters of the alphabet. The parallel between the terror of the Mansūriyya and the *Nizārīs* was also mentioned. Influences upon other extremist groups such as the Khattābiyya and the Rāwandiyya were pointed out as well. Quasi-Shī'ite groups such as the Druzes and the Ahl-i-Haqq also, in all probability, derived certain of their ideas, such as successive incarnations, from these early extremist sects.

In point of fact, what Halm conceives of as a "Kufan *Ghulāt* tradition" may be seen to have passed through these four groups into a number of later religious movements, which, although appearing in different locales, at later times, and under differing conditions, manifested many of the same beliefs and practices as the four sects investigated in the present volume. Furthermore, in each case, one also encounters strong evidence of revolutionary millenarian political, social, and religious impulses at work. After a brief excursus as to possible *Ghulāt*-Sufi linkages, the remainder of this chapter focuses upon two issues: 1) a brief examination of early-'Abbāsid Persian sects, the Khattābiyya Shī'a, the Qarmatians, the Musha'sha'iyya, and the Hurūfiyya and 2) an investigation into the millenarian features of the sects central to this study.

In addition to the evident impact of these four sects upon later Shī'ites and quasi-Shī'ites, it seems that one may also point to a relationship with the later Sufis. Marshall Hodgson probably summed it up best when he wrote:

So far as the *Ghulāt* raised problems of a more general nature regarding the spirituality of the soul and the possibility of its communion with God, they no doubt contributed to the emotional tone of later Twelver and Ismā'īlī Shī'ism. However, in this respect their evident successors were the Sufis. Though Sufism was no doubt not immediately connected with the *Ghuluw*, the mystical states of the soul, as well as the relative ranks of various mystics, have been endlessly discussed in Sufism ever since the closing of the classical period of the early *Ghulāt*; and it is among them that has been kept alive that oddly significant, so-called Christian idea, that what survives at death is the pure soul.[1]

There is the further possibility, as Mohamed Rekaya has noted, that the four groups studied here may have had an influence upon the heretical Persian movements of the early ʿAbbāsid period.[2] One of the earliest of these was under the leadership of a person known as Isḥāq the Turk. Ibn al-Nadīm informs us that Isḥāq refused to believe that Abū Muslim had died. He insisted that the latter had gone into concealment in the mountains of Rayy, from where he would emerge one day.[3] This idea is a reflection of the Mughīriyya's belief that al-Nafs al-Zakiyya had not died, but had rather gone into concealment. The same emphasis upon the hidden leader has been encountered in the doctrines of the Janāhiyya. One should note here that, as the information reveals, the Persian groups under discussion were not Shīʿite movements. Isḥāq's group appears, in fact, to have been a part of that mass movement known in some sources as the Khurramiyya. The cardinal tenet of this group was that religious and political power belonged rightfully to Abū Muslim, who was thought to be the messiah. He was expected to return to the world and spread justice and goodness.[4] The ʿAlids seem to have had no role in the religious theories of this movement. The belief in the leader's absence and his messianic return appears to have been an idea of Shīʿite origin, however.

The ideas of al-Muqannaʿ also may reflect the teaching of the extremist Shīʿites, received, perhaps, through the medium

---

[1] Hodgson, "Early Shīʿa," *JAOS*, 7 (1955), 8.

[2] Rekaya, "Khurramites," 7–57.

[3] Ibn al-Nadīm, *Fihrist*, 344. For important recent accounts of Isḥāq the Turk and other early ʿAbbāsid Iranian rebel leaders see Elton Daniel, *The Political and Social History of Khurasan under Abbasid Rule, 747–820* (Minneapolis and Chicago, 1979), 125–156; Cf. B. S. Amoretti, "Sects and Heresies," in *The Cambridge History of Iran*, IV (Cambridge, 1975), 481–519.

[4] Sadighi, *Mouvements*, 140–141.

of one of the four groups. This is reflected in his primary doctrine, according to which he was the embodiment of God, having become this by means of a succession of incarnations that started with Adam, passed through Noah, Abraham, Moses, Jesus, Muhammad, and Abū Muslim, coming finally to himself.[5] Such a doctrine, as noted previously, was of extreme importance in the beliefs of the Janāhiyya, although the individuals in whom the incarnation occurred were different. What is of interest here is that the Janāhiyya were to be found in Persia after the death of Ibn Mu'āwiya. It is quite possible, therefore, that al-Muqanna' had personal contact with them or, at any rate, was exposed to their teachings. The information that al-Muqanna' permitted his followers to kill religious opponents[6] may indicate an awareness of the teachings and practices of Abū Mansūr al-'Ijli.

One may conjecture that Bābak, the rebel against al-Ma'mūn and Mu'tasim, was similarly influenced by ideas emanating from the four groups. This is by no means certain, it should be stressed. Bābak is reported to have preached that he was the incarnation of God.[7] Ghulam Sadighi has denied this on the basis of his examination of the available evidence.[8] His argument is not convincing, however, and thus one cannot rule out the possibility that Bābak did make such a claim. Again, this idea is a reflection of the incarnation doctrine of the Janāhiyya. It is also stated that Bābak's followers taught that faith consisted of knowledge of

[5] Abū al-Rayhān Muhammad ibn Ahmad al-Bīrūnī, *al-Āthār al-Bāqiyah 'an al-Qurūn al-Khāliyah=Chronologie Orientalischer Völker* (Leipzig, 1923), 211; Muhammad ibn Ja'far al-Narshākhī, *The History of Bukhāra*, trans. R. N. Frye (Cambridge, Mass., 1954), 67–68; Sabatino Moscati, "Studi Storici sul Califfato di al-Mahdi," *Orientalia*, N. Ser. XIV (1945), 338; A. Ju. Jakubovskij, "Vosstanie Mukanny – dviženie ljudej v 'belyx odeždax,'" *Sovetskoe vostokovedenie*, V (1948), 45. Details of the revolt may be found in B. G. Gafurov, *Istorija tadžikskogo naroda v kratkom izloženii*, I (Moscow, 1955), 166–169.

[6] Sadighi, *Mouvements*, 180.

[7] Ibid., 207.

[8] Ibid., 268–269.

their religious leader; this individual absolved them of the necessity of observing religious law. A similar belief was to be found
among the tenets of the Mansūriyya and the Janāhiyya.

There is the possibility, therefore, that these Persian sects may
have derived some of their beliefs from those of the Mansūriyya
and the Janāhiyya. This is not certain, obviously, and it is clear that
these Persian movements were primarily outgrowths of Zoroastrianism, Manichaeism, and Mazdakism.[9] It is not necessary to
ascribe to a Shī'ite origin a doctrine such as transmigration of
souls, as these Iranian groups could have borrowed it directly
from Buddhism or Hinduism. One should avoid, in other words,
the temptation to connect two groups holding similar ideas,
when each may have received them individually from the same
source or from different ones. It may very well be the case, however, that the religious concepts of the four groups investigated
had an impact upon the Persian heresiarchs.

The Khattābiyya, who advocated and seemingly further developed a number of concepts and practices associated with the
Kufan *Ghulāt*, were the followers of a man by the name of Abū
al-Khattāb Muhammad b. Abī Zaynab al-Ajda' al-As'adī. Abū al-
Khattāb was a *Mawlā* of the Banū As'ad and a contemporary
and ardent partisan of the *Imām* Ja'far al-Sādiq (the sixth of the
Imāmiyya, d. 765). The precise attitude of the *Imām* Ja'far toward
Abū al-Khattāb is difficult to establish, as there are accounts in
which Ja'far repudiates him and others in which he praises him.[10]

Whatever the case, Abū al-Khattāb and his followers took up
arms against 'Isa b. Mūsā, 'Abbāsid governor of Kufa, and were
either killed in the fighting or were later executed by the 'Abbāsid
forces. Interestingly enough, the Khattābiyya are said to have

---

[9] Ibid., 208. Consult also Hassan Pirouzdjou, *Mithraisme et Émancipation: Anthropologie Sociale et Culturelle des Mouvements Populaires en Iran: au VIIIe, IXe et du
XIVe au Debut du XVIe siècle* (Montreal, 1999), 17–55.

[10] Halm, *Islamische Gnosis*, 199–206.

armed themselves with sticks or clubs in their battle with 'Isa, posing here a striking analogy with the weapons of al-Mukhtār's Khashabiyya and the Mansūriyya, noted previously.[11]

The teachings of Abū al-Khattāb are replete with concepts emanating from the earlier Kufan sects. He claimed, for instance, to be custodian of the *Imāmate* after Ja'far and then went so far as to proclaim himself to be a prophet. The Khattābiyya went him one better by asserting that both he and Ja'far were incarnations of God. Some elements of this sect also claimed divine status for Muhammad and 'Alī.[12] One recalls immediately in this case the dual-god theory of Abū Mansūr al-'Ijli. Abū al-Khattāb is even reported to have claimed divinity (*Hulūl*) for Hasan, Husayn, and al-Bāqir, another instance of the Janāhiyya's belief in the transmigration of divinity. Such pretensions to supernatural power were indicative of the often exalted rhetoric of millenarian leaders at various times.[13]

In addition to assertions of prophetic or divine status, the Khattābiyya and several of its offshoots (for example, the Mu'āmmariyya and the Bazīghiyya) taught the antinomian concept of Paradise being luxuries and pleasant things to be enjoyed and Hell consisting of unpleasant duties to be avoided. They are said to have permitted adultery and alcohol consumption, but here one may be misled by the usual spiritual libertinage accusations so often leveled against antinomians.[14]

Qādī al-Nu'mān argues that the Khattābiyya in fact considered illicit actions to be permissible. It was even legitimate for them to present false evidence in disputes. The prohibitions of Islam were cancelled, he informs us, for those who had a knowledge of

[11] Nawbakhtī, "Sectes Shi'ites," trans. Mashkūr, *Revue de l'Histoire des Religiones*, CLIV (1958), 149.
[12] anon., *'Umm' al-Kitāb*, trans. Pio Filippani-Ronconi (Naples, 1966), 20–21.
[13] al-Ash'arī al-Qummī, *Maqālāt wa al-firaq*, 50–51; Ibn Hazm, "Heterodoxies," 69; al-Rāzī, *I'tiqādāt*, 58; Isfarā'īnī, *Tabsīr*, 74.
[14] Shahrastānī, *Milal wa Nihal*, trans. A. K. Kazi and J. G. Flynn, in *Abr Nahrain*, XV (Leiden, 1975), 74–75.

and gave recognition to the *Imām*.[15] The Khattābiyya were also
allowed to shed the blood and to seize the property of their enemies, as had been the case with the Mansūriyya. Once more, these
details provide clear parallels with Cohn's millenarian adepts of
the Free Spirit in late medieval Europe.[16]

The Qarmatian revolutionaries of lower Iraq and Bahrayn
(active in the ninth and the tenth centuries) also offer many parallels with and continuations of teachings that emerged among
our four Kufan sects. The Qarmatī movement, as Madelung
showed years ago, arose from a split in the ranks of the early
Ismā'īlīs that had resuled from a new supreme leader altering
previous teachings about the *Mahdī* role of Muhammad b. Ismā'īl
b. Ja'far al-Sādiq and the number and order of *Imāms*.[17] Although
a significant issue, this factor is not our primary concern. Rather,
what is of keen interest here is the fact that the Ismā'īlīs prior to
the Qarmati origins (the work of an Ismā'īlī *dā'ī* Hamdān Qar-
mat, active in southern Iraq in the ninth century) had emphasized the expectation of the messianic advent of Muhammad b.
Ismā'īl as *Mahdī*. This doctrine was coupled with a strong commit-
ment to social justice to such an extent that, among the Qarmati
community in Bahrayn, there was communal sharing of goods.
The *Mahdī* and the other *Imāms* prior to his appearance were
thought to be of a supernatural nature, to be knowledgable about
the inner secrets of the universe, and to have spiritual insights
conferring cosmic power upon them.[18]

---

[15] Qādī al-Nu'mān, *Book of Faith* (trans. Fyzee), 58.

[16] Cohn, *Pursuit*, 163–186.

[17] Wilferd Madelung, "The Fatimids and the Qarmatīs of Bahrayn," in *Mediæval Isma'ili History and Thought*, ed. Farhad Daftary (Cambridge, 1996), 21–73.

[18] One of the clearest statements of this phenomenon is to be seen in the thesis of Abdulkareem A. al-Ghamedi, "The Qarmatians of Iraq and Arabia: A Reexam-ination," M.A. thesis (University of Arkansas, 1977), 49–53, and sources cited therein. See also the comparable work of Usama Hamid, "The Qarmatians: Society and State," M.A. thesis (American University of Beirut, August 1977), 65–66. These two theses are the only studies of Qarmatian history to be under-taken in the last forty years.

The Qarmatians were also partisans of the sort of antinomianism we have previously encountered with the Mansūriyya and the Janāhiyya and that we have also noted present in millenarian and Gnostic groups generally. The Qarmatians believed themselves to be exempt from following the dictates of Islamic law and practice. For them, such duties as prayer, fasting, payment of the alms tax, and so on could be disregarded without fear of punishment. Conversely, they are accused of having permitted proscribed practices, including homosexual relations, alcohol consumption, and incest. The problem here, of course, is the recurring issue: whether they actually engaged in spiritual libertinism or whether they were falsely accused of such by hostile witnesses and chroniclers. Whatever the case, clearly, we see another instance of a millenarian rejection or inversion of the dominant legal order.[19]

Other Qarmatian teachings already familiar to us from our Kufan groups include transmigration of souls and symbolic interpretation of the Qur'ān. The early Qarmatians, indeed, offered sometimes puzzling explications of Qur'ānic verses. As one author has written:

> Such a practice could only appeal to those who were eager, even desperate, to find relief from an intolerable situation or who were deeply concerned with arriving at a real understanding of religious truth, people to whom the mystics (Sufis) would later appeal.[20]

Like many if not most millenarian movements, the Qarmatians arose out of a sense of crisis or desperation, many of these crises examined in the excellent but unpublished study by David Waines.[21] As modern studies demonstrate, heavy taxes, 'Abbāsid neglect of irrigation and water systems, tax-farming abuses, and

---

[19] al-Ghamedi, "Qarmatians," 50–51.

[20] Ibid., 50.

[21] David F. Waines, "Caliph and Amir," Ph.D. dissertation (McGill University, 1974).

even natural catastrophes induced this sense of crisis.[22] What could be more natural, given all of this, than to turn to a supernatural redeemer who would redress grievances, institute greater justice, and punish the wicked? In the meantime, to work and to fight for his cause was meritorious, and this merit could be compounded by living in a communal, egalitarian fashion and eliminating, or, at least, reducing, social inequality, in other words, precisely the sort of regime instituted by the Qarmatians in Bahrayn.[23]

Another sectarian movement reflecting aspects of the four Kufan groups was that of the Musha'sha'iyya, which appeared in the area of Khuzistan (southwest Iran) in the fifteenth century. The name of the group is derived from an individual named Sayyid Muhammad b. Falāh (d. 1460s), a student of the noted Twelver Shī'ite cleric Ahmad b. Fahd al-Hilli.[24] As Arjomand points out in his brief but important treatment of the Musha'sha', Muhammad b. Falāh adopted the title "Musha'sha'," which apparently means the "Radiant."[25] Having put together a military force largely from Arab tribesmen in Khuzistan and various populist elements, the Musha'sha' established a sort of ministate in Khuzistan that was to last even into the Safavid period.[26]

What is germane to our discussion here is the interesting blend of ideas reminiscent especially of those of the Mughīriyya, but also evoking aspects of the militant violence of the Mansūriyya. As with al-Mughīra b. Sa'īd, so too the Musha'sha' leaders apparently made ample use of magic and hermetic teachings to mesmerize their followers. The utilization of these techniques led the

---

[22] al-Ghamedi, "Qarmatians," 19–29; Hamid, "The Qarmatians," 1–15.
[23] Hamid, "The Qarmatians," 81–89.
[24] Mazzaoui, *Origins of the Safawids*, 67–69.
[25] Arjomand, *Shadow of God*, 76–77.
[26] Ibid., 77. See the important study by Michel Mazzaoui, "Musha'sha'iyan: A Fifteenth-Century Shi'i Movement in Khuzistan and Southern Iraq," *Folia Orientalia*, XXII (1981–1984), 139–162.

Musha'sha'iyya to enter into trance states, to endure severe pain, and to accomplish such feats as leaning upon swords placed in the ground without suffering any ostensible harm.[27] Magic here, obviously, solidified the charismatic hold of Ibn Falāh and his successors over their followers, just as it had done for al-Mughīra with the Mughīriyya.[28]

One also reads that Ibn Falāh and his successors claimed to be the bearers of a new religious law.[29] The Musha'sha''s own law code seems to have been a combination of pedantic detail and intimidating controls.[30] In this instance, the millenarian prophet does not set aside *all* laws but, in fact, replaces existing religious law with a harsh and even rigid new system.

Finally, one sees again in the case of the Musha'sha'iyya the chiliastic *Mahdī* concept and even the succession of Incarnations teaching. The Musha'sha' claimed to be the *Mahdī*, and his son, Mawlā 'Alī, arrogated to himself the role of *Mahdī*, as well as the reincarnation of 'Alī, and, finally, God himself.[31] These statements, of course, echo those of Ibn Mu'āwiyya's Janāhiyya, and the *Mahdī* belief is common, as we have seen, to all four of the Kufan organizations.

By way of concluding this part of the discussion, one may point to another Iranian Shī'ite-Sufi movement, which, although it began earlier than the Musha'sha'iyya, proved to be roughly contemporary with it in its active life. The Hurūfiyya movement was created by a native of Astarabad, in northwestern Iran, one Fadl Allāh b. Abū Muhammad, who is usually referred to in the

---

[27] Qāḍī Sayyed Nūr Allāh Shūshtarī, *Majālis Mu'minīn* (Tehran, 1376), 395; Ahmad Kasrāvī, *Ta'rīkh-i Pansād Salā-yi Khuzistān* (Tehran, 1330), 10. Consult further Kamil Mustafa al-Shaibi, *Sufism and Shi'ism* (Surbiton, 1991), 243–259.

[28] One may find a useful examination of the connection between magic and millenarism in the book of Bryan Wilson, *Magic and the Millennium* (St. Albans, 1975).

[29] Werner Caskel, "Ein Mahdi des 15. Jahrhunderts: Saijid Muhammad ibn Falah und seine Nachkommen," *Islamica*, IV (1929–31), 89.

[30] Arjomand, *Shadow of God*, 77.

[31] Ibid., 77; Kasravi, *Pansād*, 19.

sources as Fadl Allāh Astarābādī. Originally a Twelver Shī'ite, he
appears to have begun somewhere around the age of forty to
enunciate ideas of a problematic nature to *Imāmī* Shī'ites. He
announced in the city of Tabriz ca. 1379 that he had come to
know the sacred and secret meaning of the Holy Books and
followed this up by claiming to be an *Imām* and then even a
prophet. Not surprisingly, his teachings attracted the attention
of the authorities, who proved to be so unsympathetic that they
put him to death in Azerbaijan in 1394.[32]

The followers he had attracted, as we have seen with Bayān and
al-Mughīra, continued to be active long after their leader's death.
Indeed, the authorities' persecution of the Hurūfiyya caused the
movement to become more politically militant, more clandes-
tine, and even heightened their expectation that their fallen
leader, Fadl Allāh, would return as the messianic *Mahdī*.[33]

When we look at the teachings attributed to Fadl Allāh and his
sectarians, we encounter once more a number of ideas already
noted among the Kufan *Ghulāt*. We know, for instance, that like
Bayān, al-Mughīra, and Abū Mansūr, Fadl Allāh claimed to be a
prophet, continuing this cyclical recurrence of such figures. He
saw himself as leading a struggle, furthermore, against evil forces.
He spoke, for example, of taking up the sword against opponents.[34] Fadl Allāh is said to have maintained that he was inau-
gurating a cycle of history in which God had become manifest
in man (especially in Fadl), whose features reflect the divine letters identified with God (in other words, the *hurūf* – the twenty-
eight letters of the Arabic alphabet or the thirty-two letters of the
Persian). One could, in other words, know God through Gnostic
interpretation of the alphabet.[35]

---

[32] Arjomand, *Shadow of God*, 72.
[33] Ibid., 72–74.
[34] Vahid Rafati, "Hurūfīs," 14.
[35] Riza Tevfiq, "Étude sur la Religion des Houroufis," in *Textes Persans Relatifs a la
Secte des Houroufis*, trans. and ed. Clement Huart (Leiden and London, 1909),
258–260; Arjomand, *Shadow of God*, 72. See also Bashir, *Fazlallāh*, passim,

What immediately comes to mind here, of course, is al-Mughīra ibn Saʿīd's speculations upon the letters of the Arabic alphabet, although it must be said that his manipulations of the letters seem decidedly crude and elementary compared to those of Fadl Allāh. It is evident, of course, that the Hurūfiyya preoccupation with alphabetical and numerical cabbalism gave the sect its name.

Similarly, one finds in Hurūfī literature spiritual interpretations given for Hell and Paradise. For the Hurūfiyya, knowledge of the Word, that is, Fadl Allāh himself, constituted Paradise. Ignorance of the Word meant being in Hell. For those who knew the Word (Fadl), religious obligations such as fasting and prayer were no longer necessary, and, on top of this, those things forbidden in Islam were made lawful to them.[36]

As the previous discussion underscores, sects of the Umayyad period, ranging from the Bayāniyya to the Janāhiyya, had spawned a body of ideas and practices that were to live long after their originators had passed into the shadows of history. All of these beliefs constituted a vocabulary, modes of behavior, and a program of action that could readily be exploited by charismatic leaders who promised to overturn whatever discredited regime and to hasten the coming of a new, righteous, and equitable world.

Millenarism and the Sects

The fundamental importance of the groups that we have examined in this study should be readily apparent by now. They were among the earliest revolutionary chiliastic, that is, millenarian, groups to appear in the Muslim world. Thanks to the

and, most recently, Karim N. Barzegar, *Intellectual Movements During Timuri and Safavi Period (1500–1700 A.D.)* (Delhi, 2005), 66–81.

[36] Rafati, "Hurūfīs," 20–21.

efforts of such scholars as Norman Cohn, Peter Worsley, Wilhelm Mühlmann, and Yonina Talmon, much has been learned within the past four decades about the general features and the nature of millenarian movements. In the remaining pages, these four groups will be evaluated within the context of these characteristics. It is only to be expected that our evidence may not correspond "perfectly" to the analytical framework employed. This should come as no surprise, however, as one rarely finds pure specimens that fit neatly into a conceptual apparatus such as the one we propose to employ here. As will be seen in the following pages, however, the evidence is of such a nature as to justify an analysis of this type.

In the preface to this book, I provided a definition of millenarism. For purposes of clarity, however, it will be repeated here. A millenarian movement is a group of individuals who expect "imminent, total, ultimate, this-worldly, collective salvation."[37] This definition reflects the basic characteristics of such a movement. The millenarian group first of all conceives of its salvation as being total; that is, the new order will be not merely an improvement but will, indeed, entail a complete transformation.[38] In all four of the groups studied there is evidence of such a feeling, although it is not stated in explicit, graphic terms. All of them included as one of their major doctrines the belief in the *Mahdī* (saviour). The *Mahdī* was to establish the reign of righteousness and justice on the earth. This establishment of right belief and equity indicated a complete transformation of society, such as the one embodied in the above definition. It is clear that the four groups, in addition, considered the new dispensation to be imminent. Through their adherence to the beliefs and

---

[37] Yonina Talmon, "Millenarism," in *International Encyclopædia of the Social Sciences*, X (2nd ed., New York, 1968), 349.

[38] Idem., "Pursuit of the Millenium: The Relation between Religious and Social Change," *Archives Européennes de Sociologie*, III (1962), 130.

practices mentioned in the previous chapters, these sects prepared themselves for the advent of the *Mahdī* and even sought to hasten it. Using older terminology, one may say that these groups were "pre-Millennialist" in orientation, that is to say, they anticipated revolutionary (abrupt) change instead of evolutionary or gradual change.[39]

The emphasis upon an apocalyptic future encompasses the view that the historical present is a time of trouble, lamentation, and oppression.[40] In the case of the Bayāniyya, Mughīriyya, Mansūriyya, and the Janāhiyya, this is another facet of the *Mahdī* concept. This figure is to transform a world that is filled with tyranny and injustice. The evil and corrupt present is to be annihilated. The new era is to be inaugurated, providing an escape from this unbearable present.[41]

An important feature of millenarism is its this-worldly orientation. Paradise is to appear on the earth. The chosen people are to receive the new blessing, not in some heavenly realm, but in this life.[42] As should be evident, the Shī'ite *Mahdī* was expected to establish a new order in *this world*. In the case of the Mughīriyya, for instance, al-Nafs al-Zakiyya was expected to emerge from a state of occultation and to "possess the earth."[43] Similarly, at least a portion of the Janāhiyya awaited the reappearance of Ibn Mu'āwiya, who would establish his rule over the world.[44] In this sense, apocalyptic ideas do not adequately convey the

[39] Henri Desroche, "Micromillenarismes et communautarisme utopique en Amérique du Nord du XVIIe au XIXe siècle," *Archives de Sociologie des Religions*, IV (1957), 87–88.

[40] Wilhelm E. Mühlmann, *Chiliasmus und Nativismus: Studien zur Psychologie, Soziologie und Historischen Kasuistik der Umsturzbewegungen* (Berlin, 1961), 282.

[41] Vittorio Lanternari, "Messianism: Its Historical Origin and Morphology," *History of Religions*, II (1962–1963), 67.

[42] Cohn, *Pursuit*, 308.

[43] al-Baghdādī, *Schisms* (trans. Halkin), 54.

[44] al-Ash'arī, *Maqālāt*, I, 95.

expectation, as they focus upon the end of the world rather than the coming of the new order.[45]

Another characteristic of millenarian movements is the belief in collective salvation.[46] The emphasis is placed upon the redemption of the group rather than upon that of the individual. This was the case with the four groups studied. The dispensation of the *Mahdī* was to apply to the sect as a whole. In the case of al-Mughīra, there seems to have been a heightened awareness of group identity.

Closely related to the collective-salvation orientation is the fundamental distinction made between followers and nonfollowers. The members of the millenarian sect consider themselves to be chosen, saintly people, engaged in a fierce and unrelenting struggle against the forces of evil, that is, those outside the group.[47] Such an attitude was common to the four groups. It is most noticeable with respect to the Mansūriyya and a later branch of the Mughīriyya, who engaged in terrorism against their opponents. In the case of these groups, as with all millenarian movements, the followers considered themselves to be in a state of grace by virtue of their devotion to the leader and the ideas

[45] For a brief but incisive discussion of apocalyptic ideas in early Islam, see the definitive new historiographical study of Fred M. Donner, *Narratives of Islamic Origins: The Beginnings of Islamic Historical Writing* (Princeton, N.J. 1998), 228–229. The standard introduction to Christian and Jewish apocalyptic ideas is that of Walter Schmithals, *The Apocalyptic Movement: Introduction and Interpretation*, trans. John E. Steely (New York, 1975). For a series of excellent essays on various aspects of apocalyptic ideas in the Middle Ages, there is Werner Verbeke, Daniel Verhelst, and Andries Welkenhuysen eds., *The Use and Abuse of Eschatology in the Middle Ages* (Louvain, 1988). Consult further Abbas Amanat and Magnus Bernhardsson, eds., *Imagining the End: Visions of Apocalypse from the Ancient Middle East to Modern America* (London, 2002). Also, John J. Collins, ed., *The Encyclopedia of Apocalypticism. II. The Origins of Apocalypticism in Judaism and Christianity* (New York, 2000).
[46] Cohn, "Medieval Millenarism," *Millennial Dreams*, ed. Thrupp, 42.
[47] Talmon, "Millenarism," in *E. Soc. Sci.*, 351.

identified with him.[48] As has been noted in the previous chapters, the members of the four groups believed that acceptance of the religious ideology legitimized struggle against their foes and conferred charisma upon both leaders and followers.[49]

Antinomian tendencies are another feature often associated with millenarian movements.[50] The antinomianism of the early extremist Shī'ites has been noted in numerous instances throughout the course of this study. The doctrine that knowledge of the religious leader exempts the members of the group from observance of ritual law was the most frequent manifestation of this idea. The allegorical interpretation of religious duties and prohibitions also had the effect of nullifying their observance. Antinomianism of this type was closely identified with the movements of Abū Mansūr and Ibn Mu'āwiya.

For some groups, the millennium is expected to come about through the working of the Deity. The new era is to result from the direct intervention of God, not from the deeds of believers. Other sects, however, believe that their members must take an activist role. In this case the coming of the new age is considered to be the result of a revolutionary, violent struggle against the groups' enemies.[51] The Bayāniyya, Mughīriyya, Mansūriyya, and Janāhiyya were of the latter persuasion. Each of these sects took up arms against their enemies, the Umayyads and their supporters, seeking to bring about the millennium. Their action took the forms of revolt or outright terroristic violence.

---

[48] Cohn, *Pursuit*, 71.

[49] I have examined elsewhere the ways in which charisma is shared by *Imāms*, sect leaders, and their rank and file followers. See Tucker, "Charismatic Leadership in Shī'ite Sectarianism," in *Islamic and Middle Eastern Societies: A Festschrift in Honor of Professor Wadie Jwaideh* (Brattleboro, Vt., 1987), 29–41.

[50] Talmon, "Millenarism," in *E. Soc. Sci.*, 351. See also, more recently, Karen Fields, "Antinomian Conduct at the Millennium: Metaphorical Conceptions of Time in Social Science and Social Life," in *The Political Dimensions of Religion*, ed. Said A. Arjomand (Albany, N.Y., 1993), 177–179.

[51] Talmon, "Pursuit," *Archives*, 131–132.

Messianism is a prominent feature of most millenarian movements. Salvation is considered the work of a messiah who is an
intermediary between God and man.[52] It should be more than
obvious by this point that the belief in a messiah was common to
each of the four groups under consideration. The messiah for
them was the *Mahdī*. In the case of the Bayāniyya, Abū Hāshim
was believed to be the messiah. Muhammad Ibn ʿAbd Allāh ibn
Hasan al-Nafs al-Zakiyya held a similar position in the doctrines
of the Mughīriyya. Abū Mansūr al-ʿIjli taught that one of his sons
would be the *Mahdī*. For the Janāhiyya, Ibn Muʿāwiya was the
awaited messianic figure. It will be recalled, furthermore, that
the Mughīriyya and the Janāhiyya believed that their messianic
heroes were in concealment and would remain so until their
establishment of the new order. As noted above, the hidden-
messiah concept is to be found among some millenarian movements of medieval Europe.[53] It was believed, for instance, that
Charlemagne had not died but was sleeping until the time of
his reappearance. A similar idea is said to have been applied to
Count Emmerich of Leiningen after his death in 1117.[54]

The leader of the messianic group is another figure of considerable importance. Such men ordinarily claim prophetic inspiration. These *prophetae* preach the new doctrines and lead the
group in the preparations for the coming of the messiah.[55]
Bayān, al-Mughīra, and Abū Mansūr each played such a role
within their movements. The situation was not the same in the
case of the Janāhiyya, however. Their leader and messiah were
embodied in a single individual, ʿAbd Allāh Ibn Muʿāwiya. Thus,
the leader as an individual distinct from the saviour figure is a millenarian concept that does not apply to the case of the Janāhiyya.

---

[52] Ibid.; Wilson Wallis, *Messias: Their Role in Civilization* (Washington, D.C., 1943),
125.
[53] Mühlmann, *Chiliasmus*, 305.
[54] Cohn, *Pursuit*, 55–57.
[55] Talmon, "Pursuit," *Archives*, 133–134.

It has been suggested that millenarian movements bring together groups that are not only separate but that were formerly even hostile to one another.[56] Although the evidence is by no means conclusive, it seems that this was the case with the sects upon which we have concentrated. All of them appear to have included both Arabs and *Mawālī* among their ranks. Some Arabs and non-Arab Muslims, as is well known, viewed each other with a mixture of contempt and animosity. A common enemy and a common sense of grievance served to bring them together in the same movement, however. The presence of *Mawālī* and Arabs in the same group is of significance, because it indicated that Shīʿism after the rebellion of al-Mukhtār did not become purely a *Mawālī* affair. Arabs continued to play a role in Shīʿite groups.

A related factor of considerable weight in millenarian-prone environments is the presence of different and potentially conflicting cultures.[57] Southern Iraq, and Kufa in particular, saw the presence of a sizable number of different ethnic and religious groups. Among others, Arabs, Persians, Aramaeans, and Jews all mingled in this diverse population, on the heels of the Muslim conquests. More importantly, this population contained an extremely wide and variegated range of religious communities. There were, as we have noted frequently, any number of religions dating from pre-Islamic times, including Mandaeans, Manichaeans, various Christian sects, Jewish groups, and Zoroastrians. To this mix was added an Islamic society in the process of self-definition and thereby giving rise to its own sectarian divisions. The lines among these various religious groupings must have been blurred at times, and the resulting tensions about one's identity probably generated unease and the potential for

[56] Peter Worsley, *The Trumpet Shall Sound: A Study of "Cargo" Cults in Melanesia* (2nd aug. ed., Schocken, N.Y., 1968), 230.
[57] One of the most important treatments of this phenomenon is Vittorio Lanternari, *The Religions of the Oppressed: A Study of Modern Messianic Cults*, trans. Lisa Sergio (New York, 1963). See also Wyatt MacGaffey, *Modern Kongo Prophets: Religion in a Plural Society* (Bloomington, Ind., 1983).

conflict. When one adds to this situation the unsettled political and psychological atmosphere in Kufa, which was, after all, a frontier city from which Islamic eastern conquests were launched, it becomes clear that sectarian leaders and movements enunciating salvationist, messianic, and millenarian ideas could flourish.[58]

Millenarian movements, in terms of organization, range from the movement with a core of leaders and zealous followers supported by an ill-defined mass following to the "fairly stable, segregated, and exclusive sect-like group."[59] The first type is ordinarily of a transitory, ephemeral nature.[60] The groups that have been examined seem to have been a combination of the two types. They included in each case a durable core of followers with sufficient organization to be termed sects. At the same time, however, there were centrifugal elements present among them. The latter were individuals who had become disaffected with the leaders or doctrines. This is particularly evident in the cases of the Mughīriyya after the death of al-Nafs al-Zakiyya and the Janāhiyya following the killing of Ibn Mu'āwiya. The principal reason for these desertions was the non-materialization of the prophecies of the sect leader, the primary weakness of the typical millenarian movement.[61]

It is necessary at this point to examine the possible reasons for the appearance of the groups upon which we have focused in this study. To a large extent, millenarism has been shown to be the religion of deprived groups. The primary cause in this case is what is known as "multiple deprivation," that is, a combination of low status, poverty, and lack of political power.[62] Low status is often the result of membership in a despised ethnic or cultural

[58] For an idea of the formation and arrangement of the population in Kufa, see the important book by Hichem Djaït, *Al-Kūfa: Naissance de la ville Islamique* (Paris, 1986), especially 227–250.

[59] Talmon, "Pursuit," *Archives*, 135.

[60] Ibid.

[61] Ibid.

[62] Ibid.

group. The *Mawālī*, at least some of those in Kufa, appear to have
been just such a disparaged group. In economic terms, there is
no doubt that they did not usually belong to the prosperous sec-
tor of the Muslim community, because, as is well known, they
received from the state a stipend lower than that given to the
Arabs. There is a sizable body of evidence, too, for the contempt
with which some Arabs looked upon them. It is said, for example, that they had to worship in mosques separate from those
of the Arabs.[63] On those occasions when they prayed together
with the Arabs, they were required to stand in the last rows.[64]
Some Arabs are even said to have believed that the prayers of
the *Mawālī* were of questionable value.[65] There were still other
acts of discrimination. *Mawālī* were forbidden to walk ahead of
an Arab in any sort of festive procession. At the table they had
to sit behind the Arabs. At the funeral of an Arab, they were
forbidden to say prayers over the deceased.[66] If a *Mawlā* made
a mistake in his Arabic, he was the target of the most offensive
mockery.[67] *Mawālī* were barred from marrying Arab women.[68]
All of the higher offices, of course, fell to the Arabs or converted
Iranian nobility.[69] This last example is indicative of the fact that
the discrimination was more of a social or economic matter than
a racial one. It also indicates something of the general economic
situation of the *Mawālī*.

The *Mawālī* belonging to the indigenous Aramaic-speaking
population of Iraq, a group known as the Nabataeans, appear

---

[63] van Vloten, *Recherches*, 14.
[64] E. A. Belyaev, *Arabs, Islam and the Arab Caliphate in the Early Middle Ages*, trans.
Adolphe Gourevitch (New York, 1969), 180.
[65] Ibid.
[66] Alfred von Kremer, *Culturgeschichtliche Streifzuge auf dem Gebiete des Islams*, trans.
S. Khuda Bukhsh, in *Contributions to the History of Islamic Civilization*, I (2nd ed.,
Calcutta, 1929), 81.
[67] Goldziher, *Muslim Studies*, I, 115.
[68] Belyaev, *Arabs, Islam*, 180.
[69] van Vloten, "Worgers," 63.

to have been especially degraded. It is said that the Arabs considered the term "Nabatī" to be an insult.[70] They believed the Nabataeans to be of a servile nature and often cited them as the typical example of the common people.[71] It is quite clear, therefore, that these people were subjected to no small degree of humiliation. They, as well as the *Mawālī* of other ethnic backgrounds, also found it demeaning to be compelled to affiliate with an Arab tribe in order to have any legal status in the Muslim community. Furthermore, there is little reason to believe that the *Mawlā* normally obtained a status equal to that of the Arabs belonging to the tribe with which he aligned himself.[72] It is quite possible that an individual in this situation would experience a pronounced feeling of insecurity with regard to his personal status. By aligning himself with a group in which belief rather than blood was the major criterion for belonging (as was the case with the four sects), he could assure himself of a more secure position. An important factor for the development of millenarism among a given group of individuals is the raising of expectations that remain unfulfilled.[73] This may have been one of the main reasons why many of the *Mawālī* gravitated to these extremist groups. Conversion to Islam had ostensibly given them membership in a community in which personal status was dependent upon the timeliness, ardor, and sincerity of one's faith. At an early date, however, it had become evident that this was only a theory. With the accession of the Umayyads, status in the Muslim state had become a matter of family, clan, and Arab blood. Thus, the anticipations of the non-Arab converts had not been realized. It

---

[70] Theodor Nöldeke, "Die Namen der Aramäischen Nation und Sprache," *ZDMG*, XXV (1871), 127.

[71] Goldziher, *Muslim Studies*, I, 145, n.1.

[72] Belyaev, *Arabs, Islam*, 179–180.

[73] D. F. Aberle, "A Note on Relative Deprivation Theory as Applied to Millenarian and Other Cult Movements," in *Millenial Dreams in Action: Essays in Comparative Study*, ed. Sylvia Thrupp (The Hague, 1962), 209–210.

is hardly surprising, then, that they turned to movements such as that of al-Mughīra and the other extremist leaders. It should not be forgotten that the messianic ideas were not new to the Persians and Aramaeans, as both groups had been exposed to such beliefs prior to the coming of the Arabs and Islam.[74]

It was indicated previously that the members of the millenarian group look upon themselves as being the truly chosen people. The group provides its adherents with a sense of personal worth. A person of formerly low status transforms himself into a member of an elite through joining the group. What is involved here is a reversal of roles.[75] As one author has aptly described it, high religious status is substituted for low social status.[76] Such was the case, clearly, in the groups dealt with in this study. They were caught up in this sense of elitism, especially pronounced in the cases of the Mughīriyya and the Janāhiyya.

The *Mawālī* were not the only element of which the four groups were composed. At least some sections of certain Arab tribes belonged to them. This would seem to contradict what has been said previously about Arab-*Mawālī* hostility. As indicated previously, however, millenarian movements may contain elements that formely upheld a tradition of animosity toward one another. The reason for this new alliance is not difficult to find, it would seem. The antagonists were driven together by hatred of a common foe. The esoteric nature of the religious doctrines doubtlessly served as the ideological bond by means of which solidarity was achieved. The members of the groups hated the Umayyads and those who recognized their dominion. The need for cooperation against a common enemy served to overcome ethnic differences. It is possible that similarity of social position

---

74 Salih, "Mahdiism in Islam," 312–376.

75 Mühlmann, *Chiliasmus*, 336.

76 Werner Stark, *The Sociology of Religion: A Study of Christendom. II: Sectarian Religion* (London, 1967), 158.

also led to the coalescence of this association. Unfortunately, one cannot be certain of this, as information about the economic and social state of those Arabs involved in the groups is simply not forthcoming. The Arabs participating in the movements were elements of the Kinda, the Bajīla, and the ʿIjl, as we have noted. We mentioned the historical background of these tribes in Chapter 4. It is necessary to review a few points here, however. In the first place, it should be recalled that the Kinda were a tribe of considerable stature. That they felt some resentment toward the Islamic state may be seen in the role they played in the *Ridda* wars (wars of Apostasy). The defeat they suffered at Muslim hands *may* have created a lasting bitterness among certain sections of the tribe. For whatever reasons, some of them viewed the Umayyad state with a great deal of hostility.[77] Members of the tribe fought with al-Mukhtār, Ibn al-Ashʿath, and Yazīd ibn Muhallab, to say nothing of al-Mughīra ibn Saʿīd and Abū Mansūr al-ʿIjli. Possibly they did so because of the ubiquitous Qays-Yamani dispute. Probably an important factor was the presence of Iraqi regional feeling against the Umayyads and their Syrian supporters. The Kinda involved in the Mughīriyya and the Mansūriyya belonged, no doubt, to the Iraqi branch of the tribe. Perhaps another reason for the Kinda involvement with these groups was resentment at being excluded from the focus of political power. Although a

---

[77] It should be noted here that the Kinda were not entirely anti-Umayyad. Illustrative of this is the fact that ʿAlī's governor in Egypt, Muhammad ibn Abi Bakr, was defeated and killed by one of Muʿāwiya's generals, Muʿāwiya ibn Khadīj or Khudayj, a Kindite. For information concerning ibn Khadīj, consult Tabarī, *Taʾrīkh*, I, passim and especially 3404–3406, II, 83 ff.; Yaʿqūbī, *Taʾrīkh*, II, 194. The army that Yazīd I sent against Ibn al-Zubayr had a Kindite, al-Husayn ibn Numayr, as the second in command. For information concerning this individual, consult Tabarī, *Taʾrīkh*, I, 2004, 2220, II, 424–427, 557–560. The chief adviser to Sulaymān ibn ʿAbd al-Mālik was a Kindite, Rajāh ibn Haywā al-Kindī. Material about this person may be found in Tabarī, *Taʾrīkh*, I, passim, II, 1341–1345; Yaʿqūbī, *Taʾrīkh*, 299, 308.

powerful and noble tribe, they were barred from ruling power by virtue of not being among the inner circle of Marwānids. Undoubtedly, a number of them were dissatisfied with the social stratification and polarization that had become all too evident in Kufa by the time of the Marwanids. For any or all of these reasons, then, members of the Kinda were among the supporters of the Shī'ite extremists examined.

Individuals from the Bajīla were also to be found among these sects.[78] Again, Qays-Yamani factional disputes, Iraqi regionalism, and dislike of Umayyad family rule may have driven them into the ranks of opposition movements. Bitterness at being deprived of booty in the campaign for Iraq may have been a continuing source of anti-government feeling, the identity of the ruling family being of little importance. In the case of the 'Ijl, Iraqi feeling plus possible Rabī'a resentment toward Mudarite rule and policies may have been the causative factors.

On the basis of the evidence available, then, it is clear that the sects that have been examined in this study can be classified without difficulty as millenarian movements. The crucial attributes of chiliastic movements were characteristic of the four groups, as indicated throughout the previous pages. By examining the sects within the context of these same attributes, we have been able to underscore their conflation of religion, politics, and social activism.

---

[78] There were also pro-Umayyad elements among the Bajīla. Probably the best example of this is Khālid al-Qasrī, Hishām's governor of Iraq, as noted above. It is necessary to recall that the Bajīla came to be identified with the yamanite faction only from the time of Khālid's grandfather and father.

Conclusion

It is by virtue of the fact that the groups examined in this study
were millenarian movements that they are of more general significance. Many scholars have studied the phenomenon of millenarism, as pointed out often in the preceding chapters. Millenarian groups, they have shown, have existed at different times
and in virtually every part of the world. Norman Cohn, years ago,
laid the groundwork for millenarian studies with his important
volume devoted to the chiliastic groups of medieval and Reformation Europe. Vittorio Lanternari, in his work *The Religions of
the Oppressed*,[1] has more recently elucidated the role of millenarism, in this case, among those nations and peoples subjected
to European colonization in the nineteenth and twentieth centuries. The universal nature of millenarism can be seen from
the range of essays appearing in the *Archives de Sociologie des Religions* (volume IV, 1957, and volume V, 1958), many of which
are referred to throughout this book. Regardless of the time or
region, millenarian movements appear to have certain features
in common, as we have seen.[2]

---

[1] Lanternari, *Religions*.
[2] In addition to the works cited throughout the course of this study, any intensive
investigation of the phenomenon of millenarian sects should be based upon the
following sources: Georges Balandier, *The Sociology of Black Africa: Social Dynamics in Central Africa*, trans. Douglas Garman (New York, 1970), see especially

In any final assessment of these sects, one must address the issue of why those interested in millenarism should study the ideas and actions of these seemingly marginal groups. The most obvious response to this query is to point out the role of millenarian groups or tendencies present in the Muslim world today. The 'Alawites (Nusayris) are clearly lineal descendants of these sectarian groups, and the 'Alawite role in Syrian political and religious life is apparent to all those having passing familiarity with contemporary Middle Eastern affairs. In addition, the Ahl-i Haqq of Kurdistan are also contemporary heirs, if indirectly, of the sects examined in this volume. Of course, one may also point to the ambiguities in the Iranian Revolution and especially the messianic role of the late Ayatollah Khomeini, which savor of millenarian utopian strains similar to those of movements analyzed in this book. One can, of course, argue that utopian and salvationist motifs figure importantly in any revolutionary movement, but it is clear that the resonances of Shī'ite *Mahdism* and social consciousness played a major role in the Iranian Revolution in a way that sets it apart from such predecessors as the French or Russian revolutions. Such factors are well underscored by Cheryl Benard and Zalmay Khalilzad in a passage from their important study, *"The Government of God" – Iran's Islamic Republic.* Speaking

410–472; Michael Barkun, *Disaster and the Millennium* (New Haven, Conn., and London, 1974); Kenelm Burridge, *New Heaven New Earth: A Study of Millenarian Activities* (Oxford, 1969); Henri Desroche, *The Sociology of Hope,* trans. Carol Martin-Sperry (London and Boston, 1979); Mark Holloway, *Heavens on Earth: Utopian Communities in America, 1680–1880* (2nd ed., New York, 1966); Hue-Tam Ho Tai, *Millenarianism and Peasant Politics in Vietnam* (Cambridge, Mass., and London, 1983); Charles Nordhoff, *The Communist Societies of the United States from Personal Visit and Observation* (New York, 1966); Audrey Wipper, *Rural Rebels: A Study of Two Protest Movements in Kenya* (Nairobi, London, and New York, 1977), particularly 77–78, 144–147; Susan Naquin, *Millenarian Rebellion in China: The Eight Trigrams Uprising of 1813* (New Haven, Conn., 1976), part 1, 7–62.

of the movement that toppled the Shah and led to the establishment of the Islamic republic, they have written:

> What emerged instead is a movement that bears some of the characteristics of a millennialist movement. It is chiliastic, orienting itself by the expected return of the Twelfth Imam. It is totalitarian, encompassing all areas of life, seeking to regulate behavior, impulses, and interactions of the private as well as the public sort and dividing the world into good and evil. Enemies are referred to in existential terms, such as the most common appellation for the U.S., "world devourers." The movement distinctly aspires to transcend worldly affairs, which are dismissed as trivial. "I cannot believe that the purpose of all these sacrifices was to have less expensive melons," Khomeini has said. The similarities of Iran's experience to a millennialist peasant uprising are evident, and again our final definition will have to be postponed; just as a revolution is contingent on its success, a millennial movement is characterized by its failure, as it gives way to the rise to dominance of elements within its membership or to the reassertion of part of the former ruling government.[3]

However much Iran has changed in recent years, it seems to me that the cogency of this analysis was amply demonstrated in the period of the Revolution and in the first years of the Republic.

More meaningfully, however, one may point to factors that illuminate aspects of the millenarian sect or social formation. For instance, at least some of these early Shī'ite groups demonstrate the exclusiveness derived from a sense of separateness or alienation from the larger community of whatever faith or political hue. There is a desire here to reject and separate from, or even to strike out at, the larger, rejected community. One sees here in a pronounced fashion the significance of the reversal of status or value. The downtrodden or persecuted are the real community of worth: true believers. Violence committed against

---

[3] Cheryl Benard and Zalmay Khalilzad, *"The Government of God" – Iran's Islamic Republic* (New York, 1984), 64–65.

the establishment or established order is not only justified, but indeed meritorious!

In this last respect, one may also note in these groups a willingness to adopt violent actions, which is reminiscent of some late medieval European protest groups or, in East Asia, the Taipeng rebels of mid-nineteenth-century China. It is difficult, if not impossible, to say why some millenarian groups eschew violence whereas others utilize it as a tactic, whether reluctantly or enthusiastically. One may conjecture, however, that the harshness of treatment meted out to some 'Alids and/or 'Alid sympathizers, for example, al-Husayn, Mukhtār, and so on, may have led these fierce 'Alid partisans to champion violence or stress terror as a modus operandi.

Another feature of the Shī'ite groups that may be of interest to scholars of millenarism is the highly symbolic and to some degree hermetic nature of their teachings. We have already seen the emphasis placed upon allegorical interpretation of scripture or religious teachings. The Gnostic character of this practice clearly suggests the elitist tinge of these groups and their hostility toward the external society. The larger society of "unbelievers" could not understand or act appropriately upon the teachings of Islam as mediated and clarified by the 'Alids or 'Alid-trusted deputies (whether actual or self-appointed deputies!). The real truth was not, and could not be, the nominally self-evident meaning!

Here one comes to a factor that is striking and important in understanding these Shī'ite extremists: their veneration of a lineage. One of the peculiarities of these groups is the fact that one may see them as radical, social-reformist "royalists." This may sound odd, but there is no doubt that the political and spiritual dominance of the descendant of 'Alī ibn Abī Tālib was the center – the *core* – of the teachings of the groups studied in this book. It is quite possible that one may encounter something similar in millenarian movements in other parts of the world at various times, but my reading of the materials utilized in this study, and mentioned in the notes and bibliography, does not yield any significant instances of this. Whether it is unique or not, it is certainly one of the facets of extremist Shī'ite beliefs that makes them worthy of attention by scholars of comparative millennialism.

In view of all this, it is to be hoped that the method of analysis employed in this study has served to add a further dimension to our knowledge of Islamic sectarianism. One may suggest modestly that comparative studies of Islamic and non-Islamic millenarism will illuminate important features of a type of religious and sociopolitical organization that has figured significantly at times in the history of religions and societies. In this way, at the very least, it may be possible to better understand the responses of social/religious groups to comparable psychological or material pressures. It is hoped that this book has, at the least, filled in the lacunae in the collected volumes on millenarism, in which one finds not one contribution on Islam, with the exception of a two-page précis by the late Marshall Hodgson, which surprisingly omitted any detailed or developed treatment of Shī'ism.[4]

[4] Marshall G. S. Hodgson, "A Note on the Millennium in Islam," in *Millennial Dreams in Action: Essays in Comparative Study*, ed. Sylvia L. Thrupp (The Hague, 1962), 218–219.

Epilogue

In the wake of the American invasion of Iraq, the election of Mahmud Ahmadinejad to the presidency of the Islamic Republic of Iran, and the rise of Hizballah (Party of God) to prominence and power in Lebanon, the Shi'ite community of the Middle East seems poised to assume a far more significant role than they have hitherto enjoyed in the region. One sees now in this respect the appearance of important books bearing such titles as *Reaching for Power: The Shi'a in the Modern Arab World* and *The Shia Revival: How Conflicts within Islam Will Shape the Future*, probably the two best-known volumes analyzing the rise of Shi'ite political and geo-strategic importance.[1] What, if anything, does this contemporary Shi'ite experience have to do with sects examined in the present study?

Notwithstanding the differences in time, place, political situations, and so on, there are clearly significant parallels between the medieval and the modern groups. First of all, however, it should be emphasized that the Shi'ite political-religious movements of today are emphatically *not* similar to *Ghulat* sects in any meaningful theological or doctrinal sense. The Shi'ite leaders

---

[1] Yitzhak Nakash, *Reaching for Power: The Shi'a in the Modern Arab World* (Princeton, N.J., 2006); Vali Nasr, *The Shia Revival: How Conflicts within Islam Will Shape the Future* (New York, 2006).

of the Iranian Islamic revolutionary groups, the Shi'ite political figures in Iraq, and the clerical leaders associated with Hizballah in Lebanon would be aghast at any suggestion that they countenance such teachings as *tanāsūkh* (transmigration of souls), *hulūl* (incarnationism), or *ibāha* (antinomianism), all ideas we have noted among our *Ghulat* sects. The irony here is that such ideas, insofar as they are still to be encountered in the Islamic world, are to be found, as noted previously, among certain Shi'ite or quasi-Shi'ite groups in the Middle East, for instance, the Ahl-i-Haqq, the Druze, the Alevis in Turkey, and the Nusayris of Syria, which are all associated today with relative political quietism and the absence of revolutionary chiliastic activism.

The improbable connection, then, is that the Twelver or *Imāmi* Shi'ites, who, out of conviction or necessity, generally eschewed revolutionary millenarianism, if one excepts the Safavid revolution and assumption of power in early sixteenth-century Iran, now seem to have assumed the mantle of the militant, militaristic messianism reminiscent of the medieval Iraqi and Iranian *Ghulat* movements. One might object that revolutionary Iran, Shi'ite groups in Iraq today, and Lebanon's Hizballah are modern political movements, parties, and so on responding to issues bound up with the Israeli-Palestinian conflict, responses to imperialism, political authoritarian regimes, and so on. Whereas this is undoubtedly true, it is also the case that symbolic language, images, and behaviors provide insight into political and religious movements, and here is where we come to the core issue.

When the president of Iran suggests that government policy should be guided by the goal of advancing the return of the concealed Twelfth Imam, and instructs his cabinet to pledge allegiance to this concealed Imam, it is clear that the messianic and millenarian impulses that arose in eighth-century Iraq are not simply a matter of "ancient history."[2] Furthermore, it is surely

---

[2] Nasr, *Shia Revival*, 133–134.

of some interest to note the name, "Mahdi Army," given to the military organization of the Iraqi Shi'ite leader Muqtada al-Sadr. Similarly, it is important to recognize the role of the pan-Islamic Mahdist state in the ideas of at least some Hizballah figures and their anticipation of the Mahdi's return to the world.[3] The ushering into existence of the new millenarian order, as with our medieval groups, seems to entail the use of force and intimidation. Whether it is the Iranian Revolutionary Guard, Hizballah, the Mahdi Army, or, for that matter, the Badr Brigade of SCIRI in Iraq, it is not simply a matter of political parties utilizing elections, political negotiations, or public opinion campaigns. Whatever the justice or merit of their programs, the issue has to do with sectarian, military organizations, analogous to the sectarian movements present in Iraq and Iran centuries ago.

Finally, another factor hearkening back to our medieval groups is the presence and role of charismatic leaders promoting the 'Alid cause to at least some degree. Whereas Ahmadinejad, Muqtada al-Sadr, and Hasan Nasrallah may very well be advancing modern national agendas, they are manifestly *Shi'ite* leaders promoting Shi'ite interests, employing language and symbols that are recognizably Shi'ite in nature. To lump their movements or parties within the larger category of modern "Islamist" movements such as al-Qaeda, Hamas, or Islamic Jihad (as examples) is to mistake the roots and the nature of their particular religious-political organizations and to mistakenly overlook the Shi'ite sectarian aspects of these leaders and those who take up arms on their behalf. In the final analysis, it is crucial to understand that these Shi'ite leaders and their faithful sense that the time of injus-

---

[3] Amal Saad-Ghorayeb, *Hizbu'llah: Politics and Religion* (London, 2002), 33–34. Among a number of other studies of Hizballah, two of the best analyses are to be found in Stephan Rosiny's excellent treatment entitled *Islamismus bei den Schiiten im Libanon: Religion im Übergang von Tradition zur Moderne* (Frankfurt, 1996); and Augustus Richard Norton's newly – published volume, *Hezbollah: A Short History* (Princeton N.J., 2007).

tice and deprivation that they and their forebears have suffered is on the verge of giving way to a new world of justice and empowerment – precisely the sort of expectation and anticipation we have noted with millenarian movements at all times and all places.

Bibliography

I. Non-Western Sources Written Prior to 1800

Abū al-Maʿālī, Muhammad al-Husaynī. *Kitāb Bayān al-Adyān*. (Teheran, 1312 H.).

[Abū Muhammad?]. *Kitāb Milal wa al-Nihal*. MS. Atif Effendi Kütübhanesi, Istanbul, no. 1373.

Abū Tammām. *An Ismaili Heresiography: The "Bāb al-Shaytān from Abū Tammām's Kitab al-Shajara*. Edited and translated by Wilferd Madelung and Paul Walker. (Leiden, 1998).

al-Akbar, Nāshi'. *Kitāb Usūl al-Nihal*. In *Frühe Muʿtazilitische Häresiographie: Zwei Werke des Nāshi' al-Akbar*. Text edited by Josef van Ess. (Beirut, 1971).

al-Ashʿarī, al-Qummī, Saʿd ibn ʿAbd Allāh ibn Abī Khalaf. *Kitāb al-Maqālāt wa al-Firaq*. (Teheran, 1964).

al-Astarābādī, Mirza Muhammad. *Minhāj al-Maqāl fī ʿIlm al-Rijāl*. (Teheran, 1313 H.).

al-Azdī, Yazīd ibn Muhammad. *Taʾrīkh al-Mawsil*. (Cairo, 1968).

al-Azdī al-Qalhātī, Abū Saʿīd Muhammad ibn Saʿīd. *Kitāb Kashf wa al-Bayān*. MS. British Library, London, Or. 2606.

al-Baghdādī, ʿAbd al-Qāhir ibn Tāhir Muhammad. *Moslem Schisms and Sects (al-Fark bain al-Firak)*. Translated by A. S. Halkin (Tel-Aviv, 1935).

————. *Moslem Schisms and Sects (al-Fark bain al-Firak)*. Translated by K. C. Seelye (New York, 1919).

————. *Usūl al-Dīn*. (Istanbul, 1928).

al-Balādhūrī, Ahmad ibn Yahyā. *Kitāb al-Ansāb wa al-Ashrāf*. V (Jerusalem, 1936).

_____. *Kitāb Futūh al-Buldān.* Translated by Philip K. Hitti as *The Origins of the Islamic State.* (2nd ed.; Beirut, 1966).

al-Barzanjī, Muhammad ibn Rasūl. *al-Nawāfid li al-Rawāfid wa al-Nawāfid.* MS. Bibliothèque Nationale, Paris, Arabe 1459.

al-Bīrūnī, Abū al-Rayhān Muhammad ibn Ahmad. *al-Āthār al-Bāqiya ʿan al-Qurūn al-Khāliya=Chronologie Orientalischer Völker.* (Leipzig, 1923).

al-Dahlāwī, Shāh ʿAbd al-ʿAzīz Ghulām al-Hakim. *Mukhtasār Tuhfa al-ʿIthnā ʿAshariyya.* Translated by Ghulām Muhammad ibn Muhyi al-Din ibn Umar al-Aslama. (Cairo, 1387 H.).

al-Dhahabī, Shams al-Dīn Muhammad ibn Ahmad. *Mizān al-Iʿtidāl fī Naqd al-Rijāl.* I (Cairo, 1325 H.).

_____. *Mizān al-Iʿtidāl fī Naqd al-Rijāl.* IV (Cairo, 1963).

_____. *Taʾrīkh al-Islām.* V (Cairo, 1369 H.).

Dīnawārī, Ahmad ibn Daʾūd Abū Hanīfa. *Akhbār al-Tiwāl.* (Cairo, 1960).

Hamdān, A'sha. Untitled Poem. *Diwan al-Aʿsha: Gedichte von Abū Bashir Maimun ibn Qais al-Aʿsha Nebst Sammlungen von Stücken anderer Dichter des Gleichen Beinammen und von al-Musayyab.* Gibb Memorial Series. New Series VI (London, 1928).

al-Himyarī, Abū Saʿīd Nashwān ibn. *Kitāb al-Hūr al-ʿIn wa Tanbīh al-Samiʿīn.* (Cairo, 1948).

Ibn ʿAbd al-Rabbīhī, Ahmad ibn Muhammad. *al-ʿIqd al-Farīd.* I (Cairo, 1884/1885).

Ibn Abī al-Dām, Shihāb al-Dīn Ibrahīm. *Dhikr Jamaʿā min Ahl al-Milal wa al-Nihal.* MS. Fatih Kütübhanesi, Istanbul, 3153.

Ibn Abī al-Hadīd, ʿAbd al-Hamīd ibn Hibāt Allāh. *Sharh Nāhj al-Balāgha.* VIII (Cairo, 1960).

Ibn Abī Ya'lā, Abū al-Husayn Muhammad ibn Muhammad. *Tabaqāt al-Hanābila.* I (Cairo, 1952).

Ibn al-Athīr, ʿIzz al-Dīn. *al-Kāmil fī al-Taʾrikh.* IV–V (Beirut, 1965).

Ibn Faqīh al-Hamadhānī, Abū Bakr Ahmad ibn Muhammad. *Mukhtasār Kitāb al-Buldān.* Bibliotheca Geographorum Arabicorum. V (Leiden, 1885).

Ibn Habīb, Abū Ja'far Muhammad. *Kitāb al-Muhabbar.* (Hyderabad, 1943).

Ibn Hajar al-ʿAsqalānī, Shihāb al-Dīn. *Lisān al-Mizān.* VI (Hyderabad, 1331 H.).

Ibn Hazm, Abū Muhammad ʿAlī ibn Ahmad ibn Saʿīd. "The Heterodoxies of the Shīʿites in the Presentation of Ibn Hazm." Translated by Israel Friedlaender. *Journal of the American Oriental Society.* 28 (1907), 1–80.

———. *Jamhārat Ansāb al-'Arab.* (Cairo, 1962).

Ibn 'Ināba, Jamāl al-Dīn Ahmad ibn 'Alī. *'Umda al-Tālib fī Ansāb Āl Abī Tālib.* (Beirut, 1963).

Ibn al-Jawzī, Abū al-Faraj 'Abd al-Rahmān. *al-Muntāzam fī Ta'rikh al-Mulūk wa al-Umām.* Aya Sofya MS. 3095. Deposited in the Suleymaniyye Kütübhanesi. Istanbul.

———. *Naqd al-'Ilm wa al-'Ulamā' = Talbīs Iblīs.* (Cairo, 1966).

———. "'The Devil's Delusion' of Ibn al-Jauzi." Translated by D. S. Margoliouth. *Islamic Culture.* IX (1935).

Ibn Jubayr, Muhammad ibn Ahmad. *The Travels of Ibn Jubayr.* Translated by R. J. C. Broadhurst. (London, 1952).

Ibn Kathīr, 'Imād al-Dīn Abū al-Fidā 'Ismā 'īl ibn 'Umar. *al-Bidāya wa al-Nihāya fī al-Ta'rīkh.* IX (Cairo, 1932).

Ibn Khaldūn, Abū Zayd 'Abd al-Rahmān. *al-'Ibar wa Diwān al-Mubtadā' wa al-Khabar fī Ayyām al-'Arab wa al-'Ajam wa al-Barbar wa man Asārahūm min Dhawī al-Sultān al-Akbār-Ta'rīkh.* III (Beirut, 1957).

Ibn al-Murtadā, al-Mahdī li Dīn Allāh Ahmad ibn Yahyā. *al-Bahr al-Zakhkhār.* MS. British Library, London, Or. 4021.

Ibn al-Nadīm, Muhammad ibn Ishāq. *Kitāb al-Fihrist.* (Beirut, 1966).

Ibn Nubāta al-Misrī, Jamāl al-Dīn Muhammad ibn Muhammad. *Sarh al-'Uyūn fī Sharh Risāla ibn Zaydūn.* (Cairo, 1964).

Ibn Qutayba, Abū Muhammad 'Abd Allāh ibn Muslim. *Kitāb al-Ma'ārif.* (Cairo, 1883).

———. *Kitāb Ta'wīl Mukhtalif al-Hadīth.* Translated by Gerard Lecomte. (Damascus, 1962).

———. *'Uyūn al-Akhbār.* II (Cairo, 1964).

Ibn Rusta, Ahmad ibn 'Umar. *Kitāb al-A'lāq al-Nafīsa.* Bibliotheca Geographorum Arabicorum. VII (2nd ed.; Leiden, 1967).

Ibn Shākir al-Kutubī, Salāh al-Dīn Muhammad. *Fawāt al-Wafayāt.* I (Cairo, 1951).

———. *'Uyūn al-Tawārīkh.* MS. Bibliothèque Nationale, Paris, 1587.

Ibn Taghrī-Birdī, Abū al-Mahāsin Yūsuf. *al-Nujūm al-Zahīra fī Mulūk Misr wa al-Qāhira.* I (Cairo, 1959).

Ibn Taymiyya, Ahmad ibn 'Abd al-Halīm. *Minhāj al-Sunna wa al-Nabawiyya.* II (Cairo, 1962).

'Ibn Tiqtaqa, Fakhr al-Dīn Muhammad ibn 'Alī. *al-Fakhrī fī Adab al-Sultāniyya.* Translated by Émile Amar. Archives Marocaine. XIV (Paris, 1910).

Ibn 'Uqda, Ahmad ibn Muhammad ibn Sa'īd al-Hamdānī. *Dhikr al-Nabī.* Translated by Nabia Abbott. *Studies in Arabic Literary Papyri. I: Historical*

Texts. University of Chicago Oriental Institute Publications. LXXV (Chicago, 1957).

al-'Iji, 'Adūd al-Dīn 'Abd al-Rahmān. *Kitāb al-Mawāqif fī 'Ilm al-Kalām.* VIII (Cairo, 1909).

al-'Irāqī al-Hanafī, Abū Muhammad 'Uthmān ibn 'Abd Allāh ibn al-Hasan. *al-Firak al- Muftariqa bayna Ahlī al-Zaygh wa al-Zandaqa.* Ankara Universitesi Ilahiyat Fakültesi Publication no. XXXII (Ankara, 1961).

al-Isbahānī, Abū Nu'aym Ahmad ibn 'Abd Allāh. *Kitāb Dhikr Akhbār Isbahān.* II (Leiden, 1934).

al-Isfahānī, Abū al-Faraj. *Kitāb al-Aghānī.* XII–XXII (Beirut, 1958–1960).

———. *Maqātil al-Tālibiyyin.* (Cairo, 1949).

al-Isfarā'īnī, Abū Muzāffar Shāhfur ibn Tāhir. *Tabsīr fī al-Dīn.* (Cairo, 1940).

al-Jāhiz, Abū 'Uthmān 'Amr ibn Bahr. *Kitāb al-Bayān wa al-Tabyīn.* I–II (Cairo, 1948–1949).

———. *Kitāb al-Hayawān.* II (2nd ed.; Cairo, 1965).

al-Jahshiyārī, Abu 'Abd Allah Muhammad ibn 'Abdūs. *Kitāb al-Wuzarā'wa al-Kuttāb.* (Cairo, 1938).

al-Jilānī, 'Abd al-Qādir. *al-Ghunya li Tālib Tarīq al-Haqq.* (1322 H.).

Jurjānī, 'Alī ibn Muhammad. *Kitāb al-Ta'rīfa.* (Istanbul, 1883).

al-Karbalā'i', Abū 'Alī Muhammad ibn Ismā'īl. *Muntahā al-Maqāl.* (Teheran, 1885).

Kashshī, Abū 'Amr Muhammad ibn 'Umar ibn 'Abd al-'Azīz. *Rijāl al-Kashshī=Ma'rifa.* (Karbala, 1963).

Khvāndāmir, Ghiyāth al-Dīn Muhammad ibn Khvāja Hamām. *Ta'rīkh Habīb al-Siyar fī Akhbār Afrād Bashāra.* II (Teheran, 1444).

al-Kirmānī, Abū al-Qāsim 'Abd al-Wāhid ibn Ahmad. "Ein Kommentar der Tradition über die 73 Sekten." Arabic text published by Sven Dedering. *Le Monde Oriental.* XXV (1931), 35–43.

anon. *Kitāb al-'Uyūn wa al-Hadā'iq fī Akhbār al-Haqā'iq.* M. de Goeje. *Fragmenta Historicum Arabicorum.* I (Leiden, 1871).

al-Kūrānī, Zayn al-'Abidīn Yūsuf ibn Muhammad. *al-Yamāniyya al-Maslūla 'alā Rawāfid al-Makhdhūla.* MS. Bibliothèque Nationale, Paris, Arabe 1462.

al-Malatī, Abū al-Husayn Muhammad ibn Ahmad. *Kitāb al-Tanbīh wa al-Radd 'alā Ahl al-Ahwā'wa al-Bida'.* (Istanbul, 1936).

al-Mamaqānī, Hājj Shaykh 'Abd Allāh. *Tanqīh al-Maqāl fī Ahwāl al-Rijāl.* I (Najaf[?], 1349 H.).

al-Maqdisī, Mutahhar ibn Tāhir. *Kitāb al-Bad'wa al-Ta'rīkh.* V (Baghdad, 1916).

al-Maqrīzī, Taqī al-Dīn. *al-Mawāʿiz wa al-Iʿtibār fī Dhikr al-Khitat wa al-Āthār.* III (Cairo, 1959).

al-Masʿūdī, Abū Hasan ʿAlī ibn Husayn. *Kitāb Tanbīh wa al-Ishrāf.* (Cairo, 1948).

_____. *Murūj al-Dhahab.* III (Beirut, 1965).

Mir Khvānd, Muhammad ibn Khvānd Shāh ibn Mahmūd. *Rawdā al-Safā fī Sīra al-Anbiyāʾwa al-Mulūk wa al-Khulafāʾ.* (Teheran, 1959–1965).

al-Mubarrad, Muhammad ibn Yazīd. *al-Kāmil.* III (Cairo, 1956).

_____. *al-Kāmil fī Lugha wa al-Adab.* (Cairo, n.d.).

al-Musāwī, Muhammad ibn (ʿAbd al-) Rasūl al-Sharīf al-Husaynī. *al-Nawāqid li al- Rawāfid wa al-Nawāfid.* MS. Library of the India Office, London, Delhi 971.

al-Narshakhī, Muhammad ibn Jaʿfar. *The History of Bukhara.* Translated by R. N. Frye. (Cambridge, Mass., 1954).

al-Nawbakhtī, al-Hasan ibn Mūsā. *Firaq al-Shīʿa.* (Najaf, 1959).

_____. "An-Nawbakhtī. Les Sectes Siʿites." Translated by M. J. Mashkūr. *Revue de l'Histoire des Religions.* CLIII (1958), 68–78, 176–214; CLIV (1958), 68–95, 146–172.

al-Nuʿmān, Abū Hanīfa Qādī b. Muhammad. *The Book of Faith from the Daʿāʾim al-Islām (Pillars of Islam) of al-Qādī al-Nuʿmān b. Muhammad al-Tamīmī.* Translated by A. A. A. Fyzee. (Bombay, 1974).

al-Rasʿānī, ʿAbd al-Razzāq. *Mukhtasār al-Farq bayn al-Firaq.* (Cairo, 1924).

al-Rāzī, Fakhr al-Dīn. *Iʿtiqādāt Firaq al-Muslimīn wa al-Mushrikīn.* (Cairo, 1949).

al-Rāzī, Murtadā ibn Dāʿī. *Tabsīra al-ʿAwām fī Maʿrifa Maqālāt al-Anām.* (Teheran, 1313 H.).

anon. *Risāla fī Bayān Firaq al-Azilla.* MS. Istanbul Universitesi Merkez Kütübhanesi, Arabic MS. 5295.

al-Saksakī al-Hānbali, Abū al-Fadl ʿAbbās ibn Mansūr ibn ʿAbbās al-Burayhī. *Kitāb al-Burhān fī Maʿrifa Aqāʿid al-Adyān.* MS. Nuri Osmaniye Kütübhanesi, Istanbul, 4919.

al-Samʿānī, ʿAbd al-Karīm ibn Muhammad. *Kitāb al-Ansāb.* II (Hyderabad, 1963).

anon. *al-Sawāʿiq al-Muhriqā li-Ikhwān al-Shayātīn wa al-Dalāl wa al-Zandaqa.* MS. Library of the India Office, London, 2167 (Delhi 916).

Shahrastānī, Muhammad ibn ʿAbd al-Karīm. *al-Milal wa al-Nihal.* I (Cairo, 1961).

_____. "Milal wa Nihal: VI. The Shīʿites." Translated by A. K. Kazi and J. G. Flynn. *Abr-Nahrain.* XV (Leiden, 1975), 50–97.

148 *Bibliography*

al-Shirwānī, Emin Sadreddin. *Untitled Treatise on the Sects of Islam.* MS. Nuri Osmaniye Kütübhanesi, Istanbul, 2144.

Shūshtarī, Qāḍī Sayyed Nūr Allāh. *Majālis Mu'minīn.* (Tehran, 1376).

Sibt ibn al-Jawzī, Shams al-Dīn. *Mir'āt al-Zamān fī Ta'rīkh al-A'yān.* MS. Bodleian Library, Oxford, Pococke 371.

al-Tabarī, Abū Ja'far Muhammad ibn Jarīr. *Ta'rīkh al-Rusūl wa al-Mulūk.* series I–III (Leiden, 1964).

———. *Ta'rīkh al-rusūl wa al-Mulūk.* Vol. 21. *The Victory of the Marwanids.* Translated by Michael Fishbein. (Albany, N.Y. 1990).

al-Tafrīshī, Mīr Mustafā al-Husaynī. *Naqd al-Rijāl.* MS. British Library, London, Or. 3640.

anon. *Ta'rīkh al-Khulafā'.* (Moscow, 1967).

anon. *Ta'rīkh-i-Sīstān.* (Teheran, 1935).

al-Tha'ālibī, Abū Mansūr 'Abd al-Malik ibn Muhammad ibn Ismā'īl. *Thimār al-Qulūb fī Mudaf wa al-Mansūb.* (Cairo, 1965).

anon. *'Umm' al-Kitāb.* Translated by Pio Filippani-Ronconi. (Naples, 1966).

al-Ya'qūbī, Abū al-'Abbās Ahmad ibn Abī Ya'qūb. *Ta'rīkh.* II (Beirut, 1960).

Yāqūt ibn 'Abd Allāh al-Rūmī. *Mu'jām al-Buldān.* II (Leipzig, 1867).

II. Near Eastern Works Since 1800

'Abd al-'Āl, Muhammad Jābir. *Harakāt al-Shī'a al-Mutatarrifīn.* (Cairo, 1954).

Abū Zāhra, Muhammad. *Ta'rīkh al-Madhāhab al-Islāmiyya.* II (Cairo, 1963 [?]).

Amīn, Muhsin. *A'yān al-Shī'a.* XIV (2nd ed.; Beirut, 1961).

Bishbishī, Mahmūd 'Alī. *al-Firaq al-Islāmiyya.* (Cairo, 1932).

Farrukh, Omar A. *Islam and the Arabs in the Eastern Mediterranean down to the Fall of the Umayyad Caliphate (132 A.H./750 C.E.).* In Arabic. (2nd ed.; Beirut, 1966).

Ghurābī, Mustafā. *Ta'rīkh al-Firaq al-Islāmiyya wa Nashā''Ilm al-Kalām 'ind al-Muslimīn.* (Cairo, n.d.).

al-Hasanī, Hāshim ibn Ma'ruf. *al-Shī'a bayna al-'Ashā'ira wa al-Mu'tazila.* (Beirut, 1964).

Iqbāl, 'Abbās. *Khāndāne Nawbakhtī.* (Teheran, 1932).

Kasrāvī, Ahmad. *Ta'rīkh-i Pansād Salā-yi Khuzistān.* (Tehran, 1330).

al-Kharbūtlī, 'Alī Husnī. *Ta'rīkh al-'Irāq fī Zill al-Hukm al-Umawī.* (Cairo, 1959).

Bibliography   149

Mahfūz, Husayn. *Ta'rīkh al-Shī`a*. (Baghdad, 1957).
al-Najjār, Muhammad Tayyib. *al-Mawālī fī al-`Asr al-Umawiyy*. (Cairo, 1949).
al-Qādī, Wadād. *al-Kaisāniyya fī Ta'rīkh wa al-Adab*. (Beirut, 1974).
al-Rāwī, Thābit. *Iraq in the Umayyad Period*. In Arabic. (Baghdad, 1965).
al-Shabībī, Muhammad Ridā. *Mua' rrikh al-`Irāq ibn al-Fuwātī*. I (Baghdad, 1950).
al-Tahānawī, Muhammad A`lā ibn `Alī. *Kashshaf Istilāhāt al-Funūn.* I (Cairo, 1963).
al-Tāmir, `Arif. *al-Imāma fī al-Islām.* (Beirut, n.d.).
al-Tustarī, Muhammad Taqī. *Qāmus al-Rijāl.* (Teheran, 1959/1960).
Ziriklī, khayr al-Dīn. *al-A`lām Qāmus Tarājim li `Ashhar al-Rijāl wa al-Nisā'min al-`Arab wa al-Musta'riba.* VIII (2nd ed.; Cairo, 1956).

III. Books in European Languages

Abd Dixon, Abd al-Ameer. *The Umayyad Caliphate 65–86/684–705 (A Political Study)*. (London, 1971).
Abu-Izzeddin, Nejla M. *The Druzes: A New Study of Their History, Faith, and Society.* (Leiden, 1984).
Agha, Salah Said. *The Revolution Which Toppled the Umayyads: Neither Arab nor Abbasid* (Leiden, 2003).
Ajami, Fouad. *The Vanished Imām: Musa al-Sadr and the Shi'a of Lebanon.* (Ithaca, N.Y., and London, 1986).
Alexander, Paul J. *The Byzantine Apocalyptic Tradition.* (Berkeley, Calif., and Los Angeles, 1985).
Alexander, Scott. "Hidden in the Books: Biobibliography and Religious Authority in the Work of an Eleventh-Century Shi'ite Jurist and Theologian." Ph.D. diss. (Columbia University, 1993).
Algar, Hamid. *Religion and State in Iran, 1785–1906: The Role of the Ulama in the Qajar Period.* (Berkeley, Calif., and Los Angeles, 1969).
Amanat, Abbas. *Resurrection and Renewal: The Making of the Babi Movement in Iran, 1844–1850* (Ithaca, N.Y., 1989).
Amir-Moezzi, Mohammad Ali. *The Divine Guide in Early Shi'ism.* Translated by David Streight. (Albany, N.Y., 1994).
Arjomand, Said Amir. *The Shadow of God and the Hidden Imām: Religion, Political Order, and Societal Change in Shi'ite Iran from the Beginning to 1890.* (Chicago and London, 1984).
———. *The Turban for the Crown: The Islamic Revolution in Iran.* (New York, 1988).

Azizi, Muhsin. *La Domination Arabe et l'Epanouissement du Sentiment National en Iran.* (Paris, 1938).

Barzegar, Karim N. *Intellectual Movements During Timuri and Safavi Period (1500–1700 A.D.).* (Delhi, 2005).

Bashir, Shahzad. *Fazlāllah Astarabadi and the Hurufis.* (Oxford, 2005).

Bausani, Alessandro. *Persia Religiosa.* (Milan, 1959).

Bayat, Mangol. *Mysticism and Dissent: Socioreligious Thought in Qajar Iran.* (Syracuse, N.Y., 1982).

Belyaev, E. A. *Arabs, Islam and the Arab Caliphate in the Early Middle Ages.* Translated by Adolphe Gourevitch. (New York, 1969).

Benard, Cheryl, and Zalmay Khalilzad. *"The Government of God"—Iran's Islamic Republic.* (New York, 1984).

Bianchi, Ugo, ed. *The Origins of Gnosticism: Colloquium of Messina 13–18 April 1966. Texts and Discussion Published by Ugo Bianchi.* (Leiden, 1967).

Blackman, E. C. *Marcion and his Influence.* (London, 1948).

Blichfeldt, Jan-Olaf. *Early Mahdism: Politics and Religion in the Formative Period of Islam.* (Leiden, 1985).

Bosworth, C. E. *Sistan under the Arabs, from the Islamic Conquest to the Rise of the Saffarids. (30–250/651–864).* (Rome, 1968).

Boyce, Mary. *Zoroastrians: Their Religious Beliefs and Practices.* (London, Boston, and Henley, 1979).

Brandon, S. G. F. *Creation Legends of the Ancient Near East.* (London, 1963).

Brockelmann, Carl. *History of the Islamic Peoples.* Translated by Joel Carmichael and Moshe Perlmann. (New York, 1960).

Burkitt, F. C. *The Religion of the Manichees.* (Cambridge, 1925).

Caetani, Leone. *Chronographia Islamica.* V (Paris, 1922).

Christensen, A. C. *L'Iran sous les Sassanides.* (2nd ed., rev.; Copenhagen, 1944).

Cole, Juan R. I. and Nikki R. Keddie. *Shi'ism and Social Protest* (New Haven, Conn., and London, 1986).

Corbin, Henri. *En Islam Iranien.* I–IV (Paris, 1971–1972).

———. *Histoire de la Philosophie Islamique.* I (Paris, 1964).

Couliano, Ioan P. *The Tree of Gnosis: Gnostic Mythology from Early Christianity to Modern Nihilism.* Translated by H. S. Wiesner and the author. (San Francisco, 1992).

Crone, Patricia. *Slaves on Horseback.* (Cambridge, 1980).

——— and G. Martin Hinds. *God's Caliph: Religious Authority in the First Centuries of Islam.* (Cambridge, 1986).

Daftary, Farhad. *The Ismāʿīlīs: Their History and Doctrines.* (Cambridge, 1990).

———, ed. *Medieval Ismāʿīlī History and Thought.* (Cambridge, 1996).

Daniel, Elton. *The Political and Social History of Khurasan under Abbasid Rule.* (Minneapolis and Chicago, 1979).

Depont, Octave and Xavier Coppolani. *Les Confréries Religieuses Musulmanes.* (Algiers, 1897).

Djaït, Hichem. *Al-Kūfa: Naissance de la ville Islamique.* (Paris, 1986).

Donner, Fred M. *Narratives of Islamic Origins: The Beginnings of Islamic Historical Writing.* (Princeton, N.J., 1998).

Drower, E. S. *The Mandaeans of Iraq and Iran.* (2nd ed.; Leiden, 1962).

Dvornik, Francis. *Early Christian and Byzantine Political Philosophy.* I (Washington, D.C., 1966).

van Ess, Josef. *Chiliastische Erwartungen und die Versuchung der Göttlichkeit: Der Kalif al-Hākim (386–411 H.).* (Heidelberg, 1977).

———. *Theologie und Gesellschaft im 2. und 3. Jahrhundert Hidschra.* 6 vols. (Berlin, 1991–1997).

de Faye, Eugène. *Gnostiques et Gnosticisme.* (2nd ed., aug.; Paris, 1925).

Fischer, Michael M. J. *Iran: From Religious Dispute to Revolution.* (Cambridge, Mass., 1980).

Fishbein, Michael. "The Life of al-Mukhtār ibn Abī ʿUbayd in some Early Arabic Historians." Ph.D diss. (The University of California at Los Angeles, 1988).

Frankfort, Henri et al. *Before Philosophy. The Intellectual Adventure of Ancient Man.* (4th ed.; Baltimore, Md., 1961).

Frazer, J. G. *The Golden Bough. III. Taboo and the Perils of the Soul.* (New York, 1935).

Frye, R. N. *Heritage of Persia.* (New York, 1962).

Gafurov, B. G. *Istorija tadikskogo naroda v kratkom izloženii.* I (Moscow, 1955).

al-Ghamedi, Abdulkareem A. "The Qarmatians of Iraq and Arabia: A Reexamination." M.A. Thesis. (University of Arkansas, 1977).

Ghirshman, Roman. *L'Iran des Origines à l'Islam.* (Paris, 1951).

Gibb, H. A. R. *Mohammedanism.* (2nd ed.; New York, 1953).

Goldziher, Ignaz. *Le Dogme et la Loi de l'Islam.* Translated by Felix Arin. (2nd ed.; Paris, 1958).

———. *Muslim Studies.* I. Translated by C. R. Barber and S. M. Stern. (Chicago, 1967).

———. *Streitschrift des Ghazali gegen die Batinijje-Sekte.* (2nd ed.; Leiden, 1956).

Grant, R. M. *Gnosticism. A Source of Heretical Writings from the Early Christian Period.* (New York, 1961).

———. *Gnosticism and Early Christianity.* (New York, 1966).

Guillaume, Alfred. *Prophecy and Divination among the Hebrews and Other Semites.* (London, 1938).

al-Haidari, Ibrahim. *Zur Soziologie des Schiitischen Chiliasmus: Ein Beitrag zur Erforschung des irakischen Passionspiels.* (Freiburg im Breisgau, 1975).

Halm, Heinz. *Die Islamische Gnosis: Die Extreme Schī`a und die `Alawiten.* (Zurich and Munich, 1982).

———. *Kosmologie und Heilslehre der Frühen Isma'iliya: Eine Studie zur Islamischen Gnosis.* (Wiesbaden, 1978).

———. *Shiism.* Translated by Janet Watson. (Edinburgh, 1991).

Hamid, Usama. "The Qarmatians: Society and State." M.A. Thesis. (American University of Beirut, August 1977).

Harnack, Adolph. *History of Dogma.* Translated from the German 3rd edition by Neil Buchanan. I (Boston, 1905).

Hawting, G. R. *The First Dynasty of Islam: The Umayyad Caliphate A.D. 661–750.* (Carbondale, Ill., and Edwardsville, Ill., 1987).

Hitti, Philip K. *History of the Arabs.* (8th ed.; New York, 1963).

Hodgson, Marshall G. S. *The Order of the Assassins.* (The Hague, 1955).

Huart, Clement. *Ancient Persia and Iranian Civilization.* (New York, 1927).

Hussain, Jassim M. *The Occultation of the Twelfth Imām.* (London, 1982).

Irenaeus. *Irenaeus Against Heresies.* Vol. I of *The Ante-Nicene Fathers.* (Buffalo, N.Y. 1887).

Jafri, S. H. M. *The Origins and Early Development of Shi'a Islam.* (London and New York, 1979).

anon. *Das Johannesbuch der Mandäer.* Translated by Mark Lidzbarski. (Berlin, 1966).

Jonas, Hans. *The Gnostic Religion.* (2nd ed., enlarged; Boston, 1963).

Keddie, Nikki. *Iran and the Muslim World: Resistance and Revolution.* (New York, 1995).

Kennedy, Hugh. *The Prophet and the Age of the Caliphates: The Islamic Near East from the Sixth to the Eleventh Centuries.* (London and New York, 1986).

———. *When Baghdad Ruled the Muslim World.* (Cambridge, Mass., 2005).

Klima, Otakar. *Mazdak.* (new ed., New York, 1979).

Klimkeit, Hans-Joachim, ed. *Gnosis on the Silk Road: Gnostic Texts from Central Asia.* (San Francisco, 1993).

Kohlberg, Etan. *Belief and Law in Imāmī Shī`ism.* (London, 1991).

Kramer, Martin, ed. *Shi'ism, Resistance, and Revolution.* (Boulder, Colo., 1987).

von Kremer, Alfred. *Culturgeschichtliche Streifzuge auf dem Gebiete des Islams.* Translated by S. Khuda Bukhsh in *Contributions to the History of Islamic Civilization.* I (2nd ed.; Calcutta, 1929).

————. *Geschichte der Herrschenden Ideen des Islams.* (Leipzig, 1868).

Lane, E. W. *Arabian Society in the Middle Ages.* (London, 1883).

Laoust, Henri. *Les Schismes dans l'Islam.* (Paris, 1965).

Le Strange, Guy. *The Lands of the Eastern Caliphate.* (New York, 1966).

————. *Palestine under the Moslems.* (Beirut, 1965).

Lewis, Bernard. *The Assassins: A Radical Sect in Islam.* (New York, 1968).

————. *Origins of Ismailism.* (Cambridge, 1940).

Lieu, Samuel N. C. *Manichaeism in the Later Roman Empire and Medieval China: A Historical Survey.* (Manchester, 1985).

————. *Manichaeism in Mesopotamia and the Roman East.* (Leiden, 1994).

————. *The Religion of Light: An Introduction to the History of Manichaeism in China.* (Hong Kong, 1979).

Litvak, Meir. *Shi'i Scholars of Nineteenth-Century Iraq: The 'Ulama' of Najaf and Karbala'.* (Cambridge, 1998).

Madelung, Wilferd. *Der Imām al-Qasim ibn Ibrahim und die Glaubenslehre der Zaiditen.* (Berlin, 1965).

anon. *Mandäische Liturgien.* Translated by Mark Lidzbarski. (Berlin, 1920).

Margherita, Michele A. "The Collected Fragments of Hisham ibn al-Hakam, Imami *Mutakallim* of the Second Century of the Hegira Together with a discussion of the Sources for and an Introduction to his Teaching." Ph.D. diss. (New York University, 1974).

Mazzaoui, Michel M. *The Origins of the Safavids: Shi'ism, Sufism, and the Ghulat.* (Wiesbaden, 1972).

Merkur, Dan. *Gnosis: An Esoteric Tradition of Mystical Visions and Unions.* (Albany, N.Y., 1993).

Modarressi Tabātabā'i, Hossein. *Crisis and Consolidation in the Formative Period of Shi'ite Islam: Abu Ja'far ibn Qiba al-Razi and His Contribution to Imamite Shi'ite Thought.* (Princeton, N.J., 1993).

————. *An Introduction to Shī'i Law.* (London, 1984).

Momen, Moojan. *An Introduction to Shi'i Islam: The History and Doctrines of Twelver Shi'ism.* (New Haven, Conn., and London, 1985).

Moosa, Matti. *Extremist Shi'ites: The Ghulat Sects.* (Syracuse, N.Y., 1988).

Morony, Michael G. *Iraq After the Muslim Conquest.* (Princeton, N.J., 1984).

Mottahedeh, Roy. *The Mantle of the Prophet: Religion and Politics in Iran.* (New York, 1985).

al-Mutairi, Rakan. "Hizbullah: (The Party of God) Origin and Ideology." M.A. Thesis. (University of Arkansas, 1994).

Nakash, Yitzhak. *The Shi'is of Iraq.* (Princeton, N.J., 1994).

———. *Reaching for Power: The Shi'a in the Modern Arab World.* (Princeton, N.J., 2006).

Nasr, Vali. *The Shi'a Revival: How Conflicts within Islam Will Shape the Future.* (New York, 2006).

Newman, Andrew. "The Development and Political Significance of the Rationalist (Usuli) and Traditionalist (Akhbari) Schools in Imami Shi'i History from the Third/Ninth to the Tenth/Sixteenth Century A.D." Ph.D. diss., parts 1 and 2. (The University of California at Los Angeles, 1986).

Nigosian, S. A. *The Zoroastrian Faith: Tradition & Modern Research.* (Montreal and Kingston, 1993).

Norton, Augustus Richard. *Amal and the Shi'a: Struggle for the Soul of Lebanon.* (Austin, Tex., 1987).

———. *Hezbollah: A Short History.* (Princeton, N.J., 2007).

al-Oraibi, Ali. "Shi'i Renaissance: A Case Study of the Theosophical School of Bahrain in the 7th/13th Century." Ph.D. diss. (Institute of Islamic Studies, McGill University, 1992).

Ort, L. J. R. *Mani: A Religio-Historical Description of His Personality.* (Leiden, 1967).

Parrinder, Geoffrey. *Jesus in the Qur'an.* (New York, 1965).

Pellat, Charles. *Le Milieu Basrien et la Formation de Djahiz.* (Paris, 1953).

Perier, Jean. *Vie d' al-Hadjdjadj ibn Yousof d'après les Sources Arabe.* (Paris, 1904).

Petrushevsky, I. P. *Islam in Iran.* Translated by Hubert Evans. (Albany, N.Y., 1985).

Pigulevskaja, N. V., Jakubovskij, A. Ju., et al. *Istorija Irana s drevnejšix vremën do konca XVIII veka.* (Leningrad, 1958).

Pipes, Daniel. *Slave Soldiers and Islam.* (New Haven, Conn., and London, 1981).

Pirouzdjou, Hassan. *Mithraisme et Émancipation: Anthropologie Sociale et Culturelle des Mouvements Populaires en Iran: au VIIIe, IXe et du XIVe au Début du XVI siècle.* (Montreal, 1999).

Poonawala, Ismail K. *Biobibliography of Ismā'īlī Literature.* (Malibu, 1977).

Puech, Henri-Charles. *Le Manicheisme. Son Fondateur. Sa Doctrine.* (Paris, 1949).

Rajkowski, W. W. "Early Shiism in Iraq." Ph.D. diss. (London University, 1955).

Ranstorp, Magnus. *Hizb'allah in Lebanon: The Politics of the Western Hostage Crisis.* (New York, 1997).

Rosiny, Stephan. *Islamismus bei den Schiiten im Libanon: Religion im Ubergang von Tradition zur Moderne.* (Frankfurt, 1996).

Rudolph, Kurt. *Gnosis: The Nature and History of Gnosticism.* Translated by P. W. Coxon and K. H. Kuhn. Translation edited by R. McLachlan Wilson. (San Francisco, 1983).

———. *Die Mandäer.* II (Göttingen, 1961).

———. *Theogonie, Kosmogonie, und Anthropogonie in den Mandäischen Schriften.* (Göttingen, 1965).

Saad-Ghorayeb, Amal. *Hizbu'llah: Politics and Religion.* (London, 2002).

Sachedina, Abdulaziz Abdulhussein. *Islamic Messianism: The Idea of the Mahdi in Twelver Shi'ism.* (Albany, N.Y., 1981).

———. *The Just Ruler (al-sultān al-ʿādil) in Shi'ite Islam.* (New York and Oxford, 1988).

de Sacy, Sylvestre. *Exposé de la Religion des Druzes.* I (Paris, 1964).

Sadighi, G. H. *Les Mouvements Religieux Iraniens au IIe et au IIIe Siècles des l'Hegire.* (Paris, 1938).

Salih, Muhammad Osman. "Mahdiism in Islam up to 260 A.H./847 A.D. and Its Relation to Zoroastrian, Jewish, and Christian Messianism." Ph.D. diss. (University of Edinburgh, 1976).

Sayed, Redwan. *Die Revolte des Ibn al-Asʿ at und die Koranleser.* (Freiburg, 1977).

Scholem, Gershom. *Major Trends in Jewish Mysticism.* (2nd ed., rev.; New York, 1946).

Schwarz, Paul. *Iran im Mittelälter nach den Arabischen Geographen.* Fasc. V (Leipzig, 1925).

Shaban, M. A. *Islamic History A.D. 600–750 (A.H. 132): A New Interpretation.* (Cambridge, 1971).

Al-Shaibi, Kamil Mustafa. *Sufism and Shi'ism.* (Surbiton, 1991).

Sharon, Moshe. *Black Banners from the East. The Establishment of the ʿAbbasid State- Incubation of a Revolt.* (Jerusalem, 1983).

Spuler, Bertold. *Iran in Früh-Islamischer Zeit (633 bis 1055).* (Wiesbaden, 1952).

Sweetman, J. W. *Islam and Christian Theology.* II, part 1 (London, 1957).

Takim, L. N. "The *Rijal* of the Shīʿi *Imāms* as depicted in *Imāmi* Biographical Literature." Ph.D. diss. (London University, SOAS, 1990).

156

Bibliography

anon. *The Thousand and Twelve Questions.* Translated by E. S. Drower. (Berlin, 1960).

Tritton, A. S. *Muslim Theology.* (London, 1947).

van Vloten, G. *De Opkomst der Abbasiden in Chorasan.* (Leiden, 1890).

———. *Recherches sur la Domination Arabe, le Chi'itisme et les Croyances Messianiques sous le Califat des Omayyades.* (Amsterdam, 1894).

Waines, David. "Caliph and Amir," Ph.D. diss. (McGill University, 1974).

Walker, Paul. *Abū Ya'qūb al-Sijistāni: Intellectual Missionary.* (London and New York, 1996).

———. *Early Philosophical Shī'ism: The Ismā'īlī Neoplatonism of Abū Ya'qūb al-Sijistānī.* (Cambridge, 1993).

Wardrop, Shona F. "The Lives of the Imāms, Muhammad al-Jawād and 'Ali al-Hādī and the Development of the Shi'ite organization." Ph.D. diss. (University of Edinburgh, 1988).

Wasserstrom, Steven. *Between Muslim and Jew: The Problem of Symbiosis under Early Islam.* (Princeton, N.J., 1995).

Waterhouse, J. W. *Zoroastrianism.* (London, 1934).

Watt, W. M. *The Formative Period of Islamic Thought.* (Edinburgh, 1973).

———. *Islam and the Integration of Society.* (Evanston, Ill., 1961).

Weil, Gustav. *Geschichte der Chalifen.* I (Mannheim, 1846).

Wellhausen, Julius. *The Arab Kingdom and its Fall.* Translated by M. G. Weir. (Beirut, 1963).

———. *Die Religiös-politischen Oppositionsparteien im Alten Islam.* Arabic translation by 'Abd al-Rahman Badawi. (Cairo, 1957).

Williams, Michael A. *Rethinking "Gnosticism": An Argument for Dismantling a Dubious Category.* (Princeton, N.J., 1966).

Zaehner, R. C. *The Dawn and Twilight of Zoroastrianism.* (New York, 1961).

———. *The Teaching of the Magi.* (New York, 1956).

IV. Articles from Periodicals and Reference Works

Alexander, H. B. "Soul (Primitive)." *Hastings Encyclopædia of Religion and Ethics.* XI (New York, 1961), 725–731.

Amoretti, B. S. "Sects and Heresies." *The Cambridge History of Iran.* IV (Cambridge, 1975), 481–519.

van Arendonk, C. "Kaisāniya." *Shorter Encyclopædia of Islam.* (Ithaca, N.Y., 1965), 208–209.

Arjomand, Said Amir. "Religion and the Diversity of Normative Orders." *The Political Dimensions of Religion.* Edited by Said A. Arjomand. (Albany, N.Y., 1993), 43–68.

_____. "Religious Extremism (*Ghuluww*), Sufism and Sunnism in Safavid Iran: 1501–1722." *Journal of Asian History*. XV (1981), 1–35.

_____. "Shīʿite Jurisprudence and Constitution Making in the Islamic Republic of Iran." *Fundamentalisms and the State: Remaking Politics, Economics, and Militance*. Edited by Martin E. Marty and R. Scott Appleby. (Chicago, 1993), 88–109.

Bacher, Wilhelm. "Shem ha-Mephorash." *Jewish Encyclopædia*. XI (New York, 1905), 262–264.

Barbier de Meynard, A. C. "le Seid Himyarite." *Journal Asiatique*. 7th Series, IV (1874), 159–258.

Bardy, G. "Mandéens." *Dictionnaire de Théologie Catholique*. IV, Part II (Paris, 1927), cols. 1480–1501.

Bausani, Alessandro. "Hurūfiyya." *Encyclopædia of Islam*. III (2nd ed.; Leiden, 1971), 600–601.

Bevan, A. A. "Manichaeism." *Hastings Encyclopædia of Religion and Ethics*. VIII (New York, 1961), 380–392.

Brandt, W. "Mandaeans." *Hastings Encyclopædia of Religion and Ethics*. VIII (New York, 1961), 383.

Browne, Edward G. "Some Notes on the Literature and Doctrines of the Hurūfī Sect." *Journal of the Royal Asiatic Society* (1898), 61–94.

Bryer, D. R. W. "The Origins of the Druze Religion." *Islam*. 52 (1975), 48–84, 239–262; 53 (1976), 4–27.

Buhl, Frants. "Alidernes Stilling til de Shiʿitske Bevaegelser under Umajjaderne." *Oversigt over Kgl. Danske Videnskabernes Selskabs Forhandlingen*. 5 (Copenhagen, 1910), 355–394.

Cahen, Claude. "Points de vue sur la Révolution ʾAbbāside." *Revue Historique*. CCVII (1963), 295–338.

Caskel, Werner. "Ein Mahdi des 15. Jahrhunderts: Saijid Muhammad ibn Falah und seine Nachkommen." *Islamica*. IV (1929–31), 48–93.

Crone, Patricia. "Were the Qays and Yemen of the Umayyad Period Political Parties?" *Der Islam*. 71 (1994), 1–57.

Dietrich, A. "al-Hadjdjādj B. Yūsuf B. al-Hakam B. ʾAkīl al-Thakafī, Abū Muhammad." *Encyclopædia of Islam*. III (2nd ed.; Leiden, 1971), 39–43.

"Docetism." *The Oxford Dictionary of the Christian Church*. (New York, 1958), 409.

Donner, Fred M. "The Bakr b. Wāʾil tribes and Politics in Northwestern Arabia on the Eve of Islam." *Studia Islamica*. 51 (1980), 5–38.

van Ess, Josef. "Dirār b. ʾAmr und die ʾCahmiye.ʾ Biographie einer vergessen Schule." *Islam*. 44 (1968), 1–70.

Fahd, T. "Djafr." *Encyclopædia of Islam.* II (2nd ed.; Leiden, 1965), 376–377.

Fortescue, Adrian. "Docetism." *Hastings Encyclopædia of Religion and Ethics.* IV (New York, 1961), 832–835.

Friedlaender, Israel. "'Abdallāh b. Sabaʾ, der Begründer der Šʾīa und sein jüdischer Ursprung." *Zeitschrift für Assyriologie.* XXIII (1909), 296–327; XXIV (1910), 1–46.

——. "The Heterodoxies of the Shīʾites in the Presentation of Ibn Hazm: Commentary." *Journal of the American Oriental Society.* 29 (1908), 1–183.

Frye, R. N. "The 'Abbasid Conspiracy' and Modern Revolutionary Theory." *Indo-Iranica.* 5iii (1952–1953), 9–14.

Gabrieli, Francesco. "Il Califfato di Hishām." *Mémoires de la Société Archéologique d'Alexandrie.* VII (1935), 1–141.

——. *La Rivolta dei Muhallabiti nel Iraq e il nuovo Baladhuri. Atti della Accademia Nazionale dei Lincei. Rendiconti: Classe Scienze Morali, Storiche e Filologiche.* Series VI, vol. XIV (1938), 199–236.

Geddes, C. L. "The Messiah in South Arabia." *Muslim World.* 57 (1967), 311–320.

de Goeje, M. J. "Al-Beladhori's Ansab al-Aschraf." *Zeitschrift der Deutschen Morgenländischen Gesellschaft.* XXXVIII (1884), 382–406.

Goldziher, Ignaz. "Badaʾ." *Shorter Encyclopædia of Islam.* (Ithaca, N.Y., 1965), 53–54.

——. "Islamisme et Parsisme." *Revue de l'Histoire des Religions.* XLIII (1901), 1–29.

——. "Neuplatonische und Gnostische Elemente im Hadit." *Zeitschrift für Assyriologie.* XXII (1909), 317–344.

Halm, Heinz. "Das 'Buch der Schatten': Die Mufāddal-Tradition der Gulāt und die Ursprünge der Nusairiertums. II. Die Stoffe." *Der Islam.* 58 (1981), 15–86.

Hamdani, Abbas. "Evolution of the Organisational Structure of the Fatimi Daʿwah." *Arabian Studies.* 3 (1976), 85–114.

de Hammer, M. J. "Tableau Généalogique des Soixante-treize sectes de l'Islam." *Journal Asiatique.* Series I, VI (1825), 321–335.

Hinds, Martin. "Kufan Political Alignments and Their Background in the Mid-Seventh Century." *International Journal of Middle East Studies.* ii (1971), 346–367.

Hodgson, Marshall G. S. "'Abdallāh ibn Sabaʾ." *Encyclopædia of Islam.* I (2nd ed.; Leiden, 1960), 51.

_____. "Bāṭiniyya." *Encyclopædia of Islam.* I (2nd ed.; Leiden, 1960), 1098–1100.

_____. "Bayān ibn Sim'ān al-Tamīmī." *Encyclopædia of Islam.* I (2nd ed.; Leiden, 1960), 1116–1117.

_____. "Ghulāt." *Encyclopædia of Islam.* II (2nd ed.; Leiden, 1965), 1093–1094.

_____. "How Did the Early Shī'a Become Sectarian." *Journal of the American Oriental Society.* 75 (1955), 1–13.

Husik, Isaac. "Ark of the Covenant." *Jewish Encyclopædia.* II (New York, 1902), 105–106.

anon. "Idjli, Abu Mansūr." *Encyclopædia of Islam.* II (Leiden, 1927), 447–448.

Ivanov, V. "Early Shī'ite Movements." *Journal of the Bombay Branch of the Royal Asiatic Society.* New Series XVIII (1941), 1–20.

_____. "Ismā'īliya." *Shorter Encyclopædia of Islam.* (Ithaca, N.Y., 1965), 179–183.

Jakubovskij, A. Ju. "Vosstanie Mukanny – dviviženie ljudej v 'belyx odeždax'." *Sovetskoe vostokovedenie.* V (1948), 35–54.

Justin. "Baruch by Justin." Translated by R. M. Grant in *Gnosticism. A Source Book of Heretical Writings from the Early Christian Period.* (New York, 1961).

Keddie, Nikki and Farah Monian. "Militancy and Religion in Contemporary Iran." *Fundamentalisms and the State.* Edited by Martin E. Marty and R. Scott Appleby. (Chicago, 1993), 511–538.

Kramer, Martin. "Hizballah: The Calculus of Jihad." *Fundamentalisms and the State.* Edited by Martin E. Marty and R. Scott Appleby. (Chicago, 1993), 539–556.

Lammens, Henri. "Ziād ibn Abīhī, vice-roi de l'Iraq." *Rivista degli Studi Orientali.* IV (1911–1912), 1–45, 199–250, 653–693.

Landau-Tasseron, Ella. "Sayf ibn 'Umar in Medieval and Modern Scholarship." *Der Islam.* 67 (1990), 1–26.

Lane, E. W. "Raj'ah." *Lane's Arabic-English Lexicon.* Book I, part III. (New York, 1961), 1040.

Lecomte, Gerard. "Ibn Kutaybah." *Encyclopædia of Islam.* III (2nd ed.; Leiden, 1968), 844–847.

Levi della Vida, G. "Il Califfato di 'Alī secondo il Kitāb Ansab al-Asraf di al-Baladuri." *Rivista degli Studi Orientali.* VI (1914–1915), 427–507.

_____. "Mukhtār." *Encyclopædia of Islam.* III (Leiden, 1936), 715–717.

Lewis, Bernard. "Abū Hāshim." *Encyclopædia of Islam.* I (2nd ed.; Leiden, 1960), 124–125.

Macdonald, D. B. "Mahdī." *Shorter Encyclopædia of Islam.* (Ithaca, N.Y., 1965), 310–313.

Madelung, Wilferd. "Apocalyptic Prophecies in Hims in the Umayyad Age." *Journal of Semitic Studies.* XXXVI, part 2 (1986), 141–185.

_____. "The Fatimids and the Qarmatīs of Bahrayn." *Mediæval Ismāʿīlī History and Thought.* Edited by Farhad Daftary. (Cambridge, 1996), 21–73.

Massignon, Louis. "Karmatians." *Shorter Encyclopædia of Islam.* (Ithaca, N.Y., 1965), 218–223.

_____. "Die Ursprunge und die Bedeutung des Gnostizismus im Islam." *Opera Minora.* I (Beirut, 1963), 499–513.

Mazzaoui, Michel. "Mushaʿshaʿiyan: A Fifteenth-Century Shiʿi Movement in Khuzistān and Southern Iraq." *Folia Orientalia.* XXII (1981–1984), 139–162.

McLean, N. "Marcionism." *Hastings Encyclopædia of Religion and Ethics.* VIII (New York, 1961), 407–409.

Minorsky, Vladimir. "Ahl-i Hakk." *Encyclopædia of Islam.* I (2nd ed.; Leiden, 1960), 260–263.

Morony, Michael G. "Status and Stratification in the Iraqi Amsar." Paper presented to the 13th Annual Meeting of the Middle East Studies Association. (Salt Lake City, Utah, November 10, 1979).

Moscati, Sabatino. "Per una Storia dell'Antica Sīʿa." *Rivista degli Studi Orientali.* XXX (1955), 251–267.

_____. "Studi di Abū Muslim. II. Propaganda e politica religiosa di Abu Muslim." *Atti della Accademia Nazionale dei Lincei. Rendiconti: Classe Scienze Morali, Storiche, e Filologiche.* Series VIII, vol. IV (1949), 474–495.

_____. "Studi Storici sul Califfato di al-Mahdi." *Orientalia.* New Series XIV (1945), 300–354.

_____. "Il Testamento di Abū Hāshim." *Rivista degli Studi Orientali.* XXVIII (1952).

Nöldeke, Theodor. "Mansūr." *Sketches from Eastern History.* Translated by J. S. Black. (Beirut, 1963), 107–145.

_____. "Die Namen der Aramäischen Nation und Sprache." *Zeitschrift der Deutschen Morgenländischen Gesellschaft.* XXV (1871), 113–171.

Nyberg, H. S. "Muʿtazila." *Shorter Encyclopædia of Islam.* (Ithaca, N.Y., 1965), 421–427.

Poonawala, Ismail K. "Ismāʿīlī taʾwīl of the Qurʾān." *Approaches to the History of the Interpretation of the Qurʾān.* Edited by A. Rippin. (Oxford, 1988), 199–222.

al-Qāḍī, Wadād. "The Development of the Term *Ghulāt* in Muslim Literature with Special Reference to the Kaysāniyya." *Akten des VII. Kongresses für Arabistik und Islamwissenschaft.* (Göttingen, 1974), 295–319.

Rafati, Vahid. "The Hurūfis: Their Main Doctrines and Works." Unpublished paper. (The University of California at Los Angeles, Winter 1976).

Rekaya, Mohamed. "Le *Khurramādin* et les mouvements Khurramites sous les ʿAbbasides." *Studia Islamica.* 60 (1984), 5–57.

Ritter, Hellmut. "Philologika III: Muhammedanische Häresiographen." *Islam.* 18 (1929), 34–55.

Sachedina, Abdulaziz A. "Activist Shiʿism in Iran, Iraq and Lebanon." *Fundamentalisms Observed.* Edited by Martin E. Marty and R. Scott Appleby. (Chicago, 1991), 403–456.

Schleifer, J. and W. M. Watt. "Hamdān." *Encyclopædia of Islam.* III (2nd ed.; Leiden, 1965), 123.

Schloessinger, Max. "Ishak ben Yaʿkub Obadiah Abū ʿIsa al-Isfahani." *Jewish Encyclopædia.* IV (New York, 1904), 646.

Shahid, Irfan. "Kinda." *Encyclopædia of Islam.* V (2nd ed.; Leiden, 1979), 118–120.

Strothmann, Rudolph. "Shīʿa." *Shorter Encyclopædia of Islam.* (Ithaca, N.Y., 1965), 534–541.

———. "Zaidiya." *Shorter Encyclopædia of Islam.* (Ithaca, N.Y., 1965), 651–653.

Tevfik, Riza. "Étude sur la Religion des Houroufis." *Textes persans relatifs a la secte Houroufis.* Edited and translated by M. Clement Huart. (Leiden and London, 1909), 221–313.

Tritton, A. S. "A Theological Miscellany." *Bulletin of the School of Oriental and African Studies.* IX (1937–1939), 923–926.

Tucker, William F. "ʿAbd Allāh ibn Muʿāwiya and the Janāhiyya: Rebels and Ideologues of the Late Umayyad Period." *Studia Islamica.* LI (1980), 39–57.

———. "Abū Manṣūr al-ʿIjli and the Mansūriyya: a Study in Medieval Terrorism." *Islam.* 54 (1977), 66–76.

———. "Bayān b. Samʿān and the Bayāniyya: Shīʿite Extremists of Umayyad Iraq." *Muslim World.* LXV (1975), 241–253.

———. "Charismatic Leadership and Shī'ite Sectarianism." *Islamic and Middle Eastern Societies: A Festschrift in Honor of Professor Wadie Jwaideh.* (Brattleboro, Vt., 1987), 29–41.

———. "Rebels and Gnostics: al-Mughīra ibn Saʿīd and the Mughīriyya." *Arabica.* XXII (1975), 33–47.

Vajda, G. "Les Zindiqs en Pays de l'Islam au début de la periode ʾAbbaside." *Rivista degli Studi Orientali.* XVIII (1938), 173–229.

Veccia Vaglieri, L. "Ibn al-Ash'ath." *Encyclopædia of Islam.* III (2nd ed.; Leiden, 1968), 715–719.

van Vloten, G. "Über einige bis jetzt nicht erkannte Münzen aus der letzen Omeijadenzeit." *Zeitschrift der Deutschen Morgenländischen Gesellschaft.* XLVI (1892), 441–444.

———. "Worgers in Iraq." *Feestbundel van Taal-Letter-, Geschied-an Aardrijkskundige Bijdragen van zijn Tachtigsten Geboortedag aan Dr. P. J. Veth.* (Leiden, 1894), 57–63.

Wasserstrom, Steven. "The Moving Finger Writes: Mughīra ibn Saʿīd's Islamic Gnosis and the Myths of its Rejection." *History of Religions.* 25 (1985), 1–29.

Watt, W. M. "Kharijite thought in the Umayyad Period." *Islam.* 36 (1961), 215–231.

———. "Shīʿism under the Umayyads." *Journal of the Royal Asiatic Society.* (1960), 158–172.

Widengren, Geo. "Manichaeism and its Iranian Background." *The Cambridge History of Iran.* III, part 2 (Cambridge, 1993), 965–990.

Zettersteen, K. V. "ʾAbd Allāh b. Muʿāwiyah." *Encyclopædia of Islam.* I (2nd ed.; Leiden, 1960), 48–49.

———. "Yūsuf ibn ʿOmar." *Encyclopædia of Islam.* III (Leiden, 1934), 1177–1178.

V. Books and Articles About Millenarism and Sectarianism

Aberle, D. F. "A Note on Relative Deprivation Theory as Applied to Millenarian and Other Cult Movements." *Millennial Dreams in Action: Essays in Comparative Study.* Edited by Sylvia Thrupp. (The Hague, 1962), 209–214.

Amanat, Abbas and Magnus Bernhardsson, eds. *Imagining the End: Visions of Apocalypse from the Ancient Middle East to Modern America.* (London, 2002).

Archives de Sociologie des Religions. IV, V (1957–1958).

Balandier, Georges. *The Sociology of Black Africa: Social Dynamics in Central Africa.* Translated by Douglas Garman. (New York, 1970).

Balch, Robert W., John Domitrovich, Barbara Lynn Mahnke, and Vanessa Morrison. "Fifteen Years of Failed Prophecy: Coping with Cognitive Dissonance in a Baha'i Sect." *Millennium, Messiahs, and Mayhem: Contemporary Apocalyptic Movements.* Edited by Thomas Robbins and Susan J. Palmer. (New York and London, 1997), 73–90.

Barkun, Michael. *Disaster and the Millennium.* (New Haven, Conn., and London, 1974).

Bastide, Roger. *The African Religions of Brazil: Toward a Sociology of the Interpenetration of Civilizations.* Translated by Helen Sebba. (Baltimore, Md., and London, 1978).

Boyer, Paul. *When Time Shall Be No More: Prophecy Belief in Modern American Culture.* (Cambridge, Mass., 1992).

Burridge, Kenelm. *New Heaven New Earth: A Study of Millenarian Activities.* (Oxford, 1969).

Cohn, Norman. *Cosmos, Chaos and the World to Come: The Ancient Roots of Apocalyptic Faith.* (New Haven, Conn., and London, 1993).

———. "Medieval Millenarism." *Millennial Dreams in Action: Essays in Comparative Study.* Edited by Sylvia Thrupp. (The Hague, 1962), 31–43.

———. *The Pursuit of the Millennium.* (2nd ed. New York, 1961).

———. *The Pursuit of the Millennium.* (Rev. ed.; New York, 1970).

Collins, John J., ed. *The Encyclopedia of Apocalypticism: III. The Origins of Apocalypticism in Judaism and Christianity.* (New York, 2000).

Desroche, Henri. "Micromillenarismes et communautarisme utopique en Amérique du Nord du XVIIe au XIXe siècle." *Archives de Sociologie des Religions.* IV (1957), 57–92.

———. *The Sociology of Hope.* Translated by Carol Martin-Sperry. (London and Boston, 1979).

Eberhardt, Jacqueline. "Messianisme en Afrique du Sud." *Archives de Sociologie des Religiones.* IV (1957), 31–56.

Fields, Karen. "Antinomian Conduct at the Millennium: Metaphorical Conceptions of Time in Social Science and Social Life." *The Political Dimensions of Religion.* Edited by Said A. Arjomand. (Albany, N.Y., 1993), 175–203.

Guiart, Jean. "Institutions religieuses traditionelles et messianismes modernes à Fiji." *Archives de Sociologie des Religions.* IV (1957), 3–30.

Hill, Christopher. *Milton and the English Revolution*. (London, 1977).
———. *The World Turned Upside Down: Radical Ideas during the English Revolution*. (Harmondsworth, 1982).
Hobsbawm, E. J. *Primitive Rebels*. (Manchester, 1959).
Holloway, Mark. *Heavens on Earth: Utopian Communities in America 1680–1880*. (New York, 1966).
Hue-Tam Ho Tai. *Millenarianism and Peasant Politics in Vietnam*. (Cambridge, Mass., and London, 1983).
Isambert, François. "Fondateurs, Papes, et Messies." *Archives de Sociologie des Religions*. V (1958), 96–98.
Isaura Pereira de Queroz, Maria. "L'influence du Milieu sociale Interne sur les mouvements messianiques brésiliens." *Archives de Sociologie des Religions*. V (1958), 3–30.
Kovalevsky, Pierre. "Messianisme et Millénarisme russes?" *Archives de Sociologie des Religions*. V (1958), 47–70.
Lanternari, Vittorio. "Messianism: Its Historical Origin and Morphology." *History of Religions*. II (1962–1963), 52–72.
———. *The Religions of the Oppressed: A Study of Modern Messianic Cults*. Translated by Lisa Sergio. (New York, 1963).
MacGaffey, Wyatt. *Modern Kongo Prophets: Religion in a Plural Society*. (Bloomington, Ind., 1983).
Metraux, Alfred. "Les Messies du l'Amérique du Sud." *Archives de Sociologie des Religions*. IV (1957), 108–112.
Mühlmann, Wilhelm. *Chiliasmus und Nativismus: Studien zur Psychologie, Soziologie und Historischen Kasuistik der Umsturzbewegungen*. (Berlin, 1961).
Naquin, Susan. *Millenarian Rebellion in China: The Eight Trigrams Uprising of 1813*. (New Haven, Conn., 1976).
Nordhoff, Charles. *The Communistic Societies of the United States from Personal Visit and Observation*. (New York, 1966).
Robbins, Thomas and Susan J. Palmer, eds. *Millennium, Messiahs, and Mayhem: Contemporary Apocalyptic Movements*. (New York and London, 1997).
Sarkisyanz, Manuel. "Culture and Politics in Vietnamese Caodaism." *The Political Dimensions of Religion*. Edited by Said A. Arjomand. (Albany, N.Y., 1993), 205–218.
———. "Lost Primeval Bliss as Re-volutionary Expectation: Millennalism of Crisis in Peru and the Philippines." *The Political Dimensions of Religion*. Edited by Said A. Arjomand. (Albany, N.Y., 1993), 157–168.

Schaer, Roland, Gregory Claeys, and Lyman Tower Sargent, eds. *Utopia: The Search for the Ideal Society in the Western World.* (New York, 2000).

Schmithals, Walter. *The Apocalyptic Movement: Introduction and Interpretation.* Translated by John E. Steely. (New York, 1975).

Seguy, Jean. "David Lazzaretti et la secte apocalyptique des Giurisdavidici." *Archives de Sociologie des Religions.* V (1958), 71–87.

Stark, Werner. *The Sociology of Religion: A Study of Christendom. II: Sectarian Religion.* (London, 1967).

van Straelen, H. "Un messianisme japonais contemporain." *Archives de Sociologie des Religions.* IV (1957), 123–132.

Sundkler, B. G. M. *Bantu Prophets in South Africa.* (London, 1948).

Talmon, Yonina. "Millenarism." *International Encyclopædia of Social Sciences.* X (2nd ed.; New York, 1968), 349–362.

———. "Pursuit of the Millennium: The Relation between Religious and Social Change." *Archives Européennes de Sociologie.* III (1962), 125–148.

Thrupp, Sylvia, ed. *Millennial Dreams in Action: Essays in Comparative Study.* (The Hague, 1962).

Verbeke, Werner, Daniel Verhelst, and Andries Welkenhuysen, eds. *The Use and Abuse of Eschatology in the Middle Ages.* (Louvain, 1988).

Wallis, Wilson. *Messias: Their Role in Civilization.* (Washington, D.C., 1943).

Wax, Murray. "Les Pawnees à la recherche du Paradis Perdu." *Archives de Sociologie des Religions.* IV (1957), 113–122.

Wilson, Bryan R. *Magic and the Millennium.* (St. Albans, 1975).

Wipper, Audrey. *Rural Rebels: A Study of Two Protest Movements in Kenya.* (Nairobi, London, and New York, 1977).

Worsley, Peter. *The Trumpet Shall Sound: A Study of "Cargo" Cults in Melanesia.* (2nd aug. ed.; New York, 1968).

VI. Books Concerning Eastern Christianity

Atiya, A. S. *A History of Eastern Christianity.* (Notre Dame, Ind., 1968).

anon. *The Book of the Himyarites.* Translated by Axel Moberg. (Leipzig, 1924).

Honigmann, Ernest. *Évêques et Evêchés Monophysites d'Asie Antérieure au VIe Siècle.* (Louvain, 1951).

Spuler, Bertold. *Die Gegenwartslage der Ostkirchen in ihrer Völkischen und Staatlichen Umwelt.* (Wiesbaden, 1948).

Thomas, Bishop of Marga. *The Book of Governors.* Translated by E. A. W. Budge. II (London, 1893).

VII. Genealogical Tables

Caskel, W. *Gamharat an-Nasab des Genealogische Werk des Hisam ibn Muhammad al-Kalbi.* I (Leiden, 1966).

Index

For EU product safety concerns, contact us at Calle de José Abascal, 56–1°,
28003 Madrid, Spain or eugpsr@cambridge.org.

 www.ingramcontent.com/pod-product-compliance
Ingram Content Group UK Ltd.
Pitfield, Milton Keynes, MK11 3LW, UK
UKHW012345130625
459647UK00009B/554